W/d

Best-Loved Poems
in Large Print

Also Available in Large Print:

Favorite Poems in Large Print
Favorite Short Stories in Large Print

Best-Loved Poems in Large Print

Edited by Virginia S. Reiser

G.K. HALL & CO.
Boston, Massachusetts
1983

Set in 16 pt Times Roman

Library of Congress Cataloging in Publication Data

Main entry under title:

Best-loved poems in large print.

   Includes index.
   1. English poetry. 2. American poetry. 3. Large
type books. I. Reiser, Virginia S.
[PR1174.B4 1983]   821'.008   83–10815
ISBN 0–8161–3575–4

Acknowledgments

The editor gratefully acknowledges permission to reproduce copyright poems in this book.

Conrad Aiken: "Music I Heard" from *Collected Poems* by Conrad Aiken. Copyright © 1953, 1970 by Conrad Aiken; renewed 1981 by Mary Aiken. Reprinted by permission of Oxford University Press, Inc.

Hart Crane: "My Grandmother's Love Letters" and "To Brooklyn Bridge" from *The Complete Poems and Selected Letters and Prose of Hart Crane*, edited by Brom Weber, reprinted by permission of Liveright Publishing Corporation. Copyright 1933, © 1958, 1966 by Liveright Publishing Corporation. Reprinted in the British Commonwealth by permission of Laurence Pollinger Ltd.

E. E. Cummings: "what if a much of a which of a wind" from *Complete Poems 1913–1962* by E. E. Cummings. Copyright 1944 by E. E. Cummings, renewed 1972 by Nancy T. Andrews. Reprinted by permission of Harcourt Brace Jovanovich. Reprinted in the British Commonwealth by permission of E. E. Cummings Trust.

Walter de la Mare: "The Listeners" reprinted by permission of The Society of Authors as the representative of The Literary Trustees of Walter de la Mare.

Emily Dickinson: "A Bird Came Down the Walk"; " 'Hope' Is the Thing with Feathers"; "I Died for Beauty—But Was Scarce"; "I Never Lost as Much But Twice"; "I Years Had Been from Home"; "The Pedigree of Honey"; "The Soul Selects Her Own Society"; and "There's a Certain Slant of Light" reprinted by permission of the publishers and The Trustees of Amherst College from *The Poems of Emily Dickinson*, edited by Thomas H. Johnson, Cambridge, Mass.: The Belknap Press of Harvard University Press, Copyright © 1951, 1955, 1979 by the President and Fellows of Harvard College.

Sam Walter Foss: "The House by the Side of the Road" courtesy of Lothrop, Lee and Shepard Books (A Division of William Morrow and Company).

Robert Frost: "Design"; "Directive"; "Mowing"; "My November Guest"; "The Pasture"; "The Silken Tent"; "To Earthward"; "Tree at My Window"; "Two Tramps in Mud Time"; and "West-Running Brook" from *The Poetry of Robert Frost*, edited by Edward Connery Lathem. Copyright 1923, 1928, 1934, 1939, 1947, © 1967, 1969 by Holt, Rinehart and Winston. Copyright 1936, 1942, 1951, © 1956, 1962 by Robert Frost. Copyright © 1964, 1970, 1975 by Lesley Frost Ballantine. Reprinted by permission of Holt, Rinehart, and Winston, Publishers.

John Galsworthy: "So Might It Be" from *The Collected Poems of John Galsworthy*. Copyright 1934, 1962 Charles Scribner's Sons. Reprinted by permission of Charles Scribner's Sons. Reprinted in the British Commonwealth by permission of The Society of Authors as the literary representative of the Estate of John Galsworthy.

Edgar A. Guest: "Becoming a Dad"; "A Friend's Greeting"; "Home"; "Lord, Make a Regular Man Out of Me"; "Myself"; and "Out Fishin' " from *Collected Verse of Edgar A.*

For Gary
with love

Contents

A Note from the Editor xxv

Stories and Ballads

The Destruction of Sennacherib/
   George Gordon, Lord Byron 3
The Main-Truck; Or a Leap for Life/
   George P. Morris 5
The Skeleton in Armor/
   Henry Wadsworth Longfellow 6
Maud Muller/*John Greenleaf Whittier* 12
The Lady of Shalott/
   Alfred, Lord Tennyson 18
The Pied Piper of Hamelin/
   Robert Browning 24
How They Brought the Good News from
   Ghent to Aix/*Robert Browning* 35
Cleopatra Dying/
   Thomas Stephens Collier 39
Yussouf/*James Russell Lowell* 41
The First Snowfall/*James Russell Lowell* 43
Aux Italiens/*Robert Bulwer-Lytton* 44
Back to Griggsby's Station/
   James Whitcomb Riley 50
Curfew Must Not Ring Tonight/
   Rose Hartwick Thorpe 53

Christmas at Sea/*Robert Louis Stevenson*   57
The Ballad of East and West/
   Rudyard Kipling   60
Ballad of the Tempest/*James T. Fields*   66
The Cremation of Sam McGee/
   Robert W. Service   67
The Spell of the Yukon/
   Robert W. Service   72
Darius Green and His Flying-Machine/
   John Townsend Trowbridge   75
The Barrel-Organ/*Alfred Noyes*   94

Love and Friendship

Love Not Me/*Unknown*   97
My Love in Her Attire/*Unknown*   97
Sonnet/*Edmund Spenser*   98
One Day I Wrote Her Name/
   Edmund Spenser   98
Loving in Truth/*Sir Philip Sidney*   99
Farewell to Love/*Michael Drayton*   100
Helen/*Christopher Marlowe*   101
Who Ever Loved, That Loved Not at First
   Sight?/*Christopher Marlowe*   102
Who Is Silvia?/*William Shakespeare*   102
Not Marble, Nor the Gilded Monuments/
   William Shakespeare   103
When I Have Seen by Time's Fell Hand/
   William Shakespeare   104
When in the Chronicle of Wasted Time/
   William Shakespeare   105
When I Consider Everything That Grows/
   William Shakespeare   106
The Flea/*John Donne*   106

A Valediction Forbidding Mourning/
    John Donne 108
The Canonization/*John Donne* 109
The Hour Glass/*Ben Jonson* 111
Sweet Disorder/*Robert Herrick* 112
To Electra/*Robert Herrick* 112
On a Girdle/*Edmund Waller* 113
To My Dear and Loving Husband/
    Anne Bradstreet 113
The Definition of Love/*Andrew Marvell* 114
The Garden/*Andrew Marvell* 115
Auld Lang Syne/*Robert Burns* 118
She Was a Phantom of Delight/
    William Wordsworth 119
So, We'll Go No More A-Roving/
    George Gordon, Lord Byron 120
The Indian Serenade/*Percy Bysshe Shelley* .. 121
Love's Philosophy/*Percy Bysshe Shelley* 122
One Word Is Too Often Profaned/
    Percy Bysshe Shelley 122
When I Have Fears That I May Cease to Be/
    John Keats 123
Bright Star, Would I Were Steadfast as
    Thou Art/*John Keats* 124
First Time He Kissed Me/
    Elizabeth Barrett Browning 125
Go From Me/*Elizabeth Barrett Browning* 126
For Annie/*Edgar Allan Poe* 126
To One in Paradise/*Edgar Allen Poe* 130
Song/*Alfred, Lord Tennyson* 131
A Woman's Last Word/*Robert Browning* 132
My Love/*James Russell Lowell* 134
The Blessed Damozel/
    Dante Gabriel Rossetti 136
Mid-Rapture/*Dante Gabriel Rossetti* 141
A Birthday/*Christina Georgina Rossetti* 142

The First Day/
Christina Georgina Rossetti 143
Rondel/Algernon Charles Swinburne 143
I Will Not Let Thee Go/Robert Bridges 144
When She Comes Home/
James Whitcomb Riley...................... 146
Romance/Robert Louis Stevenson 146
Kashmiri Song/Laurence Hope 147
Light/Francis W. Bourdillon.................. 151
Will You Love Me When I'm Old?/
Unknown 151
New Friends and Old Friends/
Joseph Parry.................................. 152
Spring Night/Sara Teasdale.................. 153
Love Song/Elinor Wylie 154
A Friend's Greeting/Edgar A. Guest 155
Music I Heard/Conrad Aiken 156
Ashes of Life/Edna St. Vincent Millay 157
My Grandmother's Love Letters/
Hart Crane.................................... 158

Nature and the Seasons

The Wild Honey Suckle/Philip Freneau 163
To Spring/William Blake 164
Flow Gently, Sweet Afton/Robert Burns 165
It Is a Beauteous Evening, Calm and Free/
William Wordsworth 167
Composed Upon Westminster Bridge/
William Wordsworth 167
Tintern Abbey/William Wordsworth 168
The Sea/George Gordon, Lord Byron 175
The Cloud/Percy Bysshe Shelley 178
The Yellow Violet/William Cullen Bryant ... 182
Ode to a Nightingale/John Keats.............. 183

Autumn/*Thomas Hood* 187
The Snow-Storm/*Ralph Waldo Emerson* 190
Fable/*Ralph Waldo Emerson* 191
Hymn to the Night/
    Henry Wadsworth Longfellow 192
The Fire of Drift-Wood/
    Henry Wadsworth Longfellow 193
The Tide Rises, the Tide Falls/
    Henry Wadsworth Longfellow 195
Blow, Bugle, Blow/
    Alfred, Lord Tennyson 196
Break, Break, Break/
    Alfred, Lord Tennyson 197
Pippa's Song/*Robert Browning* 198
Nature/*Henry David Thoreau* 198
The Blue-Bird/*Herman Melville* 199
What Is So Rare As a Day in June/
    James Russell Lowell 200
A Noiseless Patient Spider/*Walt Whitman* ... 202
Grass/*Walt Whitman* 203
A Bird Came Down the Walk/
    Emily Dickinson 205
The Wind/*Christina Georgina Rossetti* 206
October's Bright Blue Weather/
    Helen Hunt Jackson 206
My Garden/*Thomas Edward Brown* 208
Inversnaid/*Gerard Manley Hopkins* 208
Loveliest of Trees/*A. E. Housman* 209
Lilacs/*Amy Lowell* 210
The Pasture/*Robert Frost* 214
Mowing/*Robert Frost* 215
Tree at My Window/*Robert Frost* 216
My November Guest/*Robert Frost* 216
Thirteen Ways of Looking at a Blackbird/
    Wallace Stevens 217

Queen-Ann's-Lace/
   William Carlos Williams 220
God's World/*Edna St. Vincent Millay* 221

Home and Family

A Thanksgiving to God for His House/
   Robert Herrick............................. 225
Old Age/*Edmund Waller*........................ 227
Nurse's Song/*William Blake* 227
We Are Seven/*William Wordsworth* 228
On His Seventy-Fifth Birthday/
   Walter Savage Landor...................... 231
Youth and Age/*Samuel Taylor Coleridge* 232
Long, Long Be My Heart with Such
   Memories Filled/*Thomas Moore* 233
Oft in the Stilly Night/*Thomas Moore*........ 235
Sweet and Low/*Alfred, Lord Tennyson* 236
The Old Man Dreams/
   Oliver Wendell Holmes...................... 237
Young and Old/*Charles Kingsley* 239
A Child's Laughter/
   Algernon Charles Swinburne 240
My Dog/*John Kendrick Bangs*.................. 241
The Power of the Dog/*Rudyard Kipling*...... 242
A Prayer for My Daughter/
   William Butler Yeats........................ 244
Home/*Edgar A. Guest*.......................... 247
Becoming a Dad/*Edgar A. Guest*.............. 249
Piano/*D, H. Lawrence* 252
Prayer for This House/*Louis Untermeyer* 253
The Hand That Rocks the Cradle Is the
   Hand That Rules the World/
   William Ross Wallace 253
Roofs/*Joyce Kilmer*............................ 255

My Mother/*Jane Taylor* 256
Rock Me to Sleep/*Elizabeth Akers Allen* 258
Home Is Where There Is One to Love Us/
  Charles Swain 260
Suppose/*Phoebe Cary* 261
My Mother's Garden/*Alice E. Allen* 263

Grief and Death

Even Such Is Time/*Sir Walter Raleigh* 267
Death the Leveller/*James Shirley* 267
They Are All Gone/*Henry Vaughan* 268
On His Deceased Wife/*John Milton* 270
Vital Spark of Heavenly Flame/
  Alexander Pope 271
A Slumber Did My Spirit Seal/
  William Wordsworth 272
Desideria/*William Wordsworth* 272
Prospice/*Robert Browning* 273
Remembrance/*Emily Brontë* 274
The Death of the Flowers/
  William Cullen Bryant 276
Along the Road/
  Robert Browning Hamilton 278
Telling the Bees/*John Greenleaf Whittier* 279
Verses Written in 1872/
  Robert Louis Stevenson 282
Not Thou But I/*Philip Bourke Marston* 283
So Might It Be/*John Galsworthy* 284
To an Athlete Dying Young/
  A. E. Housman 284
The House with Nobody in It/
  Joyce Kilmer 286
Should You Go First/*A. K. Rowswell* 288
Tract/*William Carlos Williams* 289

A Refusal to Mourn the Death, by Fire, of
a Child in London/*Dylan Thomas* 292

Patriotism and War

The Harp That Once Through Tara's Halls/
Thomas Moore 297
Concord Hymn/*Ralph Waldo Emerson* 298
Emily Geiger/*Unknown* 299
The March into Virginia/
Herman Melville 301
The Blue and the Gray/
Frances Miles Finch 303
The Fighting Race/*Joseph I. C. Clarke* 305
England, My England/
William Ernest Henley 308
America for Me/*Henry Van Dyke* 310
I Have Loved England/*Alice Duer Miller* 312
Grass/*Carl Sandburg* 312

Faith and Inspiration

Psalm 23: The Lord Is My Shepherd 317
Batter My Heart/*John Donne* 318
At the Round Earth's Imagined Corners/
John Donne 318
His Litany to the Holy Spirit/
Robert Herrick 319
The Collar/*George Herbert* 321
Prayer/*George Herbert* 323
Wise Men and Shepherds/
Sidney Godolphin 324
The Retreat/*Henry Vaughan* 325
My Spirit Longeth for Thee/*John Byrom* 326

The Lamb/*William Blake* 327
Auguries of Innocence/*William Blake* 328
To a Waterfowl/*William Cullen Bryant* 331
Lead, Kindly Light/*John Henry Newman* 333
Inspiration/*Henry David Thoreau* 334
There Is No God/*Arthur Hugh Clough* 335
Evening Contemplation/
   George Washington Doane 336
God's Grandeur/*Gerard Manley Hopkins* 337
Optimism/*Ella Wheeler Wilcox* 338
How the Great Guest Came/
   Edwin Markham 339
A Creed/*Edwin Markham* 342
The Hound of Heaven/*Francis Thompson* ... 342
Recessional/*Rudyard Kipling* 350
Pray Without Ceasing/
   Ophelia Guyon Browning 351
Rocked in the Cradle of the Deep/
   Emma Willard 353
Opportunity/*Walter Malone* 354
The House by the Side of the Road/
   Sam Walter Foss 355
A Prayer/*Max Ehrmann* 357
Turn Again to Life/*Mary Lee Hall* 359

Reflection and Contemplation

Hyacinths to Feed Thy Soul/
   Gulistan of Moslih 363
My Mind to Me a Kingdom Is/
   Sir Edward Dyer 363
They That Have Power to Hurt/
   William Shakespeare 364
When Forty Winters/
   William Shakespeare 365

On Time/*John Milton* 366
Know Then Thyself/*Alexander Pope* 367
Ode on a Distant Prospect of Eton College/
    Thomas Gray 370
Night/*William Blake* 373
Ode (Intimations of Immortality from
    Recollections of Early Childhood)/
    William Wordsworth 375
Hymn to Intellectual Beauty/
    Percy Bysshe Shelley 384
Thanatopsis/*William Cullen Bryant* 388
The Mermaid Tavern/*John Keats* 392
Each and All/*Ralph Waldo Emerson* 393
The Village Blacksmith/
    Henry Wadsworth Longfellow 395
Is It Too Late!/
    Henry Wadsworth Longfellow 397
The Lost Occasion/
    John Greenleaf Whittier 397
A Dream Within a Dream/
    Edgar Allan Poe 400
The Visionary/*Emily Brontë* 401
Myself/*Walt Whitman* 403
To Think of Time/*Walt Whitman* 404
I Never Lost as Much But Twice/
    Emily Dickinson 408
I Years Had Been from Home/
    Emily Dickinson 408
A Certain Slant of Light/*Emily Dickinson* ... 409
The Soul Selects Her Own Society/
    Emily Dickinson 410
The Pedigree of Honey/*Emily Dickinson* 411
I Died for Beauty—But Was Scarce/
    Emily Dickinson 411
"Hope" Is the Thing with Feathers/
    Emily Dickinson 412

The Garden of Proserpine/
   Algernon Charles Swinburne 412
You Never Can Tell/*Ella Wheeler Wilcox* 416
The Two Glasses/*Ella Wheeler Wilcox* 417
The Man with the Hoe/*Edwin Markham* 419
Victory in Defeat/*Edwin Markham* 422
Lord, Make a Regular Man Out of Me/
   Edgar A. Guest 422
Myself/*Edgar A. Guest* 423
Tell Him So/*Unknown* 424
Sculpture/*Unknown* 425
The Measure of a Man/*Unknown* 426
Design/*Robert Frost* 427
Two Tramps in Mud Time/*Robert Frost* 427
West-Running Brook/*Robert Frost* 430
To Earthward/*Robert Frost* 434
The Silken Tent/*Robert Frost* 435
Prophecy/*Elinor Wylie* 436
What Are Years?/*Marianne Moore* 436

Humor

Drinking/*Abraham Cowley* 441
Sally in Our Alley/*Henry Carey* 442
The Mad Gardener's Song/*Lewis Carroll* 444
The Game of Life/*John Godfrey Saxe* 446
Early Rising/*John Godfrey Saxe* 448
The Preacher's Vacation/*Unknown* 451
To a Thesaurus/*Franklin P. Adams* 455
A Chronicle/*Unknown* 456
When Father Carves the Duck/
   Ernest Vincent Wright 458
Methuselah/*Unknown* 459
The Jumblies/*Edward Lear* 460
Mr. and Mrs. Discobbolos/*Edward Lear* 463

The Nutcrackers and the Sugar-Tongs/
  Edward Lear 467
The Goat/*Unknown* 470
If I Should Die To-Night/*Ben King* 471
An Overworked Elocutionist/
  Carolyn Wells 472
Antigonish/*Hughes Mearnes* 474
Very Like a Whale/*Ogden Nash* 474
Reflections on Ice-Breaking/*Ogden Nash* 476
So That's Who I Remind Me Of/
  Ogden Nash 477
Portrait of the Artist as a Prematurely Old
  Man/*Ogden Nash* 478

Various Themes

They Flee from Me/*Sir Thomas Wyatt* 483
A Thing of Beauty/*John Keats* 484
On Seeing the Elgin Marbles/*John Keats* 485
The Solitary Reaper/*William Wordsworth* ... 486
Ulalume/*Edgar Allan Poe* 487
Israfel/*Edgar Allan Poe* 491
The Conqueror Worm/*Edgar Allen Poe* 493
Ring Out, Wild Bells/
  Alfred, Lord Tennyson 495
Locksley Hall/*Alfred, Lord Tennyson* 496
Days of Birth/*Unknown* 509
Rabbi Ben Ezra/*Robert Browning* 509
Echoes/*William Ernest Henley* 518
With Rue My Heart Is Laden/
  A. E. Housman 519
A Minuet on Reaching the Age of Fifty/
  George Santayana 520
The Second Coming/*William Butler Yeats* ... 522

Among School Children/
    William Butler Yeats 523
The Listeners/*Walter De La Mare* 526
The Forgotten Man/*Edwin Markham* 527
The Vampire/*Rudyard Kipling* 529
George Crabbe/
    Edwin Arlington Robinson 531
Mr. Flood's Party/
    Edwin Arlington Robinson 531
The Red Wheelbarrow/
    William Carlos Williams 534
The Men That Don't Fit In/
    Robert W. Service 534
Cargoes/*John Masefield* 536
Out Fishin'/*Edgar A. Guest* 537
Peregrine/*Elinor Wylie* 538
Little Things/*Julia A. Fletcher* 542
Directive/*Robert Frost* 542
Chicago/*Carl Sandburg* 545
Cool Tombs/*Carl Sandburg* 547
Sunday Morning/*Wallace Stevens* 548
what if a much of a which of a wind/
    E. E. Cummings 552
To Brooklyn Bridge/*Hart Crane* 553
The End of the World/
    Archibald MacLeish 556
The force that through the green fuse drives the
    flower/*Dylan Thomas* 557
Poetry/*Marianne Moore* 558

Index of Authors 561

Index of Titles 566

Index of First Lines 575

A Note from the Editor

Poetry is our bond with the ages—and with each other. A poem can satisfy our souls and renew our spirits as no novel or short story can. In the past, Large Print readers have been denied this experience. There simply was little or no poetry available in a format they could read. I hope this collection of favorite poems will bring as much joy to the Large Print reader as compiling it has brought to me.

For the reader's convenience, the poems are arranged in categories, chronologically within each category.

I would like to express my appreciation to all those at G. K. Hall who make Large Print possible. Thank you, Amy Pastan, Pru Schofield, Lynn Harmet and, most of all, Pinky Chin who really gave her heart to this project.

Virginia Reiser
Boston, Mass.

Stories and Ballads

The Destruction of Sennacherib

The Assyrian came down like the wolf on
   the fold,
And his cohorts were gleaming in purple and
   gold;
And the sheen of their spears was like stars
   on the sea,
When the blue wave rolls nightly on deep
   Galilee.

Like the leaves of the forest when summer is
   green,
That host with their banners at sunset were
   seen;
Like the leaves of the forest when autumn
   hath blown,
That host on the morrow lay wither'd and
   strown.

For the Angel of Death spread his wings on
   the blast,
And breathed in the face of the foe as he
   pass'd;
And the eyes of the sleepers wax'd deadly
   and chill,

And their hearts but once heaved, and for
  ever grew still!

And there lay the steed with his nostril all
  wide,
But through it there roll'd not the breath of
  his pride;
And the foam of his gasping lay white on
  the turf,
And cold as the spray of the rock-beating
  surf.

And there lay the rider distorted and pale,
With the dew on his brow and the rust on
  his mail;
And the tents were all silent, the banners
  alone,
The lances unlifted, the trumpet unblown.

And the widows of Ashur are loud in their
  wail;
And the idols are broke in the temple of
  Baal;
And the might of the Gentile, unsmote by
  the sword,
Hath melted like snow in the glance of the
  Lord!

George Gordon, Lord Byron

The Main-Truck; Or a Leap for Life

Old Ironsides at anchor lay,
 In the harbor of Mahon;
A dead calm rested on the bay —
 The waves to sleep had gone;
When little Jack, the captain's son,
 With gallant hardihood,
Climb'd shroud and spar — and then upon
 The main-truck rose and stood!

A shudder shot through every vein —
 All eyes were turn'd on high!
There stood the boy, with dizzy brain,
 Between the sea and sky!
No hold had he above — below.
 Alone he stood in air!
At that far height none dared to go —
 No aid could reach him there.

We gazed — but not a man could speak! —
 With horror all aghast
In groups, with pallid brow and cheek,
 We watch'd the quivering mast.
The atmosphere grew thick and hot,
 And of a lurid hue,
As, riveted unto the spot,
 Stood officers and crew.

THE FATHER CAME ON DECK! — He gasp'd,
 "O God, thy will be done!"

Then suddenly a rifle grasp'd,
  And aimed it at his son!
"Jump — far out, into the wave,
  Jump, or I fire," he said:
"That only chance your life can save!
  Jump — jump, boy!" — He obey'd.

He sunk — he rose — he lived — he
    moved —
  He for the ship struck out!
On board we hail'd the lad beloved,
  With many a manly shout,
His father drew, in silent joy,
  Those wet arms round his neck,
Then folded to his heart his boy,
  And fainted on the deck.

George P. Morris

The Skeleton in Armor

"Speak! speak! thou fearful guest!
Who, with thy hollow breast
Still in rude armor drest,
  Comest to daunt me!
Wrapt not in Eastern balms,
But with thy fleshless palms
Stretched, as if asking alms,
  Why dost thou haunt me?"

Then from those cavernous eyes
Pale flashes seemed to rise,

As when the Northern skies
  Gleam in December;
And, like the water's flow
Under December's snow,
Came a dull voice of woe
  From the heart's chamber.

"I was a Viking old!
My deeds, though manifold,
No Skald in song has told,
  No Saga taught thee!
Take heed that in thy verse
Thou dost the tale rehearse,
Else dread a dead man's curse;
  For this I sought thee.

"Far in the Northern Land,
By the wild Baltic's strand,
I, with my childish hand,
  Tamed the gerfalcon;
And, with my skates fast-bound,
Skimmed the half-frozen Sound,
That the poor whimpering hound
  Trembled to walk on.

"Oft to his frozen lair
Tracked I the grisly bear,
While from my path the hare
  Fled like a shadow;
Oft through the forest dark
Followed the were-wolf's bark,

7

Until the soaring lark
   Sang from the meadow.

"But when I older grew,
Joining a corsair's crew,
O'er the dark sea I flew
   With the marauders.
Wild was the life we led;
Many the souls that sped,
Many the hearts that bled,
   By our stern orders.

"Many a wassail-bout
Wore the long Winter out;
Often our midnight shout
   Set the cocks crowing,
As we the Berserk's tale
Measured in cups of ale,
Draining the oaken pail
   Filled to o'erflowing.

"Once as I told in glee
Tales of the stormy sea,
Soft eyes did gaze on me,
   Burning yet tender;
And as the white stars shine
On the dark Norway pine,
On that dark heart of mine
   Fell their soft splendor.

"I wooed the blue-eyed maid,
Yielding, yet half afraid,

And in the forest's shade
  Our vows were plighted.
Under its loosened vest
Fluttered her little breast,
Like birds within their nest
  By the hawk frighted.

"Bright in her father's hall
Shields gleamed upon the wall,
Loud sang the minstrels all,
  Chanting his glory;
When of old Hildebrand
I asked his daughter's hand,
Mute did the minstrels stand
  To hear my story.

"While the brown ale he quaffed,
Loud then the champion laughed,
And as the wind-gusts waft
  The sea-foam brightly,
So the loud laugh of scorn,
Out of those lips unshorn,
From the deep drinking-horn
  Blew the foam lightly.

"She was a Prince's child,
I but a Viking wild,
And though she blushed and smiled,
  I was discarded!
Should not the dove so white
Follow the sea-mew's flight?

Why did they leave that night
    Her nest unguarded?

"Scarce had I put to sea,
Bearing the maid with me, —
Fairest of all was she
    Among the Norsemen! —
When on the white sea-strand,
Waving his armèd hand,
Saw we old Hildebrand,
    With twenty horsemen.

"Then launched they to the blast,
Bent like a reed each mast,
Yet we were gaining fast,
    When the wind failed us;
And with a sudden flaw
Came round the gusty Skaw,
So that our foe we saw
    Laugh as he hailed us.

"And as to catch the gale
Round veered the flapping sail,
'Death!' was the helmsman's hail,
    'Death without quarter!'
Midships with iron keel
Struck we her ribs of steel;
Down her black hull did reel
    Through the black water!

"As with his wings aslant,
Sails the fierce cormorant,
Seeking some rocky haunt,

With his prey laden,
So toward the open main,
Beating to sea again,
Through the wild hurricane,
    Bore I the maiden.

"Three weeks we westward bore,
And when the storm was o'er,
Cloud-like we saw the shore
    Stretched to leeward;
There for my lady's bower
Built I the loft tower,
Which, to this very hour,
    Stands looking seaward.

"There lived we many years;
Time dried the maiden's tears;
She had forgot her fears,
    She was a mother;
Death closed her mild blue eyes;
Under that tower she lies;
Ne'er shall the sun arise
    On such another.

"Still grew my bosom then
Still as a stagnant fen!
Hateful to me were men,
    The sunlight hateful!
In the vast forest here,
Clad in my warlike gear,
Fell I upon my spear,
    Oh, death was grateful!

"This, seamed with many scars,
Bursting these prison bars,
Up to its native stars
    My soul ascended!
There from the flowing bowl
Deep drinks the warrior's soul,
Skoal! to the Northland! *skoal!*"
    Thus the tale ended.
            Henry Wadsworth Longfellow

Maud Muller

Maud Muller on a summer's day
Raked the meadow sweet with hay.

Beneath her torn hat glowed the wealth
Of simple beauty and rustic health.

Singing, she wrought, and her merry glee
The mock-bird echoed from his tree.

But when she glanced to the far-off town,
White from its hill-slope looking down,

The sweet song died, and a vague unrest
And a nameless longing filled her breast, —

A wish that she hardly dared to own,
For something better than she had known

The Judge rode slowly down the lane,
Smoothing his horse's chestnut mane.

He drew his bridle in the shade
Of the apple-trees, to greet the maid,

And asked a draught from the spring that
    flowed
Through the meadow across the road.

She stooped where the cool spring bubbled
    up,
And filled for him her small tin cup,

And blushed as she gave it, looking down
On her feet so bare, and her tattered gown.

"Thanks!" said the Judge; "a sweeter
    draught
From a fairer hand was never quaffed."

He spoke of the grass and flowers and trees,
Of the singing birds and the humming bees;

Then talked of the haying, and wondered
    whether
The cloud in the west would bring foul
    weather.

And Maud forgot her brier-torn gown,
And her graceful ankles bare and brown;

And listened, while a pleased surprise
Looked from her long-lashed hazel eyes.

At last, like one who for delay
Seeks a vain excuse, he rode away.

Maud Muller looked and sighed: ''Ah me!
That I the Judge's bride might be!

''He would dress me up in silks so fine,
And praise and toast me at his wine.

''My father should wear a broadcloth coat;
My brother should sail a painted boat.

''I'd dress my mother so grand and gay,
And the baby should have a new toy each
   day.

''And I'd feed the hungry and clothe the
   poor,
And all should bless me who left our door.''

The Judge looked back as he climbed the
   hill,
And saw Maud Muller standing still.

''A form more fair, a face more sweet,
Ne'er hath it been my lot to meet.

''And her modest answer and graceful air

Show her wise and good as she is fair.

"Would she were mine, and I to-day,
Like her, a harvester of hay;

"No doubtful balance of rights and wrongs,
Not weary lawyers with endless tongues,

"But low of cattle and song of birds,
And health and quiet and loving words."

But he thought of his sisters, proud and
    cold,
And his mother, vain of her rank and gold.

So, closing his heart, the Judge rode on,
And Maud was left in the field alone.

But the lawyers smiled that afternoon,
When he hummed in court an old love-tune;

And the young girl mused beside the well
Till the rain on the unraked clover fell.

He wedded a wife of richest dower,
Who lived for fashion, as he for power.

Yet oft, in his marble hearth's bright glow,
He watched a picture come and go;

And sweet Maud Muller's hazel eyes
Looked out in their innocent surprise.

Oft, when the wine in his glass was red,
He longed for the wayside well instead;

And closed his eyes on his garnished rooms
To dream of meadows and clover-blooms.

And the proud man sighed, with a secret
    pain,
''Ah, that I were free again!

''Free as when I rode that day,
Where the barefoot maiden raked her hay.''

She wedded a man unlearned and poor,
And many children played round her door.

But care and sorrow, and childbirth pain,
Left their traces on heart and brain.

And oft, when the summer sun shone hot
Of the new-mown hay in the meadow lot,

And she heard the little spring brook fall
Over the roadside, through the wall,

In the shade of the apple-tree again
She saw a rider draw his rein;

And, gazing down with timid grace,
She felt his pleased eyes read her face.

Sometimes her narrow kitchen walls
Stretched away into stately halls;

The weary wheel to a spinet turned,
The tallow candle an astral burned,

And for him who sat by the chimney lug,
Dozing and grumbling o'er pipe and mug,

A manly form at her side she saw,
And joy was duty and love was law.

Then she took up her burden of life again,
Saying only, "It might have been."

Alas for maiden, alas for Judge,
For rich repiner and household drudge!

God pity them both! and pity us all,
Who vainly the dreams of youth recall.

For of all sad words of tongue or pen,
The saddest are these: "It might have
   been!"

Ah, well! for us all some sweet hope lies
Deeply buried from human eyes;

And, in the hereafter, angels may
Roll the stone from its grave away!
                          John Greenleaf Whittier

The Lady of Shalott

Part I

On either side the river lie
Long fields of barley and of rye,
That clothe the wold and meet the sky;
And through the field the road runs by
   To many-towered Camelot;
And up and down the people go,
Gazing where the lilies blow
Round an island there below,
   The island of Shalott.

Willows whiten, aspens quiver,
Little breezes dusk and shiver
Through the wave that runs for ever
By the island in the river
   Flowing down to Camelot.
Four gray walls, and four gray towers,
Overlook a space of flowers,
And the silent isle imbowers
   The Lady of Shalott.

By the margin, willow-veiled,
Slide the heavy barges trailed
By slow horses; and unhailed
The shallop flitteth silken-sailed
   Skimming down to Camelot:
But who hath seen her wave her hand?
Or at the casement seen her stand?
Or is she known in all the land,
   The Lady of Shalott?

Only reapers, reaping early
In among the bearded barley,
Hear a song that echoes cheerly
From the river winding clearly,
   Down to towered Camelot:
And by the moon the reaper weary,
Piling sheaves in uplands airy,
Listening, whispers, 'Tis the fairy
   Lady of Shalott.'

Part II

There she weaves by night and day
A magic web with colours gay.
She has heard a whisper say,
A curse is on her if she stay
   To look down to Camelot.
She knows not what the curse may be,
And so she weaveth steadily,
And little other care hath she,
   The Lady of Shalott.

And moving through a mirror clear
That hangs before her all the year,
Shadows of the world appear.
There she sees the highway near
   Winding down to Camelot:
There the river eddy whirls,
And there the surly village-churls,
And the red cloaks of market girls,
   Pass onward from Shalott.

Sometimes a troop of damsels glad,
An abbot on an ambling pad,
Sometimes a curly shepherd-lad,
Or long-haired page in crimson clad,
  Goes by to towered Camelot;
And sometimes through the mirror blue
The knights come riding two and two:
She hath no loyal knight and true,
  The Lady of Shalott.

But in her web she still delights
To weave the mirror's magic sights,
For often through the silent nights
A funeral, with plumes and lights
  And music, went to Camelot:
Or when the moon was overhead,
Came two young lovers lately wed;
'I am half sick of shadows,' said
  The Lady of Shalott.

Part III

A bow-shot from her bower-eaves,
He rose between the barley-sheaves
The sun came dazzling through the leaves,
And flamed upon the brazen greaves
  Of bold Sir Lancelot.
A red-cross knight for ever kneeled
To a lady in his shield,
That sparkled on the yellow field,
  Beside remote Shalott.

The gemmy bridle glittered free,
Like to some branch of stars we see
Hung in the golden Galaxy.
The bridle bells rang merrily
　　As he rose down to Camelot:
And from his blazoned baldric slung
A mighty silver bugle hung,
And as he rode his armour rung,
　　Beside remote Shalott.

All in the blue unclouded weather
Thick-jewelled shone the saddle-leather,
The helmet and the helmet-feather
Burned like one burning flame together,
　　As he rode down to Camelot.
As often through the purple night,
Below the starry clusters bright,
Some bearded meteor, trailing light,
　　Moves over still Shalott.

His broad clear brow in sunlight glowed;
On burnished hooves his war-horse trode;
From underneath his helmet flowed
His coal-black curls as on he rode,
　　As he rode down to Camelot.
From the bank and from the river
He flashed into the crystal mirror,
'Tirra lirra,' by the river
　　Sang Sir Lancelot.

She left the web, she left the loom,
She made three paces through the room,

She saw the water-lily bloom,
She saw the helmet and the plume,
   She looked down to Camelot.
Out flew the web and floated wide;
The mirror cracked from side to side;
'The curse is come upon me,' cried
   The Lady of Shalott.

Part IV

In the stormy east-wind straining,
The pale yellow woods were waning,
The broad stream in his banks complaining,
Heavily the low sky raining
   Over towered Camelot;
Down she came and found a boat
Beneath a willow left afloat,
And round about the prow she wrote
   The Lady of Shalott.

And down the river's dim expanse
Like some bold seer in a trance,
Seeing all his own mischance —
With a glassy countenance
   Did she look to Camelot.
And at the closing of the day
She loosed the chain, and down she lay;
The broad stream bore her far away,
   The Lady of Shalott.

Lying, robed in snowy white
That loosely flew to left and right —
The leaves upon her falling light —

Through the noises of the night
    She floated down to Camelot:
And as the boat-head wound along
The willowy hills and fields among,
They heard her singing her last song,
    The Lady of Shalott.

Heard a carol, mournful, holy,
Chanted loudly, chanted lowly,
Till her blood was frozen slowly,
And her eyes were darkened wholly,
    Turned to towered Camelot.
For ere she reached upon the tide
The first house by the water-side,
Singing in her song she died,
    The Lady of Shalott.

Under tower and balcony,
By garden-wall and gallery,
A gleaming shape she floated by,
Dead-pale between the houses high,
    Silent into Camelot.
Out upon the wharfs they came,
Knight and burgher, lord and dame,
And round the prow they read her name,
    The Lady of Shalott.

Who is this? and what is here?
And in the lighted palace near
Died the sound of royal cheer;
And they crossed themselves for fear,
    All the knights at Camelot:

But Lancelot mused a little space;
He said, 'She has a lovely face;
God in his mercy lend her grace,
    The Lady of Shalott.'

                    Alfred, Lord Tennyson

The Pied Piper of Hamelin

Hamelin Town's in Brunswick,
By famous Hanover city;
    The river Weser, deep and wide,
    Washes its wall on the southern side;
    A pleasanter spot you never spied;
But, when begins my ditty,
    Almost five hundred years ago,
    To see the townsfolk suffer so
From vermin was a pity.

        Rats!
They fought the dogs, and kill'd the cats,
    And bit the babies in the cradles,
And ate the cheeses out of the vats,
    And lick'd the soup from the cook's own
        ladles,
Split open the kegs of salted sprats,
Made nests inside men's Sunday hats,
And even spoil'd the women's chats,
        By drowning their speaking
        With shrieking and squeaking
In fifty different sharps and flats.

At last the people in a body
    To the Town Hall came flocking:
" 'Tis clear," cried they, "our Mayor's a
      noddy;
    And as for our Corporation — shocking
To think we buy gowns lined with ermine
For dolts that can't or won't determine
What's best to rid us of our vermin!
You hope, because you're old and obese,
To find in the furry civic robe ease?
Rouse up, sirs! Give your brains a racking
To find the remedy we're lacking,
Or, sure as fate, we'll send you packing!"
At this the Mayor and Corporation
Quaked with a mighty consternation.

An hour they sate in counsel,
    At length the Mayor broke silence:
"For a guilder I'd my ermine gown sell;
    I wish I were a mile hence!
It's easy to bid one rack one's brain —
I'm sure my poor head aches again,
I've scratch'd it so, and all in vain.
Oh for a trap, a trap, a trap!"
Just as he said this, what should hap
At the chamber-door but a gentle tap?
"Bless us!" cried the Mayor, "what's
      that?"
(With the Corporation as he sat,
Looking little though wondrous fat;
Nor brighter was his eye, nor moister

Than a too long-open'd oyster,
Save when at noon his paunch grew
        mutinous
For a plate of turtle, green and glutinous)
"Only a scraping of shoes on the mat?
Anything like the sound of a rat
Makes my heart go pit-a-pat!"

"Come in!" — the Mayor cried, looking
        bigger:
And in did come the strangest figure!
His queer long coat from heel to head
Was half of yellow and half of red;
And he himself was tall and thin,
With sharp blue eyes, each like a pin,
And light loose hair, yet swarthy skin,
No tuft on cheek nor beard on chin,
But lips where smiles went out and in —
There was no guessing his kith and kin!
And nobody could enough admire
The tall man and his quaint attire:
Quoth one: "It's as my great-grandsire,
Starting up at the Trump of Doom's tone,
Had walk'd this way from his painted
        tombstone!"

He advanced to the council-table:
And, "Please your honors," said he, "I'm
        able,
By means of a secret charm, to draw
All creatures living beneath the sun,
That creep, or swim, or fly, or run,

After me so as you never saw!
And I chiefly use my charm
On creatures that do people harm,
The mole, and toad, and newt, and viper;
And people call me the Pied Piper.''
(And here they noticed round his neck
A scarf of red and yellow stripe,
To match with his coat of the selfsame
    check;
And at the scarf's end hung a pipe;
And his fingers, they noticed, were ever
    straying
As if impatient to be playing
Upon this pipe, as low it dangled
Over his vesture so old-fangled.)
''Yet,'' said he, ''poor piper as I am,
In Tartary I freed the Cham,
Last June, from his huge swarm of gnats;
I eased in Asia the Nizam
Of a monstrous brood of vampyre bats;
And, as for what your brain bewilders —
If I can rid your town of rats,
Will you give me a thousand guilders?''
''One? fifty thousand!'' was the exclamation
Of the astonish'd Mayor and Corporation.

Into the street the piper stept,
    Smiling first a little smile,
As if he knew what magic slept
    In his quiet pipe the while;
Then, like a musical adept,
To blow the pipe his lips he wrinkled,

And green and blue his sharp eyes twinkled,
Like a candle-flame where salt is sprinkled;
And ere three shrill notes the pipe utter'd,
You heard as if an army mutter'd;
And the muttering grew to a grumbling;
And the grumbling grew to a mighty
    rumbling;
And out of the houses the rats came
    tumbling.
Great rats, small rats, lean rats, brawny rats,
Brown rats, black rats, gray rats, tawny rats,
Grave old plodders, gay young friskers,
    Fathers, mothers, uncles, cousins,
Cocking tails and pricking whiskers,
    Families by tens and dozens,
Brothers, sisters, husbands, wives —
Follow'd the piper for their lives.
From street to street he piped advancing,
And step for step they follow'd dancing,
Until they came to the river Weser,
Wherein all plunged and perish'd,
Save one who, stout as Julius Cæsar,
Swam across and lived to carry
(As the manuscript he cherish'd)
To Rat-land home his commentary,
Which was, ''At the first shrill notes of the
    pipe,
I heard a sound as of scraping tripe,
And putting apples, wondrous ripe,
Into a cider press's gripe:
And a moving away of pickle-tub boards,
And a leaving ajar of conserve-cupboards,

And a drawing the corks of train-oil flasks,
And a breaking the hoops of butter-casks;
And it seemed as if a voice
(Sweeter far than by harp or by psaltery
Is breathed) call'd out, O rats, rejoice!
The world is grown to one vast drysaltery!
So munch on, crunch on, take your
    nuncheon,
Breakfast, supper, dinner, luncheon!
And just as a bulky sugar-puncheon,
All ready staved, like a great sun shone
Glorious scarce an inch before me,
Just as methought it said, Come, bore me!
I found the Weser rolling o'er me.''

You should have heard the Hamelin people
Ringing the bells till they rock'd the steeple;
''Go,'' cried the Mayor, ''and get long
    poles!
Poke out the nests and block up the holes!
Consult with carpenters and builders,
And leave in our town not even a trace
Of the rats!'' — when suddenly up the face
Of the piper perk'd in the market-place,
With a, ''First, if you please, my thousand
    guilders!''

A thousand guilders! The Mayor look'd
    blue;
So did the Corporation too.
For council dinners made rare havoc
With Claret, Moselle, Vin-de-Grave, Hock;

And half the money would replenish
Their cellar's biggest butt with Rhenish.
To pay this sum to a wandering fellow
With a gypsy coat of red and yellow!
"Beside," quoth the Mayor, with a knowing
    wink,
"Our business was done at the river's brink;
We saw with our eyes the vermin sink,
And what's dead can't come to life, I think.
So, friend, we're not the folks to shrink
From the duty of giving you something for
    drink,
And a matter of money to put in your poke;
But, as for the guilders, what we spoke
Of them, as you very well know, was in
    joke.
Beside, our losses have made us thrifty;
A thousand guilders! Come, take fifty!"

The piper's face fell and he cried,
"No trifling! I can't wait! beside,
I've promised to visit by dinner-time
Bagdat, and accept the prime
Of the Head Cook's pottage, all he's rich in,
For having left, in the Caliph's kitchen,
Of a nest of scorpions no survivor ——
With him I proved no bargain-driver.
With you, don't think I'll bate a stiver!
And folks who put me in a passion
May find me pipe to another fashion."

"How?" cried the Mayor, "d'ye think I'll
    brook
Being worse treated than a Cook?
Insulted by a lazy ribald
With idle pipe and vesture piebald?
You threaten us, fellow? Do your worst,
Blow your pipe there till you burst!"

Once more he stept into the street;
    And to his lips again
Laid his long pipe of smooth straight cane;
    And ere he blew three notes (such sweet
Soft notes as yet musician's cunning
  Never gave the enraptured air)
There was a rustling, that seem'd like a
        bustling
Of merry crowds justling at pitching and
        hustling,
Small feet were pattering, wooden shoes
        clattering,
Little hands clapping, and little tongues
        chattering,
And, like fowls in a farm-yard when barley
    is scattering,
Out came the children running.
All the little boys and girls,
With rosy cheeks and flaxen curls,
And sparkling eyes and teeth like pearls,
Tripping and skipping, ran merrily after
The wonderful music with shouting and
        laughter.

The Mayor was dumb, and the Council
        stood
As if they were changed into blocks of
        wood,
Unable to move a step, or cry
To the childen merrily skipping by —
And could only follow with the eye
That joyous crowd at the Piper's back.
But how the Mayor was on the rack,
And the wretched Council's bosoms beat,
As the Piper turn'd from the High Street
To where the Weser roll'd its waters
Right in the way of their sons and
        daughters!
However, he turned from south to west,
And to Koppelberg Hill his steps address'd,
And after him the children press'd;
Great was the joy in every breast.
"He never can cross that mighty top!
He's forced to let the piping drop,
And we shall see our children stop!"
When, lo, as they reach'd the mountain's
        side,
A wondrous portal open'd wide,
As if a cavern was suddenly hollow'd;
And the Piper advanced and the children
        follow'd,
And when all were in to the very last,
The door in the mountain-side shut fast.
Did I say all? No! one was lame,
And could not dance the whole of the way,
And in after years, if you would blame

His sadness, he was used to say,
"It's dull in our town since my playmates
        left!
I can't forget that I'm bereft
Of all the pleasant sights they see,
Which the Piper also promised me,
For he led us, he said, to a joyous land,
Joining the town and just at hand,
Where waters gush'd and fruit trees grew,
And flowers put forth a fairer hue,
And everything was strange and new;
The sparrows were brighter than peacocks
        here,
And the dogs outran our fallow deer,
And honey-bees had lost their stings,
And horses were born with eagles' wings;
And just as I became assured
My lame foot would be speedily cured,
The music stopp'd, and I stood still,
And found myself outside the Hill,
Left alone against my will,
To go now limping as before,
And never hear of that country more!"

Alas, alas for Hamelin!
    There came into many a burgher's pate
    A text which says that Heaven's Gate
    Opes to the rich at as easy rate
As the needle's eye takes a camel in!
The Mayor sent east, west, north, and south
To offer the Piper by word of mouth,
    Wherever it was men's lot to find him,

33

Silver and gold to his heart's content,
If he'd only return the way he went,
    And bring the children behind him.
But when they saw 'twas a lost endeavor,
And Piper and dancers were gone for ever,
They made a decree that lawyers never
    Should think their records dated duly
If, after the day of the month and year,
These words did not as well appear:
"And so long after what happen'd here
    On the twenty-second of July,
    Thirteen hundred and Seventy-six;"
And the better in memory to fix
The place of the children's last retreat,
They call'd it the Pied Piper's Street,
Where any one playing on pipe or tabor
Was sure for the future to lose his labor.
Nor suffer'd they hostelry or tavern
    To shock with mirth a street so solemn,
But opposite the place of the cavern
    They wrote the story on a column,
And on the great church-window painted
The same, to make the world acquainted
How their children were stolen away,
And there it stands to this very day.
And I must not omit to say
That in Transylvania there's a tribe
Of alien people that ascribe
The outlandish ways and dress
On which their neighbors lay such stress,
To their fathers and mothers having risen
Out of some subterranean prison,

Into which they were trepann'd
Long time ago in a mighty band
Out of Hamelin town in Brunswick land,
But how or why, they don't understand.

So, Willy, let you and me be wipers
Of scores out with all men — especially
    pipers;
And, whether they pipe us free, from rats or
    from mice,
If we've promised them aught, let us keep
    our promise.

Robert Browning

How They Brought the Good News
from Ghent to Aix

I sprang to the stirrup, and Joris, and he;
I gallop'd, Dirck gallop'd, we gallop'd all
    three;
"Good speed!" cried the watch, as the gate-
    bolts undrew;
"Speed!" echo'd the wall to us galloping
    through;
Behind shut the postern, the lights sank to
    rest,
And into the midnight we gallop'd abreast.

Not a word to each other; we kept the great
    pace

Neck by neck, stride by stride, never
  changing our place;
I turn'd in my saddle and made its girths
  tight,
Then shorten'd each stirrup, and set the
  pique right,
Rebuckled the check-strap, chain'd slacker
  the bit,
Nor gallop'd less steadily Roland a whit.

'Twas moonset at starting; but while we
  drew near
Lokeren, the cocks crew and twilight
  dawn'd clear;
At Boom, a great yellow star came out to
  see;
At Düffeld, 'twas morning as plain as could
  be;
And from Mecheln church-steeple we heard
  the half-chime,
So Joris broke silence with, ''Yet there is
  time!''

At Aerschot, up leap'd of a sudden the sun,
And against him the cattle stood black every
  one,
To stare through the mist at us galloping
  past,
And I saw my stout galloper Roland at last,
With resolute shoulders, each butting away
The haze, as some bluff river headland its
  spray.

And his low head and crest, just one sharp
    ear bent back
For my voice, and the other prick'd out on
    his track;
And one eye's black intelligence, — ever
    that glance
O'er its white edge at me, his own master,
    askance!
And the thick heavy spume flakes which aye
    and anon
His fierce lips shook upward in galloping
    on.

By Hasselt, Dirck groan'd; and cried Joris,
    "Stay spur!
Your Roos gallop'd bravely, the fault's not
    in her;
We'll remember at Aix —" for one heard
    the quick wheeze
Of her chest, saw the stretch'd neck, and
    staggering knees,
And sunk tail, and horrible heave of the
    flank,
As down on her haunches she shudder'd and
    sank.

So we were left galloping, Joris and I,
Past Looz and past Tongres, no cloud in the
    sky;
The broad sun above laugh'd a pitiless
    laugh,

'Neath our feet broke the brittle bright
  stubble like chaff;
Till over by Dalhem a dome-spire sprang
  white,
And "Gallop," gasp'd Joris, "for Aix is in
  sight!

"How they'll greet us!" — and all in a
  moment his roan
Roll'd neck and croup over, lay dead as a
  stone;
And there was my Roland to bear the whole
  weight
Of the news which alone could save Aix
  from her fate,
With his nostrils like pits full of blood to the
  brim,
And with circles of red for his eye-sockets'
  rim.

Then I cast loose my buff coat, each holster
  let fall,
Shook off both my jack-boots, let go belt
  and all,
Stood up in the stirrup, lean'd, patted his
  ear,
Call'd my Roland his pet-name, my horse
  without peer;
Clapp'd my hands, laugh'd and sang, any
  noise, bad or good,
Till at length into Aix Roland gallop'd and
  stood.

38

And all I remember is, friends flocking
    round
As I sate with his head 'twixt my knees on
    the ground,
And no voice but was praising this Roland
    of mine,
As I pour'd down his throat our last measure
    of wine,
Which (the burgesses voted by common
    consent)
Was no more than his due who brought good
    news from Ghent.

Robert Browning

Cleopatra Dying

Sinks the sun below the desert,
    Golden glows the sluggish Nile;
Purple flame crowns Spring and Temple,
    Lights up every ancient pile
Where the old gods now are sleeping;
    Isis and Osiris great,
Guard me, help me, give me courage
    Like a Queen to meet my fate.

"I am dying, Egypt, dying,"
    Let the Caesar's army come —
I will cheat him of his glory,
    Though beyond the Styx I roam;
Shall he drag this beauty with him —

While the crowd his triumph sings?
No, no, never! I will show him
    What lies in the blood of Kings.

Though he hold the golden scepter,
    Rule the Pharaoh's sunny land,
Where old Nilus rolls resistless
    Through the sweeps of silvery sand —
He shall never say I met him
    Fawning, abject, like a slave —
I will foil him, though to do it
    I must cross the Stygian wave.

Oh, my hero, sleeping, sleeping —
    Shall I meet you on the shore
Of Plutonian shadows? Shall we
    In death meet and love once more?
See, I follow in your footsteps —
    Scorn the Caesar in his might;
For your love I will leap boldly
    Into realms of death and night.

Down below the desert sinking,
    Fades Apollo's brilliant car;
And from out the distant azure
    Breaks the bright gleam of a star.
Venus, Queen of Love and Beauty,
    Welcomes me to death's embrace,
Dying, free, proud, and triumphant,
    The last sovereign of my race.

Dying, dying! I am coming,

Oh, my hero, to your arms;
You will welcome me, I know it —
  Guard me from all rude alarms.
Hark! I hear the legions coming,
  Hear the cries of triumph swell,
But, proud Caesar, dead I scorn you —
  Egypt, Antony, farewell.
                    Thomas Stephens Collier

Yussouf

A stranger came one night to Yussouf's tent,
Saying, "Behold one outcast and in dread,
Against whose life the bow of power is bent,
Who flies, and hath not where to lay his
    head;
I come to thee for shelter and for food,
To Yussouf, called through all our tribes
    'The Good.'"

"This tent is mine," said Yussouf, "but no
    more
Than it is God's; come in, and be at peace;
Freely shalt thou partake of all my store
As I of His who buildeth over these
Our tents his glorious roof of night and day,
And at whose door none ever yet heard
    Nay."

So Yussouf entertained his guest that night,

And, waking him ere day, said: "Here is
   gold;
My swiftest horse is saddled for thy flight;
Depart before the prying day grow bold."
As one lamp lights another, nor grows less,
So nobleness enkindleth nobleness.

That inward light the stranger's face made
   grand,
Which shines from all self-conquest;
   kneeling low,
He bowed his forehead upon Yussouf's
   hand,
Sobbing: "O Sheik, I cannot leave thee so;
I will repay thee; all this thou hast done
Unto that Ibrahim who slew thy son!"

"Take thrice the gold," said Yussouf, "for
   with thee
Into the desert, never to return,
My one black thought shall ride away from
   me;
First-born, for whom by day and night I
   yearn,
Balanced and just are all of God's decrees;
Thou art avenged, my first-born, sleep in
   peace!"

James Russell Lowell

The First Snowfall

The snow had begun in the gloaming,
  And busily all the night
Had been heaping field and highway
  With a silence deep and white.

Every pine and fir and hemlock
  Wore ermine too dear for an earl,
And the poorest twig on the elm-tree
  Was ridged inch deep with pearl.

From sheds new-roofed with Carrara
  Came Chanticleer's muffled crow,
The stiff rails were softened to swan's-
    down,
  And still fluttered down the snow.

I stood and watched by the window
  The noiseless work of the sky,
And the sudden flurries of snow-birds,
  Like brown leaves whirling by.

I thought of a mound in sweet Auburn
  Where a little headstone stood;
How the flakes were folding it gently,
  As did robins the babes in the wood.

Up spoke our own little Mabel,
  Saying, "Father, who makes it snow?"
And I told of the good All-father
  Who cares for us here below.

Again I looked at the snow-fall,
　　And thought of the leaden sky
That arched o'er our first great sorrow,
　　When that mound was heaped so high.

I remembered the gradual patience
　　That fell from that cloud-like snow,
Flake by flake, healing and hiding
　　The scar of our deep-plunged woe.

And again to the child I whispered,
　　"The snow that husheth all,
Darling, the merciful Father
　　Alone can make it fall!"

Then, with eyes that saw not, I kissed her;
　　And she, kissing back, could not know
That *my* kiss was given to her sister,
　　Folded close under deepening snow.
　　　　　　　　　　　James Russell Lowell

Aux Italiens

At Paris it was, at the opera there; —
　　And she look'd like a queen in a book that
　　　night,
With the wreath of pearl in her raven hair,
　　And the brooch on her breast so bright.

44

Of all the operas that Verdi wrote,
    The best, to my taste, is the Trovatore;
And Mario can soothe, with a tenor note,
    The souls in purgatory.

The moon on the tower slept soft as snow;
    And who was not thrill'd in the strangest
        way,
As we heard him sing, while the gas burn'd
        low,
    "Non ti scordar di me?" *

The emperor there, in his box of state,
    Look'd grave, as if he had just then seen
The red flag wave from the city gate,
    Where his eagles in bronze had been.

The empress, too, had a tear in her eye:
    You'd have said that her fancy had gone
        back again,
For one moment, under the old blue sky,
    To the old glad life in Spain.

Well, there in our front-row box we sat
    Together, my bride betroth'd and I;
My gaze was fixed on my opera hat,
    And hers on the stage hard by.

And both were silent, and both were sad;

* Do not forget me.

Like a queen she lean'd on her full white
    arm,
With that regal, indolent air she had,
    So confident of her charm!

I have not a doubt she was thinking then
    Of her former lord, good soul that he was,
Who died the richest and roundest of men,
    The Marquis of Carabas.

I hope that, to get to the kingdom of heaven,
    Through a needle's eye he had not to
        pass;
I wish him well, for the jointure given
    To my lady of Carabas.

Meanwhile, I was thinking of my first love,
    As I had not been thinking of aught for
        years,
Till over my eyes there began to move
    Something that felt like tears.

I thought of the dress that she wore last
    time,
    When we stood 'neath the cypress trees
        together,
In that lost land, in that soft clime,
    In the crimson evening weather;

Of that muslin dress (for the eve was hot),
    And her warm white neck in its golden
        chain,

And her full, soft hair, just tied in a knot,
  And falling loose again;

And the jasmine flower in her fair young
    breast,
  (Oh, the faint, sweet smell of that jasmine
    flower!)
And the one bird singing alone to his nest,
  And the one star over the tower.

I thought of our little quarrels and strife,
  And the letter that brought me back my
    ring;
And it all seem'd then, in the waste of life,
  Such a very little thing!

For I thought of her grave below the hill,
  Which the sentinel cypress tree stands
    over,
And I thought, "Were she only living still,
  How I could forgive her, and love her!"

And I swear, as I thought of her thus, in that
    hour,
  And of how, after all, old things were
    best,
That I smelt the smell of that jasmine flower
  Which she used to wear in her breast.

It smelt so faint, and it smelt so sweet,
  It made me creep, and it made me cold;

Like the scent that steals from the crumbling
    sheet
    Where a mummy is half unroll'd.

And I turn'd and look'd: she was sitting
    there,
    In a dim box over the stage, and drest
In that muslin dress, with that full, soft hair,
    And that jasmine in her breast.

I was here: and she was there:
    And the glittering horseshoe curved
    between,
From my bride betroth'd, with her raven
    hair,
    And her sumptuous, scornful mien,

To my early love, with her eyes downcast,
    And over her primrose face the shade.
(In short, from the future back to the past
    There was but a step to be made.)

To my early love from my future bride
    One moment I look'd. Then I stole to the
    door,
I traversed the passage, and down at her side
    I was sitting, a moment more.

My thinking of her, or the music's strain,
    Or something which never will be exprest,
Had brought her back from the grave again,
    With the jasmine in her breast.

She is not dead, and she is not wed,
　　But she loves me now, and she loved me
　　　　then!
And the very first word that her sweet lips
　　said,
　　My heart grew youthful again.

The marchioness there, of Carabas.
　　She is wealthy, and young, and handsome
　　　　still;
And but for her — well, we'll let that pass;
　　She may marry whomever she will.

But I will marry my own first love,
　　With her primrose face, for old things are
　　　　best;
And the flower in her bosom, I prize it
　　above
　　The brooch in my lady's breast.

The world is filled with folly and sin,
　　And love must cling where it can, I say:
For beauty is easy enough to win;
　　But one isn't loved every day.

And I think, in the lives of most women and
　　men,
　　There's a moment when all would go
　　　　smooth and even,
If only the dead could find out when
　　To come back and be forgiven.

But O, the smell of that jasmine flower!
　And O, that music! and O, the way
That voice rang out from the donjon tower,
　　Non ti scordar di me,
　　　Non ti scordar di me!

Robert Bulwer-Lytton

Back to Griggsby's Station

Pap's got his patent right, and rich as all
　　creation;
　But where's the peace and comfort that
　　we all had had before?
Let's go a-visitin' back to Griggsby's
　　Station —
　Back where we ust to be so happy and so
　　pore!

The likes of us a-livin' here! It's jest a
　　mortal pity
　To see us in this great big house with
　　carpets on the stairs
And the pump right in the kitchen! And the
　　city, city, city!
　And nothin' but the city around us
　　everywhere.

Climb clean above the roof and look out
　　from the steeple,

And never see a robin, nor a beech nor
    elm tree!
Right there in earshot of at least a thousand
    people,
    And none that neighbors with us, or we
    want to go and see.

Let's go a-visitin' back to Griggsby's
    Station —
    Back where the latch string's a-hangin'
    from the door,
And every neighbor around the place as dear
    as a relation —
    Back where we ust to be so happy and so
    pore!

I want to see the Wiggenses, the whole kit
    and bilin',
    A-driven' up from Shaller Ford to stay the
    Sunday thru;
And I want to see them hitchin' at their son-
    in-law's and pilin'
    Out there at Liza Ellen's like they ust to
    do!

I want to see the piece-quilts the Jones girls
    is makin';
    And I want to pester Laura 'bout their
    freckled hired hand,
And joke her 'bout the widower she came
    pert nigh a-takin',

Till her pap got his pension 'lowed in
   time to save his land.

Let's go a-visitin' back to Griggsby's
      Station,
   Back where there's nothin' to aggrivate us
      any more,
Shet away safe about the whole location —
   Back where we ust to be so happy and so
      pore!

I want to see Mirandy and help her with her
      sewin',
   And hear her talk so lovin' of her man
      that's dead and gone,
And stand up with Emanuel and to show
      how he's a-growin',
   And smile as I have seen her 'fore she put
      her mounin' on.

What's in all this grand life and high
      situation,
   And nary a pink nor hollyhawk bloomin'
      at the door?
Let's go a-visitin' back to Griggsby's
      Station —
   Back where we ust to be so happy and so
      pore!

                              James Whitcomb Riley

52

Curfew Must Not Ring Tonight

Slowly England's sun was setting o'er the
    hilltops far away,
Filling all the land with beauty at the close
    of one sad day;
And the last rays kissed the forehead of a
    man and maiden fair,
He with footsteps slow and weary, she with
    sunny floating hair;
He with bowed head, sad and thoughtful,
    she with lips all cold and white,
Struggling to keep back the murmur,
    "Curfew must not ring tonight!"

"Sexton," Bessie's white lips faltered,
    pointing to the prison old,
With its turrets tall and gloomy, with its
    walls, dark, damp and cold —
"I've a lover in the prison, doomed this
    very night to die
At the ringing of the curfew, and no earthly
    help is nigh.
Cromwell will not come till sunset"; and her
    face grew strangely white
As she breathed the husky whisper,
    "Curfew must not ring tonight!"

"Bessie," calmly spoke the sexton — and
    his accents pierced her heart

Like the piercing of an arrow, like a deadly
    poisoned dart —
"Long, long years I've rung the curfew
    from that gloomy, shadowed tower;
Every evening, just at sunset, it has told the
    twilight hour;
I have done my duty ever, tried to do it just
    and right —
Now I'm old I still must do it: Curfew, girl,
    must ring tonight!"

Wild her eyes and pale her features, stern
    and white her thoughtful brow,
And within her secret bosom Bessie made a
    solemn vow.
She had listened while the judges read,
    without a tear or sigh,
"At the ringing of the curfew, Basil
    Underwood must die."
And her breath came fast and faster, and her
    eyes grew large and bright,
As in undertone she murmured, "Curfew
    must not ring tonight!"

With quick step she bounded forward,
    sprang within the old church door,
Left the old man threading slowly paths he'd
    often trod before;
Not one moment paused the maiden, but
    with eye and cheek aglow
Mounted up the gloomy tower, where the
    bell swung to and fro

As she climbed the dusty ladder, on which
  fell no ray of light,
Up and up, her white lips saying, "Curfew
  shall not ring tonight!"

She has reached the topmost ladder, o'er her
  hangs the great dark bell;
Awful is the gloom beneath her like the
  pathway down to hell;
Lo, the ponderous tongue is swinging. 'Tis
  the hour of curfew now,
And the sight has chilled her bosom,
  stopped her breath and paled her brow;
Shall she let it ring? No, never! Flash her
  eyes with sudden light,
And she springs and grasps it firmly:
  "Curfew shall not ring tonight!"

Out she swung, far out; the city seemed a
  speck of light below;
She 'twixt heaven and earth suspended as
  the bell swung to and fro;
And the sexton at the bell rope, old and
  deaf, heard not the bell,
But he thought it still was ringing fair young
  Basil's funeral knell.
Still the maiden clung more firmly, and,
  with trembling lips and white,
Said, to hush her heart's wild beating,
  "Curfew shall not ring tonight!"

It was o'er; the bell ceased swaying, and the
    maiden stepped once more
Firmly on the dark old ladder, where for
    hundred years before
Human foot had not been planted; but the
    brave deed she had done
Should be told long ages after — often as
    the setting sun
Should illume the sky with beauty, aged
    sires, with heads of white,
Long should tell the little children, "Curfew
    did not ring that night."

O'er the distant hills came Cromwell; Bessie
    sees him, and her brow,
Full of hope and full of gladness, has no
    anxious traces now.
At his feet she tells her story, shows her
    hands all bruised and torn;
And her face so sweet and pleading, yet
    with sorrow pale and worn,
Touched his heart with sudden pity — lit his
    eye with misty light;
"Go, your lover lives!" said Cromwell;
    "Curfew shall not ring tonight!"

Rose Hartwick Thorpe

Christmas at Sea

The sheets were frozen hard, and they cut
  the naked hand;
The decks were like a slide, where a seaman
  scarce could stand;
The wind was a nor'-wester, blowing
  squally off the sea;
And cliffs and spouting breakers were the
  only things a-lee.

They heard the surf a-roaring before the
  break of day;
But 'twas only with the peep of light we saw
  how ill we lay.
We tumbled every hand on deck instanter,
  with a shout,
And we gave her the maintops'l, and stood
  by to go about.

All day we tacked and tacked between the
  South Head and the North;
All day we hauled the frozen sheets, and got
  no further forth;
All day as cold as charity, in bitter pain and
  dread,
For very life and nature we tacked from
  head to head.

We gave the South a wider berth, for there
  the tide-race roared;

But every tack we made brought the North
    Head close aboard;
So's we saw the cliffs and houses, and the
    breakers running high,
And the coastguard in his garden, with his
    glass against his eye.

The frost was on the village roofs as white
    as ocean foam;
The good red fires were burning bright in
    every 'longshore home;
The windows sparkled clear, and the
    chimneys volleyed out;
And I vow we sniffed the victuals as the
    vessel went about.

The bells upon the church were rung with a
    mighty jovial cheer;
For it's just that I should tell you how (of all
    days in the year)
This day of our adversity was blessèd
    Christmas morn,
And the house above the coastguard's was
    the house where I was born.

O well I saw the pleasant room, the pleasant
    faces there,
My mother's silver spectacles, my father's
    silver hair;
And well I saw the firelight, like a flight of
    homely elves,

Go dancing round the china-plates that stand
  upon the shelves.

And well I knew the talk they had, the talk
  that was of me,
Of the shadow on the household and the son
  that went to sea;
And O the wicked fool I seemed, in every
  kind of way,
To be here and hauling frozen ropes on
  blessèd Christmas Day.

They lit the high sea-light, and the dark
  began to fall.
"All hands to loose topgallant sails," I
  heard the captain call.
"By the Lord, she'll never stand it," our
  first mate, Jackson, cried.
"It's the one way or the other, Mr.
  Jackson," he replied.

She staggered to her bearings, but the sails
  were new and good,
And the ship smelt up to windward, just as
  though she understood.
As the winter's day was ending, in the entry
  of the night,
We cleared the weary headland, and passed
  below the light.

And they heaved a mighty breath, every soul
  on board but me,

As they saw her nose again pointing
    handsome out to sea;
But all that I could think of, in the darkness
    and the cold,
Was just that I was leaving home and my
    folks were growing old.

Robert Louis Stevenson

The Ballad of East and West

Oh East is East, and West is West, and
    never the twain shall meet,
Till Earth and Sky stand presently at God's
    great Judgment Seat;
But there is neither East nor West, Border,
    nor Breed, nor Birth,
When two strong men stand face to face,
    tho' they come from the ends of the earth!

Kamal is out with twenty men to raise the
    Border side,
And he has lifted the Colonel's mare that is
    the Colonel's pride:
He has lifted her out of the stable-door
    between the dawn and the day,
And turned the calkins upon her feet, and
    ridden her far away.
Then up and spoke the Colonel's son that
    led a troop of the Guides:
"Is there never a man of all my men can say
    where Kamal hides?"

Then up and spoke Mahommed Khan, the
    son of the Ressaldar,
"If ye know the track of the morning-mist,
    ye know where his pickets are.
"At dusk he harries the Abazai — at dawn
    he is into Bonair,
"But he must go by Fort Bukloh to his own
    place to fare,
"So if ye gallop to Fort Bukloh as fast as a
    bird can fly,
"By the favor of God ye may cut him off,
    ere he win to the Tongue of Jagai,
"But if he be passed the Tongue of Jagai,
    right swiftly turn ye then,
"For the length and the breadth of that
    grisly plain is sown with Kamal's men.
"There is rock to the left, and rock to the
    right, and low, lean thorn between,
"And ye may hear a breech bolt snick where
    never a man is seen."
The Colonel's son has taken a horse, and a
    raw rough dun was he,
With the mouth of a bell and the heart of
    Hell, and the head of the gallows-tree.
The Colonel's son to the Fort has won, they
    bid him stay to eat —
Who rides at the tail of a Border thief, he
    sits not long at his meat.
He's up and away from Fort Bukloh as fast
    as he can fly,
Till he was aware of his father's mare in the
    gut of the Tongue of Jagai,

Till he was aware of his father's mare with
   Kamal upon her back,
And when he could spy the white of her
   eye, he made the pistol crack.
He has fired once, he has fired twice, but
   the whistling ball went wide.
"Ye shoot like a soldier," Kamal said.
   "Show now if ye can ride."
It's up and over the Tongue of Jagai, as
   blown dust-devils go,
The dun he fled like a stag of ten, but the
   mare like a barren doe.
The dun he leaned against the bit and
   slugged his head above,
But the red mare played with the snaffle-
   bars, as a maiden plays with a glove.
There was rock to the left and rock to the
   right, and low lean thorn between,
And thrice he heard a breech-bolt snick tho'
   never a man was seen.
They have ridden the low moon out of the
   sky, their hoofs drum up the dawn,
The dun he went like a wounded bull, but
   the mare like a new-roused fawn.
The dun he fell at a water-course — in a
   woful heap fell he,
And Kamal has turned the red mare back,
   and pulled the rider free.
He has knocked the pistol out of his hand —
   small room was there to strive,
" 'Twas only by favor of mine," quoth he,
   "ye rode so long alive:

"There was not a rock for twenty miles,
    there was not a clump of tree,
"But covered a man of my own men with
    his rifle cocked on his knee.
"If I had raised my bridle-hand, as I have
    held it low,
"The little jackals that flee so fast, were
    feasting all in a row:
"If I had bowed my head on my breast, as I
    have held it high,
"The kite that whistles above us now were
    gorged till she could not fly."
Lightly answered the Colonel's son: "Do
    good to bird and beast,
"But count who come for the broken meats
    before thou makest a feast.
"If there should follow a thousand swords to
    carry my bones away,
"Belike the price of a jackal's meal were
    more than a thief could pay.
"They will feed their horse on the standing
    crop, their men on the garnered grain,
"The thatch of the byres will serve their
    fires when all the cattle are slain.
"But if thou thinkest the price be fair, —
    thy brethen wait to sup,
"The hound is kin to the jackal-spawn, —
    howl, dog, and call them up!
"And if thou thinkest the price be high, in
    steer and gear and stack,
"Give me my father's mare again, and I'll
    fight my own way back!"

Kamal has gripped him by the hand and set
   him upon his feet.
"No talk shall be of dogs," said he, "when
   wolf and gray wolf meet.
"May I eat dirt if thou hast hurt of me in
   deed or breath;
"What dam of lances brought thee forth to
   jest at the dawn with Death?"
Lightly answered the Colonel's son: "I hold
   by the blood of my clan:
"Take up the mare for my father's gift —
   by God, she has carried a man!"
The red mare ran to the Colonel's son, and
   nuzzled against his breast;
"We be two strong men," said Kamal then,
   "but she loveth the younger best.
"So she shall go with a lifter's dower, my
   turquoise-studded rein,
"My broidered saddle and saddle-cloth, and
   silver stirrups twain."
The Colonel's son a pistol drew and held it
   muzzle-end,
"Ye have taken the one from a foe," said
   he; "will ye take the mate from a
   friend?"
"A gift for a gift," said Kamal straight; "a
   limb for the risk of a limb.
"Thy father has sent his son to me, I'll send
   my son to him!"
With that he whistled his only son, that
   dropped from a mountain-crest —

He trod the ling like a buck in spring, and
    he looked like a lance in rest.
"Now here is thy master," Kamal said,
    "who leads a troop of the Guides,
"And thou must ride at his left side as
    shield on shoulder rides.
"Till Death or I cut loose the tie, at camp
    and board and bed,
"Thy life is his — thy fate is to guard him
    with thy head.
"So thou must eat the White Queen's meat,
    and all her foes are thine,
"And thou must harry thy father's hold for
    the peace of the Borderline,
"And thou must make a trooper tough and
    hack thy way to power —
"Belike they will raise thee to Ressaldar
    when I am hanged in Peshawur."
They have looked each other between the
    eyes, and there they have found no fault,
They have taken the Oath of the Brother-in-
    Blood on leavened bread and salt;
They have taken the Oath of the Brother-in-
    Blood on fire and fresh-cut sod,
On the hilt and the haft of the Khyber knife,
    and the Wondrous Names of God.
The Colonel's son he rides the mare and
    Kamal's boy the dun,
And two have come back to Fort Bukloh
    where there went forth but one.
And when they drew to the Quarter-Guard,
    full twenty swords flew clear —

There was not a man but carried his feud
    with the blood of the mountaineer.
"Ha' done! ha' done!" said the Colonel's
    son. "Put up the steel at your sides!
"Last night ye had struck at a Border thief
    — tonight 'tis a man of the Guides!"

Oh East is East and West is West, and never
    the twain shall meet,
Till Earth and Sky stand presently at God's
    great Judgment Seat;
But there is neither East nor West, Border,
    nor Breed, nor Birth,
When two strong men stand face to face,
    tho' they come from the end of the earth.
                      Rudyard Kipling

Ballad of the Tempest

We were crowded in the cabin,
    Not a soul would dare to sleep, —
It was midnight on the waters,
    And a storm was on the deep.

'Tis a fearful thing in Winter
    To be shattered in the blast,
And to hear the rattling trumpet
    Thunder: "Cut away the mast!"

So we shuddered there in silence, —
    For the stoutest held his breath,

While the hungry sea was roaring,
  And the breakers talked with Death.

As thus we sat in darkness,
  Each one busy in his prayers,
"We are lost!" the captain shouted
  As he staggered down the stairs.

But his little daughter whispered,
  As she took his icy hand:
"Isn't God upon the ocean
  Just the same as on the land?"

Then we kissed the little maiden,
  And we spoke in better cheer,
And we anchored safe in harbor
  When the morn was shining clear.
                              James T. Fields

The Cremation of Sam McGee

*There are strange things done in the
  midnight sun
By the men who moil for gold;
The Arctic trails have their secret tales
That would make your blood run cold;
The Northern Lights have seen queer sights,
But the queerest they ever did see
Was the night on the marge of Lake Lebarge
I cremated Sam McGee.*

Now Sam McGee was from Tennessee,
   where the cotton blooms and blows,
Why he left his home in the South to roam
   'round the Pole, God only knows.
He was always cold, but the land of gold
   seemed to hold him like a spell;
Though he'd often say in his homely way
   that "he'd sooner live in hell."

On a Christmas day we were mushing our
   way over the Dawson trail.
Talk of your cold! through the parka's fold
   it stabbed like a driven nail.
If our eyes we'd close, then the lashes froze
   till sometimes we couldn't see;
It wasn't much fun, but the only one to
   whimper was Sam McGee.

And that very night, as we lay packed tight
   in our robes beneath the snow,
And the dogs were fed, and the stars
   o'erhead were dancing heel and toe,
He turned to me, and "Cap," says he, "I'll
   cash in this trip, I guess;
And if I do, I'm asking that you won't
   refuse my last request."

Well, he seemed so low that I couldn't say
   no; then he says with a sort of moan:
"It's the cursed cold, and it's got right hold
   till I'm chilled clean through to the bone.

Yet 'tain't being dead — it's my awful
  dread of the icy grave that pains;
So I want you to swear that, foul or fair,
  you'll cremate my last remains.''

A pal's last need is a thing to heed, so I
  swore I would not fail;
And we started on at the streak of dawn; but
  God! he looked ghastly pale.
He crouched on the sleigh, and he raved all
  day of his home in Tennessee;
And before nightfall a corpse was all that
  was left of Sam McGee.

There wasn't a breath in that land of death,
  and I hurried, horror-driven,
With a corpse half hid that I couldn't get
  rid, because of a promise given;
It was lashed to the sleigh, and it seemed to
  say: ''You may tax your brawn and
  brains,
But you promised true, and it's up to you to
  cremate these last remains.''

Now a promise made is a debt unpaid, and
  the trail has its own stern code.
In the days to come, though my lips were
  dumb, in my heart how I cursed that load.
In the long, long night, by the lone firelight,
  while the huskies, round in a ring,
Howled out their woes to the homeless
  snows — O God! how I loathed the thing.

And every day that quiet clay seemed to
   heavy and heavier grow;
And on I went, though the dogs were spent
   and the grub was getting low;
The trail was bad, and I felt half mad, but I
   swore I would not give in;
And I'd often sing to the hateful thing, and
   it hearkened with a grin.

Till I came to the marge of Lake Lebarge,
   and a derelict there lay;
It was jammed in the ice, but I saw in a
   trice it was called the "Alice May."
And I looked at it, and I thought a bit, and I
   looked at my frozen chum;
Then "Here," said I, with a sudden cry, "is
   my cre-ma-to-re-um."

Some planks I tore from the cabin floor, and
   I lit the boiler fire;
Some coal I found that was lying around,
   and I heaped the fuel higher;
The flames just soared, and the furnace
   roared — such a blaze you seldom see;
And I burrowed a hole in the glowing coal,
   and I stuffed in Sam McGee.

Then I made a hike, for I didn't like to hear
   him sizzle so;
And the heavens scowled, and the huskies
   howled, and the wind began to blow.

It was icy cold, but the hot sweat rolled
  down my cheeks, and I don't know why;
And the greasy smoke in an inky cloak went
  streaking down the sky.

I do not know how long in the snow I
  wrestled with grisly fear;
But the stars came out and they danced
  about ere again I ventured near;
I was sick with dread, but I bravely said:
  "I'll just take a peep inside.
I guess he's cooked, and it's time I
  looked," . . . . then the door I opened
  wide.

And there sat Sam, looking cold and calm,
  in the heart of the furnace roar;
And he wore a smile you could see a mile,
  and he said: "Please close that door.
It's fine in here, but I greatly fear you'll let
  in the cold and storm —
Since I left Plumtree down in Tennessee, it's
  the first time I've been warm."

There are strange things done in the
  midnight sun
By the men who moil for gold;
The Arctic trails have their secret tales
That would make your blood run cold;
The Northern Lights have seen queer sights,
But the queerest they ever did see

Was that night on the marge of Lake Lebarge
I cremated Sam McGee!

Robert W. Service

The Spell of the Yukon

I wanted the gold, and I sought it;
   I scrabbled and mucked like a slave.
Was it famine or scurvy — I fought it;
   I hurled my youth into a grave.
I wanted the gold, and I got it —
   Came out with a fortune last fall —
Yet somehow life's not what I thought it,
   And somehow the gold isn't all.

No! There's the land. (Have you seen it?)
   It's the cussedest land that I know,
From the big, dizzy mountains that screen it
   To the deep, deathlike valleys below.
Some say God was tired when He made it;
   Some say it's a fine land to shun;
Maybe; but there's some as would trade it
   For no land on earth — and I'm one.

You come to get rich (damned good reason);
   You feel like an exile at first;
You hate it like hell for a season,
   And then you are worse than the worst.
It grips you like some kinds of sinning;

It twists you from foe to a friend;
It seems it's been since the beginning;
It seems it will be to the end.

I've stood in some mighty-mouthed hollow
That's plumb-full of hush to the brim;
I've watched the big, husky sun wallow
In crimson and gold, and grow dim,
Till the moon set the pearly peaks gleaming,
And the stars tumbled out, neck and crop;
And I've thought that I surely was
dreaming,
With the peace o' the world piled on top.

The summer — no sweeter was ever;
The sunshiny woods all athrill;
The grayling aleap in the river,
The bighorn asleep on the hill.
The strong life that never knows harness;
The wilds where the caribou call;
The freshness, the freedom, the farness —
O God! how I'm stuck on it all.

The winter! the brightness that blinds you,
The white land locked tight as a drum,
The cold fear that follows and finds you,
The silence that bludgeons you dumb.
The snows that are older than history,
The woods where the weird shadows
slant;
The stillness, the moonlight, the mystery,
I've bade 'em good-bye — but I can't.

There's a land where the mountains are
    nameless,
  And the rivers all run God knows where;
There are lives that are erring and aimless,
  And deaths that just hang by a hair;
There are hardships that nobody reckons;
  There are valleys unpeopled and still;
There's a land — oh, it beckons and
    beckons,
  And I want to go back — and I will.

They're making my money diminish;
  I'm sick of the taste of champagne.
Thank God! when I'm skinned to a finish
  I'll pike to the Yukon again.
I'll fight — and you bet it's no sham-fight;
  It's hell! — but I've been there before;
And it's better than this by a damsite —
  So me for the Yukon once more.

There's gold, and it's haunting and haunting;
  It's luring me on as of old;
Yet it isn't the gold that I'm wanting
  So much as just finding the gold.
It's the great, big, broad land 'way up
    yonder,
  It's the forests where silence has lease;
It's the beauty that thrills me with wonder,
  It's the stillness that fills me with peace.

Robert W. Service

Darius Green and His Flying-Machine

If ever there lived a Yankee lad,
Wise or otherwise, good or bad,
Who, seeing the birds fly, didn't jump
With flapping arms from stake or stump,
   Or, spreading the tail
   Of his coat for a sail
Take a soaring leap from post or rail,
   And wonder why
   He couldn't fly,
And flap and flutter and wish and try —
If ever you knew a country dunce
Who didn't try that as often as once,
All I can say is, that's a sign
He never would do for a hero of mine.

An aspiring genius was D. Green:
The son of a farmer, age fourteen;
His body was long and lank and lean —
Just right for flying, as will be seen;
He had two eyes as bright as a bean,
And a freckled nose that grew between,
A little awry — for I must mention
That he riveted his attention
Upon his wonderful invention,
Twisting his tongue as he twisted the
   strings,
And working his face as he worked the
   wings,
And with every turn of gimlet and screw

Turning and screwing his mouth round, too,
  Till his nose seemed bent
  To catch the scent,
Around some corner, of new-baked pies,
And his wrinkled cheeks and his squinting
   eyes
Grew puckered into a queer grimace,
That made him look very droll in the face,
  And also very wise.

And wise he must have been, to do more
Than ever a genius did before,
Excepting Dædalus of yore
And his son Icarus, who wore
  Upon their backs
  Those wings of wax
He had read of in the old almanacs.
Darius was clearly of the opinion
That the air was also man's dominion,
And that, with paddle or fin or pinion,
  We soon or late shall navigate
The azure as now we sail the sea.
The thing looks simple enough to me;
  And if you doubt it,
Hear how Darius reasoned about it:

  "The birds can fly an' why can't I?
  Must we give in," says he with a grin,
  "That the bluebird an' phoebe
  Are smarter'n we be?
Jest fold our hands an' see the swaller
An' blackbird an' catbird beat us holler?

Does the little chatterin', sassy wren,
No bigger'n my thumb, know more than
    men?
    Jest show me that!
    Ur prove't the bat
Hez got more brains than's in my hat,
An' I'll back down, an' not till then!''

He argued further: ''Nur I can't see
What's the use o' wings to a bumble-bee,
Fur to get a livin' with, more'n to me; —
    Ain't my business
    Important's his'n is?
    That Icarus
    Made a perty muss —
Him an' his daddy Dædalus
They might 'a' knowed wings made o' wax
Wouldn't stand sun-heat an' hard whacks.
    I'll make mine o' luther,
    Or suthin' or other.''

And he said to himself as he tinkered and
    planned:
''But I ain't goin' to show my hand
To nummies that never can understand
    The fust idee that's big an' grand.''
They'd 'a' laft an' made fun
O' Creation itself afore 'twas done!''
So he kept his secret from all the rest,
Safely buttoned within his vest;
And in the loft above the shed
Himself he locks, with thimble and thread

And wax and hammer and buckles and
    screws,
And all such things as geniuses use; —
Two bats for a pattern, curious fellows!
A charcoal-pot and a pair of bellows;
An old hoop-skirt or two, as well as
Some wire and several old umbrellas;
A carriage cover, for tail and wings;
A piece of harness; and straps and strings;
    And a big strong box,
    In which he locks
These and a hundred other things.

His grinning brothers, Reuben and Burke
And Nathan and Jotham and Solomon, lurk
Around the corner and see him work —
Sitting cross-legged, like a Turk,
Drawing the wax-end through with a jerk,
And boring the holes with a comical quirk
Of his wise old head, and a knowing smirk.
But vainly they mounted each other's backs,
And poked through knot-holes and pried
    through cracks;
With wood from the pile and straw from the
    stacks
He plugged the knot-holes and caulked the
    cracks;
And a dipper of water, which one would
    think
He had brought up in the loft to drink
    When he chanced to be dry,
    Stood always nigh,

For Darius was sly!
And whenever at work he happened to spy
At chink or crevice a blinking eye,
He let the dipper of water fly.

"Take that! an' ef ever ye get a peep,
Guess ye'll ketch a weasel asleep!"
    And he sings as he locks
    His big strong box:
        "The weasel's head is small and trim,
        An' he's little an' long an' slim,
        An' quick of motion an' nimble of
        limb,
            An' ef you'll be
            Advised by me,
        Keep wide awake when you're ketchin'
        him!"

    So day after day
He stitched and tinkered and hammered
        away,
    Till at last 'twas done —
The greatest invention under the sun!
"An' now," says Darius, "hooray fur some
    fun!"

    'Twas the Fourth of July,
    And the weather was dry,
And not a cloud was on all the sky,
Save a few light fleeces, which here and
        there,
    Half mist, half air,

Like foam on the ocean went floating by —
Just as lovely a morning as ever was seen
For a nice little trip in a flying-machine.

Thought cunning Darius: "Now I shan't go
Along 'ith the fellers to see the show.
I'll say I've got sich a terrible cough!
And then, when the folks 'ave all gone off
I'll have full swing fur to try the thing,
An' practice a little on the wing."

"Ain't goin' to see the celebration?"
Says brother Nate. "No: botheration!
I've got such a cold — a toothache — I —
My gracious! feel's though I should fly!"
    Said Jotham, "Sho!
    Guess ye better go."
    But Darius said, "No!
Shouldn't wonder 'f you might see me,
        though,
'Long 'bout noon, if I get red
O' this jumpin', thumpin' pain 'n my
        head."
For all the while to himself he said:
    "I tell ye what!
I'll fly a few times around the lot,
To see how't seems, then soon's I've got
The hang o' the thing, ez likely's not,
    I'll astonish the nation,
    An' all creation,
By flyin' over the celebration!
    Over their heads I'll sail like an eagle;

80

I'll balance myself on my wings like a sea-
    gull.
I'll dance on the chimbleys; I'll stand on the
    steeple;
I'll flop up to windows and scare the people!
I'll light on the liberty-pole an' crow;
An' I'll say to the gawpin' fools below,
    'What world's this 'ere
    That I've come near?'
Fur I'll make 'em b'lieve I'm a chap f'm the
    moon;
An' I'll try a race 'ith their ol' balloon!''

    He crept from his bed;
And, seeing the others were gone, he said,
''I'm gittin' over the cold'n my head.''
    Away he sped,
To open the wonderful box in the shed.

His brothers had walked but a little way,
When Jotham to Nathan chanced to say,
''What is the feller up to, hey?''
''Don'o' — the's suthin' ur other to pay,
Ur he wouldn't 'a' stayed to hum today.''
Says Burke, ''His toothache's all'n his eye!
He never'd miss a F'oth-o-July
Ef he hadn't got some machine to try.''
Then Sol, the little one, spoke: ''By darn!
Le's hurry back an' hide'n the barn,
An' pay him fur tellin' us that yarn!''
''Agreed!'' Through the orchard they creep
    back,

Along by the fences, behind the stack,
And one by one, through a hole in the wall,
Dressed in their Sunday garments and all;
And a very astonishing sight was that,
When each in his cobwebbed coat and hat
Came up through the floor like an ancient
     rat.

    And there they hid;
    And Reuben slid
The fastenings back, and the door undid.
"Keep dark!" said he,
"While I squint an' see what the' is to
     see."

As knights of old put on their mail —
    From head to foot an iron suit,
Iron jacket and iron boot,
Iron breeches, and on the head
No hat, but an iron pot instead,
    And under the chin the bail,
(I believe they call the thing a helm),
Then sallied forth to overwhelm
The dragons and pagans that plague the
     realm —
    So this *modern* knight
    Prepared for flight,
Put on his wings and strapped them tight;
Jointed and jaunty, strong and light —
Buckled them fast to shoulder and hip;
Ten feet they measured from tip to tip!
And a helmet had he, but that he wore,

Not on his head, like those of yore,
  But more like the helm of a ship.

  "Hush!" Reuben said,
  "He's up in the shed!
He's opened the winder — I see his head!
He stretches it out, an' pokes it about,
Lookin' to see 'f the coast is clear,
  An' nobody near —
Guess he don'o' who's hid in here!
He's riggin' a spring-board over the sill!
Stop laffin', Solomon! Burke, keep still!
He's a-climbin' out now — Of all the
    things!
What's he got on? I van, it's wings!
An' that 'tother thing? I vum, it's a tail!
An' there he sets like a hawk on a rail!
Steppin' careful, he travels the length
Of his spring-board, and teeters to try its
    strength,
Now he stretches his wings, like a
    monstrous bat;
Peeks over his shoulder, this way an' that,
Fur to see 'f the' 's any one passin' by;
But the' 's on'y a ca'f an' a goslin' nigh.
They turn up at him a wonderin' eye,
To see — The Dragon! he's goin' to fly!
Away he goes! Jimminy! what a jump!
  Flop — flop — an' plump
  To the ground with a thump!
Flutt'rin' an' flound'rin', all'n a lump!"

As a demon is hurled by an angel's spear,
Heels over head, to his proper sphere —
Heels over head, and head over heels,
Dizzily down the abyss he wheels —
So fell Darius. Upon his crown,
In the midst of the barn-yard he came down,
In a wonderful whirl of tangled strings,
Broken braces and broken springs,
Broken tail and broken wings,
Shooting stars, and various things;
Barn-yard litter of straw and chaff,
And much that wasn't so sweet by half.
Away with a bellow fled the calf,
And what was that? Did the gosling laugh?
'Tis a merry roar from the old barn-door,
And he hears the voice of Jotham crying,
"Say, Darius! how do you like flyin'?"
Slowly, ruefully where he lay,
Darius just turned and looked that way,
As he staunched his sorrowful nose with his
        cuff.
"Wal, I like flyin' well enough,"
He said; "but the' ain't sich a thunderin'
        sight
O' fun in't when ye come to light."

I have just room for the moral here:
And this is the moral — Stick to your sphere.
Or if you insist, as you have a right,
On spreading your wings for a loftier flight,
The moral is — Take care how you light.
John Townsend Trowbridge

The Barrel-Organ

There's a barrel-organ caroling across a
      golden street
   In the City as the sun sinks low;
And the music's not immortal; but the world
      has made it sweet
   And fulfilled it with the sunset glow;
And it pulses through the pleasures of the
      City and the pain
   That surround the singing organ like a
      large eternal light;
And they've given it a glory and a part to
      play again
   In the Symphony that rules the day and
      night.
And now it's marching onward through the
      realms of old romance,
   And trolling out a fond familiar tune,
And now it's roaring cannon down to fight
      the King of France,
   And now it's prattling softly to the moon.
And all around the organ there's a sea
      without a shore
   Of human joys and wonders and regrets;
To remember and to recompense the music
      evermore
   For what the cold machinery forgets . . .

      Yes; as the music changes,
         Like a prismatic glass,

It takes the light and ranges
　　Through all the moods that pass:
Dissects the common carnival
　　Of passions and regrets,
And gives the world a glimpse of all
　　The colors it forgets.

And there *La Traviata* sighs
　　Another sadder song;
And there *Il Trovatore* cries
　　A tale of deeper wrong;
And bolder knights to battle go
　　With sword and shield and lance,
Than ever here on earth below
　　Have whirled into — a dance! —

Go down to Kew in lilac-time, in lilac-time,
　　in lilac-time;
　　Go down to Kew in lilac-time (it isn't far
　　from London!)
And you shall wander hand in hand with
　　love in summer's wonderland;
　　Go down to Kew in lilac-time (it isn't far
　　from London!)

The cherry-trees are seas of bloom and soft
　　perfume and sweet perfume,
　　The cherry-trees are seas of bloom (and
　　oh, so near to London!)
And there they say, when dawn is high and
　　all the world's a blaze of sky

The cuckoo, though he's very shy, will
   sing a song for London.

The nightingale is rather rare and yet they
   say you'll hear him there
   At Kew, at Kew in lilac-time (and oh, so
   near to London!)
The linnet and the throstle, too, and after
   dark the long halloo
   And golden-eyed *tu-whit, tu-whoo* of owls
   that ogle London.

For Noah hardly knew a bird of any kind
   that isn't heard
   At Kew, at Kew in lilac-time (and oh, so
   near to London!)
And when the rose begins to pout and all the
   chestnut spires are out
   You'll hear the rest without a doubt, all
   chorusing for London: —

Come down to Kew in lilac-time, in lilac-
   time, in lilac-time;
   Come down to Kew in lilac-time (it isn't
   far from London!)
And you shall wander hand in hand with
   love in summer's wonderland;
   Come down to Kew in lilac-time (it isn't
   far from London!)

And then the troubadour begins to thrill the
   golden street,

In the City as the sun sinks low;
And in all the gaudy busses there are scores
　　of weary feet
Marking time, sweet time, with a dull
　　mechanic beat,
And a thousand hearts are plunging to a love
　　they'll never meet,
Through the meadows of the sunset, through
　　the poppies and the wheat,
　In the land where the dead dreams go.

Verdi, Verdi, when you wrote *Il Trovatore*
　　did you dream
　Of the City when the sun sinks low,
Of the organ and the monkey and the many-
　　colored stream
On the Piccadilly pavement, of the myriad
　　eyes that seem
To be litten for a moment with a wild Italian
　　gleam
As *A che la morte* parodies the world's
　　eternal theme
　And pulses with the sunset-glow?

There's a thief, perhaps, that listens with a
　　face of frozen stone
　In the City as the sun sinks low;
There's a portly man of business with a
　　balance of his own,
There's a clerk and there's a butcher of a
　　soft reposeful tone,

And they're all of them returning to the
    heavens they have known:
They are crammed and jammed in busses
    and — they're each of them alone
    In the land where the dead dreams go.

There's a very modish woman and her smile
    is very bland
    In the City as the sun sinks low;
And her hansom jingles onward, but her
    little jeweled hand
Is clenched a little tighter and she cannot
    understand
What she wants or why she wanders to that
    undiscovered land,
For the parties there are not at all the sort of
    thing she planned,
    In the land where the dead dreams go.

There's a rowing man that listens and his
    heart is crying out
    In the City as the sun sinks low;
For the barge, the eight, the Isis, and the
    coach's whoop and shout,
For the minute-gun, the counting and the
    long dishevelled rout,
For the howl along the tow-path and a fate
    that's still in doubt,
For a roughened oar to handle and a race to
    think about
    In the land where the dead dreams go.

There's a laborer that listens to the voices of
	the dead
	In the City as the sun sinks low;
And his hand begins to tremble and his face
	is rather red
As he sees a loafer watching him and —
	there he turns his head
And stares into the sunset where his April
	love is fled,
For he hears her softly singing and his
	lonely soul is led
	Through the land where the dead dreams
	go . . .

There's an old and haggard demi-rep, it's
	ringing in her ears,
	In the City as the sun sinks low;
With the wild and empty sorrow of the love
	that blights and sears,
Oh, and if she hurries onward, then be sure,
	be sure she hears,
Hears and bears the bitter burden of the
	unforgotten years,
And her laugh's a little harsher and her eyes
	are brimmed with tears
	For the land where the dead dreams go.

There's a barrel-organ caroling across a
	golden street
	In the City as the sun sinks low;
Though the music's only Verdi there's a
	world to make it sweet

Just as yonder yellow sunset where the earth
    and heaven meet
Mellows all the sooty City! Hark, a hundred
    thousand feet
Are marching on to glory through the
    poppies and the wheat
In the land where the dead dreams go.

    So it's Jeremiah, Jeremiah,
      What have you to say
    When you meet the garland girls
      Tripping on their way?
    All around my gala hat
      I wear a wreath of roses
    (A long and lonely year it is
      I've waited for the May!)
    If any one should ask you,
      The reason why I wear it is —
    My own love, my true love, is
      coming home today.

And it's buy a bunch of violets for the lady
    (It's lilac-time in London; it's lilac-
    time in London!)
Buy a bunch of violets for the lady;
    While the sky burns blue above:

On the other side the street you'll find it
    shady
    (It's lilac-time in London; it's lilac-
    time in London!)
But buy a bunch of violets for the lady,

And tell her she's your own true love.
There's a barrel-organ caroling across a
  golden street
  In the City as the sun sinks glittering
    and slow;
And the music's not immortal; but the
    world has made it sweet
And enriched it with the harmonies that
    make a song complete
In the deeper heavens of music where
    the night and morning meet,
  As it dies into the sunset glow;
And it pulses through the pleasures of
    the City and the pain
  That surround the singing organ like a
    large eternal light,
And they've given it a glory and a part
    to play again
  In the Symphony that rules the day
    and night.

And there, as the music changes,
  The song runs round again;
Once more it turns and ranges
  Through all its joy and pain:
Dissects the common carnival
  Of passions and regrets;
And the wheeling world remembers all
  The wheeling song forgets.
Once more *La Traviata* sighs
  Another sadder song:

Once more *Il Trovatore* cries
    A tale of deeper wrong;
Once more the knights to battle go
    With sword and shield and lance
Till once, once more, the shattered foe
    Has whirled into — a dance!

Come down to Kew in lilac-time, in lilac-
    time, in lilac-time;
Come down to Kew in lilac-time (it isn't far
    from London!)
And you shall wander hand in hand with
    Love in summer's wonderland,
Come down to Kew in lilac-time (it isn't far
    from London!)

                    Alfred Noyes

Love and Friendship

Love Not Me

Love not me for comely grace,
For my pleasing eye or face,
Nor for any outward part:
No, nor for a constant heart!
For these may fail or turn to ill:
   So thou and I shall sever.
Keep therefore a true woman's eye,
And love me still, but know not why!
So hast thou the same reason still
   To doat upon me ever.

Unknown

My Love in Her Attire

My love in her attire doth show her wit,
   It doth so well become her:
For every season she hath dressings fit,
   For winter, spring, and summer.
No beauty she doth miss,
When all her robes are on:
But Beauty's self she is,
When all her robes are gone.

Unknown

Sonnet

Men call you fair, and you do credit it,
For that yourself ye daily such do see:
But the true fair, that is the gentle wit
And virtuous mind, is much more praised of
    me:
For all the rest, however fair it be,
Shall turn to naught and lose that glorious
    hue;
But only that is permanent and free
From frail corruption that doth flesh ensue.
That is true beauty; that doth argue you
To be divine, and born of heavenly seed;
Derived from that fair Spirit from whom all
    true
And perfect beauty did at first proceed:
  He only fair, and what he fair hath made;
  All other fair, like flowers, untimely fade.
                        Edmund Spenser

One Day I Wrote Her Name

One day I wrote her name upon the strand,
But came the waves and washed it away:
Again I wrote it with a second hand,
But came the tide and made my pains his
    prey.
"Vain man," said she, "that dost in vain
    essay

A mortal thing so to immortalize;
For I myself shall like to this decay,
And eke my name be wipèd out likewise.''
''Not so,'' quoth I; ''let baser things devise
To die in dust, but you shall live by fame;
My verse your virtues rare shall eternize,
And in the heavens write your glorious
    name:
Where, whenas Death shall all the world
    subdue,
Our love shall live, and later life renew.''
                   Edmund Spenser

Loving in Truth

Loving in truth, and fain in verse my love to
    show,
That she, dear she, might take some
    pleasure of my pain,
Pleasure might cause her read, reading might
    make her know,
Knowledge might pity win, and pity grace
    obtain, —
I sought fit words to paint the blackest face
    of woe;
Studying inventions fine, her wits to
    entertain,
Oft turning others' leaves to see if thence
    would flow
Some fresh and fruitful showers upon my
    sun-burned brain.

But words came halting forth, wanting
    invention's stay;
Invention, nature's child, fled step-dame
    Study's blows,
And others' feet still seemed but strangers in
    my way.
Thus, great with child to speak, and helpless
    in my throes,
Biting my truant pen, beating myself for
    spite,
Fool, said my muse to me, look in thy heart
    and write.

                    Sir Philip Sidney

Farewell to Love

Since there's no help, come let us kiss and
    part;
Nay I have done, you get no more of me;
And I am glad, yea, glad with all my heart,
That thus so cleanly I myself can free;
Shake hands for ever, cancel all our vows,
And when we meet at any time again,
Be it not seen in either of our brows
That we one jot of former love retain.
Now at the last gasp of love's latest breath,
When his pulse failing, passion speechless
    lies,
When faith is kneeling by his bed of death,
And innocence is closing up his eyes,

Now if thou would'st, when all have given
   him over,
From death to life thou might'st him yet
   recover.

                      Michael Drayton

Helen

Was this the face that launched a thousand
   ships,
And burned the topless towers of Ilium? —
Sweet Helen, make me immortal with a
   kiss! —
Her lips suck forth my soul: see where it
   flees! —
Come, Helen, come, give me my soul again.
Here will I dwell, for heaven is in these
   lips,
And all is dross that is not Helena.
I will be Paris, and for love of thee,
Instead of Troy, shall Wittenberg be sacked,
And I will combat with weak Menelaus,
And wear thy colours on my plumèd crest;
Yes, I will wound Achilles in the heel,
And then return to Helen for a kiss.
Oh, thou art fairer than the evening air
Clad in the beauty of a thousand stars;
Brighter art thou than flaming Jupiter
When he appeared to hapless Semele;
More lovely than the monarch of the sky

In wanton Arethusa's azured arms;
And none but thou shalt be my paramour!

From
*The Tragical History
of Dr. Faustus*
Christopher Marlowe

Who Ever Loved, That Loved Not at First Sight?

It lies not in our power to love or hate,
For will in us is overruled by fate.
When two are stripped, long ere the course
  begin,
We wish that one should lose, the other win;
And one especially do we affect
Of two gold ingots, like in each respect:
The reason no man knows; let it suffice
What we behold is censured by our eyes.
Where both deliberate, the love is slight:
Who ever loved, that loved not at first sight?

From *Hero and Leander*
Christopher Marlowe

Who Is Silvia?

Who is Silvia? what is she,
  That all our swains commend her?
Holy, fair, and wise is she;

The heaven such grace did lend her,
That she might admiréd be.

Is she kind as she is fair?
For beauty lives with kindness.
Love doth to her eyes repair,
To help him of his blindness,
And, being help'd, inhabits there.

Then to Silvia let us sing,
That Silvia is excelling;
She excels each mortal thing
Upon the dull earth dwelling:
To her let us garlands bring.

William Shakespeare

Not Marble, nor the Gilded Monuments

Not marble, nor the gilded monuments
Of princes, shall outlive this powerful
rhyme;
But you shall shine more bright in these
contents
Than unswept stone besmear'd with sluttish
time.
When wasteful war shall statues overturn,
And broils root out the work of masonry,
Nor Mars his sword nor war's quick fire
shall burn
The living record of your memory.

'Gainst death and all-oblivious enmity
Shall you pace forth; your praise shall still
   find room
Even in the eyes of all posterity
That wears this world out to the ending
   doom.
So, till the judgment that yourself arise,
You live in this, and dwell in lovers' eyes.
                  William Shakespeare

When I Have Seen by Time's Fell Hand

When I have seen by Time's fell hand
   defaced
The rich proud cost of outworn buried age;
When sometime lofty towers I see down-
   razed
And brass eternal slave to mortal rage;
When I have seen the hungry ocean gain
Advantage on the kingdom of the shore,
And the firm soil win of the watery main,
Increasing store with loss and loss with
   store;

When I have seen such interchange of state,
Or state itself confounded to decay;
Ruin hath taught me thus to ruminate,
That Time will come and take my love
   away.

This thought is as a death, which cannot
    choose
But weep to have that which it fears to lose.
                    William Shakespeare

When in the Chronicle of Wasted Time

When in the chronicle of wasted time
I see descriptions of the fairest wights,
And beauty making beautiful old rhyme
In praise of ladies dead and lovely knights,
Then, in the blazon of sweet beauty's best,
Of hand, of foot, of lip, of eye, of brow,
I see their antique pen would have express'd
Even such a beauty as you master now.
So all their praises are but prophecies
Of this our time, all you prefiguring;
And, for they look'd but with divining eyes,
They had not skill enough your worth to
        sing:
    For we, which now behold these present
        days,
    Have eyes to wonder, but lack tongues to
        praise.
                    William Shakespeare

When I Consider Everything That Grows

When I consider every thing that grows
Holds in perfection but a little moment,
That this huge stage presenteth naught but
    shows
Whereon the stars in secret influence
    comment;
When I perceive that men as plants increase,
Cheerèd and checked even by the self-same
    sky,
Vaunt in their youthful sap, at height
    decrease,
And wear their brave state out of memory:
Then the conceit of this inconstant stay
Sets you most rich in youth before my sight.
Where wasteful Time debateth with Decay,
To change your day of youth to sullied night;
    And all in war with Time for love of you,
    As he takes from you, I engraft you new.
                   William Shakespeare

The Flea

Mark but this flea, and mark in this,
How little that which thou deny'st me is;
It sucked me first, and now sucks thee,
And in this flea our two bloods mingled be;

Thou know'st that this cannot be said
A sin, nor shame, nor loss of maidenhead;
   Yet this enjoys before it woo,
   And pampered swells with one blood
     made of two,
   And this, alas, is more than we would do.

Oh stay, three lives in one flea spare,
Where we almost, yea, more than married
     are.
This flea is you and I, and this
Our marriage bed, and marriage temple is;
Though parents grudge, and you, w' are
     met,
And cloistered in these living walls of jet.
   Though use make you apt to kill me,
   Let not to that, self-murder added be,
   And sacrilege, three sins in killing three.

Cruel and sudden, hast thou since
Purpled thy nail in blood of innocence?
Wherein could this flea guilty be,
Except in that drop which it sucked from
     thee?
Yet thou triumph'st and say'st that thou
Find'st not thyself, nor me the weaker now;
   'Tis true, then learn how false fears be:
   Just so much honor, when thou yield'st to
     me,
   Will waste, as this flea's death took life
     from thee.

John Donne

A Valediction Forbidding Mourning

As virtuous men pass mildly away,
   And whisper to their souls to go,
Whilst some of their sad friends do say,
   The breath goes now, and some say, No:

So let us melt, and make no noise,
   No tear-floods, nor sigh-tempests move;
'Twere profanation of our joys
   To tell the laity our love.

Moving of th' earth brings harms and fears,
   Men reckon what it did, and meant;
But trepidation of the spheres,
   Though greater far, is innocent.

Dull sublunary lovers' love
   — Whose soul is sense — cannot admit
Absence, because it doth remove
   Those things which elemented it.

But we by a love so much refined
   That ourselves know not what it is,
Inter-assurèd of the mind,
   Care less eyes, lips and hands to miss.

Our two souls therefore, which are one,
   Though I must go, endure not yet
A breach, but an expansion,
   Like gold to airy thinness beat.

If they be two, they are two so
　　As stiff twin compasses are two;
Thy soul, the fix'd foot, makes no show
　　To move, but doth, if th' other do.

And though it in the centre sit,
　　Yet, when the other far doth roam,
It leans, and hearkens after it,
　　And grows erect, as that comes home.

Such wilt thou be to me, who must,
　　Like th' other foot, obliquely run;
Thy firmness makes my circle just,
　　And makes me end where I begun.

John Donne

The Canonization

For God's sake hold your tongue, and let me
　　　love,
　　Or chide my palsy, or my gout,
My five gray hairs, or ruined fortune flout;
With wealth your state, your mind with arts
　　　improve;
　　Take you a course, get you a place,
　　Observe his Honour, or his Grace,
And the King's real, or his stamped face
　　Contemplate; what you will, approve,
　　　So you will let me love.

Alas, alas, who's injured by my love?
    What merchant's ships have my sighs
            drowned?
Who says my tears have overflowed his
            ground?
When did my colds a forward spring
            remove?
    When did the heats which my veins fill
    Add one man to the plaguy Bill?
Soldiers find wars, and lawyers find out still
    Litigious men, which quarrels move,
        Though she and I do love.

Call us what you will, we're made such by
            love;
    Call her one, me another fly,
We're tapers too, and at our own cost die,
And we in us find the Eagle and the Dove;
    The Phoenix riddle hath more wit
    By us; we two, being one, are it,
So, to one neutral thing both sexes fit.
    We die and rise the same, and prove
        Mysterious by this love.

We can die by it, if not live by love,
    And if unfit for tombs or hearse
Our legend be, it will be fit for verse;
And if no piece of chronicle we prove,
    We'll build in sonnets pretty rooms;
    As well a well-wrought urn becomes

The greatest ashes, as half-acre tombs;
   And by these hymns all shall approve
     Us canonized for love;

And thus invoke us: 'You, whom reverend
     Love
   Made one another's hermitage;
You, to whom love was peace, that now is
     rage;
Who did the whole world's soul extract, and
     drove
   Into the glasses of your eyes,
   So made such mirrors, and such spies,
That they did all to you epitomize,
   Countries, towns, courts: beg from above
     A pattern of your love!'

John Donne

The Hour Glass

Consider this small dust, here in the glass,
   By atoms moved:
Could you believe that this the body was
   Of one that loved;
And in his mistress' flame playing like a fly,
Was turned to cinders by her eye:
Yes; and in death, as life unblessed,
   To have it expressed,
Even ashes of lovers find no rest.

Ben Jonson

Sweet Disorder

A sweet disorder in the dress
Kindles in clothes a wantonness:
A lawn about the shoulders thrown
Into a fine distraction —
An erring lace, which here and there
Enthrals the crimson stomacher —
A cuff neglectful, and thereby
Ribbands to flow confusedly —
A winning wave, deserving note,
In the tempestuous petticoat —
A careless shoe-string, in whose tie
I see a wild civility —
Do more bewitch me than when art
Is too precise in every part.

Robert Herrick

To Electra

I dare not ask a kiss,
   I dare not beg a smile,
Lest having that, or this,
   I might grow proud the while.

No, no, the utmost share
   Of my desire shall be
Only to kiss that air
   That lately kissèd thee.

Robert Herrick

On a Girdle

That which her slender waist confined,
Shall now my joyful temples bind;
No monarch but would give his crown,
His arms might do what this has done.

It was my heaven's extremest sphere,
The pale which held that lovely deer.
My joy, my grief, my hope, my love,
Did all within this circle move!

A narrow compass! and yet there
Dwelt all that's good, and all that's fair;
Give me but what this ribband bound,
Take all the rest the sun goes round.

Edmund Waller

To My Dear and Loving Husband

If ever two were one, then surely we.
If ever man were loved by wife, then thee;
If ever wife was happy in a man,
Compare with me ye women if you can.
I prize thy love more than whole mines of
    gold,
Or all the riches that the East doth hold.
My love is such that rivers cannot quench,
Nor ought but love from thee give
    recompense.

113

Thy love is such I can no way repay;
The heavens reward thee manifold, I pray.
Then while we live, in love let's so
    persever,
That when we live no more we may live
    ever.

Anne Bradstreet

The Definition of Love

My love is of a birth as rare
As 'tis for object strange and high:
It was begotten by Despair
Upon Impossibility.

Magnanimous Despair alone
Could show me so divine a thing,
Where feeble Hope could ne'er have flown
But vainly flapped its tinsel wing.

And yet I quickly might arrive
Where my extended soul is fixed,
But Fate does iron wedges drive,
And always crowds itself betwixt.

For Fate with jealous eye does see
Two perfect loves, nor lets them close:
Their union would her ruin be,
And her tyrannic power depose.

And therefore her decrees of steel
Us as the distant poles have placed
(Though love's whole world on us doth
   wheel)
Not by themselves to be embraced,

Unless the giddy heaven fall,
And earth some new convulsion tear,
And, us to join, the world should all
Be cramped into a planisphere.

As lines, so loves oblique may well
Themselves in every angle greet;
But ours, so truly parallel,
Though infinite, can never meet.

Therefore the love which us doth bind,
But fate so enviously debars,
Is the conjunction of the mind,
And opposition of the stars.

Andrew Marvell

The Garden

How vainly men themselves amaze
To win the palm, the oak, or bays;
And their incessant labours see
Crowned from some single herb, or tree,
Whose short and narrow-vergèd shade
Does prudently their toils upbraid;

While all flowers and all trees do close
To weave the garlands of repose!

Fair Quiet, have I found thee here,
And Innocence, thy sister dear?
Mistaken long, I sought you then
In busy companies of men.
Your sacred plants, if here below,
Only among the plants will grow;
Society is all but rude
To this delicious solitude.

No white nor red was ever seen
So amorous as this lovely green.
Fond lovers, cruel as their flame,
Cut in these trees their mistress' name:
Little, alas! they know or heed
How far these beauties hers exceed!
Fair trees! wheres'e'er your barks I wound
No name shall but your own be found.

When we have run our passion's heat,
Love hither makes his best retreat.
The gods, that mortal beauty chase,
Still in a tree did end their race;
Apollo hunted Daphne so,
Only that she might laurel grow;
And Pan did after Syrinx speed,
Not as a nymph, but for a reed.

What wondrous life is this I lead!
Ripe apples drop about my head;

The luscious clusters of the vine
Upon my mouth do crush their wine;
The nectarine, and curious peach,
Into my hands themselves do reach;
Stumbling on melons, as I pass,
Ensnared with flowers, I fall on grass.

Meanwhile, the mind, from pleasure less,
Withdraws into its happiness:
The mind, that ocean where each kind
Does straight its own resemblance find;
Yet it creates, transcending these,
Far other worlds, and other seas;
Annihilating all that's made
To a green thought in a green shade.

Here at the fountain's sliding foot,
Or at some fruit-tree's mossy root,
Casting the body's vest aside,
My soul into the boughs does glide:
There like a bird it sits, and sings,
Then whets and combs its silver wings;
And, till prepared for longer flight,
Waves in its plumes the various light.

Such was that happy garden-state,
While man there walked without a mate:
After a place so pure and sweet,
What other help could yet be meet?
But 'twas beyond a mortal's share
To wander solitary there:

Two paradises 'twere in one,
To live in paradise alone.

How well the skillful gardener drew
Of flowers, and herbs, this dial new;
Where, from above, the milder sun
Does through a fragrant zodiac run;
And, as it works, the industrious bee
Computes its time as well as we.
How could such sweet and wholesome hours
Be reckoned but with herbs and flowers!

Andrew Marvell

Auld Lang Syne

Should auld acquaintance be forgot,
   And never brought to mind?
Should auld acquaintance be forgot,
   And auld lang syne?

For auld lang syne, my dear,
   For auld lang syne,
We'll tak a cup o' kindness yet
   For auld lang syne!

And surely ye'll be your pint-stowp,
   And surely I'll be mine,
And we'll tak a cup o' kindness yet
   For auld lang syne!

We twa hae run about the braes
   And pou'd the gowans fine,

But we've wandered monie a weary fit
   Sin' auld lang syne.

We two hae paidl'd in the burn
   Frae morning sun till dine,
But seas between us braid hae roared
   Sin' auld lang syne.

Robert Burns

She Was a Phantom of Delight

She was a Phantom of delight
When first she gleamed upon my sight;
A lovely Apparition, sent
To be a moment's ornament;
Her eyes as stars of Twilight fair;
Like Twilight's, too, her dusky hair;
But all things else about her drawn
From May-time and the cheerful Dawn;
A dancing Shape, an Image gay,
To haunt, to startle, and way-lay.

I saw her upon nearer view,
A Spirit, yet a Woman too!
Her household motions light and free,
And steps of virgin-liberty;
A countenance in which did meet
Sweet records, promises as sweet;
A Creature not too bright or good
For human nature's daily food;

For transient sorrows, simple wiles,
Praise, blame, love, kisses, tears, and
  smiles.

And now I see with eye serene
The very pulse of the machine;
A Being breathing thoughtful breath,
A Traveller between life and death;
The reason firm, the temperate will,
Endurance, foresight, strength, and skill;
A perfect Woman, nobly planned,
To warn, to comfort, and command;
And yet a Spirit still, and bright
With something of angelic light.

William Wordsworth

So, We'll Go No More A-Roving

So, we'll go no more a-roving
  So late into the night,
Though the heart be still as loving,
  And the moon be still as bright.

For the sword outwears its sheath,
  And the soul wears out the breast,
And the heart must pause to breathe,
  And Love itself have rest.

Though the night was made for loving,
  And the day returns too soon,

Yet we'll go no more a-roving
   By the light of the moon.
                    George Gordon, Lord Byron

The Indian Serenade

I arise from dreams of thee
In the first sweet sleep of night,
When the winds are breathing low,
And the stars are shining bright:
I arise from dreams of thee,
And a spirit in my feet
Hath led me — who knows how?
To thy chamber window, Sweet!

The wandering airs they faint
On the dark, the silent stream —
The Champak odors fail
Like sweet thoughts in a dream;
The nightingale's complaint,
It dies upon her heart; —
As I must on thine,
Oh, belovèd as thou art!

Oh lift me from the grass!
I die! I faint! I fail!
Let thy love in kisses rain
On my lips and eyelids pale.
My cheek is cold and white, alas!
My heart beats loud and fast; —

Oh! press it to thine own again,
Where it will break at last.
Percy Bysshe Shelley

Love's Philosophy

The fountains mingle with the river,
And the rivers with the ocean;
The winds of heaven mix forever,
With a sweet emotion;
Nothing in the world is single;
All things by a law divine
In one another's being mingle: —
Why not I with thine?

See! the mountains kiss high heaven,
And the waves clasp one another;
No sister flower would be forgiven
If it disdained its brother;
And the sunlight clasps the earth,
And the moonbeams kiss the sea: —
What are all these kissings worth,
If thou kiss not me?
Percy Bysshe Shelley

One Word Is Too Often Profaned

One word is too often profaned
For me to profane it;
One feeling too falsely disdain'd

For thee to disdain it;
One hope is too like despair
   For prudence to smother;
And pity from thee more dear
   Than that from another.

I can give not what men call love:
   But wilt thou accept not
The worship the heart lifts above
   And the heavens reject not,
The desire of the moth for the star,
   Of the night for the morrow,
The devotion to something afar
   From the sphere of our sorrow?
                Percy Bysshe Shelley

When I Have Fears That
I May Cease to Be

When I have fears that I may cease to be
Before my pen has gleaned my teeming
   brain,
Before high-pilèd books, in charact'ry,
Hold like rich garners the full-ripened grain;
When I behold, upon the night's starred
   face,
Huge cloudy symbols of a high romance,
And think that I may never live to trace
Their shadows, with the magic hand of
   chance;

And when I feel, fair creature of an hour!
That I shall never look upon thee more,
Never have relish in the faery power
Of unreflecting love; — then on the shore
Of the wide world I stand alone, and think,
Till Love and Fame to nothingness do sink.

John Keats

Bright Star, Would I Were Steadfast as Thou Art

Bright star, would I were steadfast as thou
    art —
Not in lone splendor hung aloft the night,
And watching, with eternal lids apart,
Like Nature's patient sleepless Eremite,
The moving waters at their priestlike task
Of pure ablution round earth's human
    shores,
Or gazing on the new soft fallen mask
Of snow upon the mountains and the
    moors —
No — yet still steadfast, still unchangeable,
Pillowed upon my fair love's ripening
    breast,
To feel for ever its soft fall and swell,
Awake for ever in a sweet unrest,
Still, still to hear her tender-taken breath,
And so live ever — or else swoon to death.

John Keats

First Time He Kissed Me

First time he kissed me, he but only kiss'd
  The fingers of this hand wherewith I
    write;
  And ever since, it grew more clean and
    white,
Slow to world-greetings, quick with its
    "Oh, list,"
When the angels speak. A ring of amethyst
  I could not wear here, plainer to my sight,
  Than that first kiss. The second pass'd in
    height
The first, and sought the forehead, and half
    miss'd,
Half falling on the hair. Oh, beyond meed!
  That was the chrism of love, which love's
    own crown,
With sanctifying sweetness, did precede.
  The third upon my lips was folded down
In perfect, purple state; since when, indeed,
  I have been proud, and said, "My love,
    my own!"

Elizabeth Barrett Browning

125

Go From Me

Go from me. Yet I feel that I shall stand
Henceforward in thy shadow. Nevermore
Alone upon the threshold of my door
Of individual life, I shall command
The uses of my soul, nor lift my hand
Serenely in the sunshine as before,
Without the sense of that which I
    forbore, . . .
Thy touch upon the palm. The widest land
Doom takes to part us, leaves thy heart in
    mine
With pulses that beat double. What I do
And what I dream include thee, as the wine
Must taste of its own grapes. And when I
    sue
God for myself, he hears that name of thine,
And sees within my eyes the tears of two.
Elizabeth Barrett Browning

For Annie

Thank Heaven! the crisis —
    The danger is past,
And the lingering illness
    Is over at last —
And the fever called "Living"
    Is conquered at last.

Sadly, I know
　　I am shorn of my strength,
And no muscle I move
　　As I lie at full length —
But no matter! — I feel
　　I am better at length.

And I rest so composedly,
　　Now, in my bed,
That any beholder
　　Might fancy me dead —
Might start at beholding me,
　　Thinking me dead.

The moaning and groaning,
　　The sighing and sobbing,
Are quieted now,
　　With that horrible throbbing
At heart: — ah, that horrible,
　　Horrible throbbing!

The sickness — the nausea —
　　The pitiless pain —
Have ceased, with the fever
　　That maddened my brain —
With the fever called "Living"
　　That burned in my brain.

And oh! of all tortures
　　That torture the worst
Has abated — the terrible
　　Torture of thirst

For the napthaline river
  Of Passion accurst: —
I have drank of a water
  That quenches all thirst: —

She tenderly kissed me,
  She fondly caressed.
And then I fell gently
  To sleep on her breast —
Deeply to sleep
  From the heaven of her breast.

When the light was extinguished,
  She covered me warm,
And she prayed to the angels
  To keep me from harm —
To the queen of the angels
  To shield me from harm.

And I lie so composedly,
  Now, in my bed,
(Knowing her love)
  That you fancy me dead —
And I rest so contentedly,
  Now in my bed,
(With her love at my breast)
  That you fancy me dead —
That you shudder to look at me,
  Thinking me dead: —

But my heart it is brighter
  Than all of the many

128

Stars in the sky,
    For it sparkles with Annie —
It glows with the light
    Of the love of my Annie —
With the thought of the light
    Of the eyes of my Annie.

Of a water that flows,
    With a lullaby sound,
From a spring but a very few
    Feet under ground —
From a cavern not very far
    Down under ground.

And ah! let it never
    Be foolishly said
That my room it is gloomy
    And narrow my bed;
For man never slept
    In a different bed —
And, to *sleep,* you must slumber
    In just such a bed.

My tantalized spirit
    Here blandly reposes,
Forgetting, or never
    Regretting its roses —
Its old agitations
    Of myrtles and roses:

For now, while so quietly
    Lying, it fancies

A holier odor
   About it, of pansies —
A rosemary odor,
   Commingled with pansies —
With rue and the beautiful
   Puritan pansies.

And so it lies happily,
   Bathing in many
A dream of the truth
   And the beauty of Annie —
Drowned in a bath
   Of the tresses of Annie.

Edgar Allan Poe

To One in Paradise

Thou wast all that to me, love,
   For which my soul did pine:
A green isle in the sea, love,
   A fountain and a shrine
All wreathed with fairy fruits and flowers,
   And all the flowers were mine.

Ah, dream too bright to last!
   Ah, starry Hope, that didst arise
But to be overcast!
   A voice from out of the Future cries,
"On! on!" — but o'er the Past
   (Dim gulf!) my spirit hovering lies
Mute, motionless, aghast.

For, alas! alas! with me
　　The light of Life is o'er!
No more — no more — no more —
(Such language holds the solemn sea
　　To the sands upon the shore)
Shall bloom the thunder-blasted tree,
　　Or the stricken eagle soar.

And all my days are trances,
　　And all my nightly dreams
Are where thy dark eye glances,
　　And where thy footstep gleams —
In what ethereal dances,
　　By what eternal streams.

　　　　　　　　　　Edgar Allan Poe

Song

Now sleeps the crimson petal, now the white;
Nor waves the cypress in the palace walk;
Nor winks the gold fin in the porphyry font:
The firefly wakens: waken thou with me.

　　Now droops the milkwhite peacock like a
　　　　ghost,
And like a ghost she glimmers on to me.
　　Now lies the earth all Danaë to the stars,
And all thy heart lies open unto me.

Now slides the silent meteor on, and
    leaves
A shining furrow, as thy thoughts in me.

Now folds the lily all her sweetness up,
And slips into the bosom of the lake:
So fold thyself, my dearest, thou, and slip
Into my bosom and be lost in me.
                Alfred, Lord Tennyson

A Woman's Last Word

Let's contend no more, Love,
    Strive nor weep:
All be as before, Love,
    — Only sleep!

What so wild as words are?
    I and thou
In debate, as birds are,
    Hawk on bough!

See the creature stalking
    While we speak!
Hush and hide the talking,
    Cheek on cheek!

What so false as truth is,
    False to thee?
Where the serpent's tooth is
    Shun the tree —

Where the apple reddens
  Never pry —
Lest we lose our Edens,
  Eve and I!

Be a god and hold me
  With a charm!
Be a man and fold me
  With thine arm!

Teach me, only teach, Love!
  As I ought
I will speak thy speech, Love,
  Think thy thought —

Meet, if thou require it,
  Both demands,
Laying flesh and spirit
  In thy hands.

That shall be to-morrow
  Not to-night:
I must bury sorrow
  Out of sight:

— Must a little weep, Love.
  (Foolish me!)
And so fall asleep, Love
  Loved by thee.
                    Robert Browning

My Love

Not as all other women are
Is she that to my soul is dear;
Her glorious fancies come from far,
Beneath the silver evening-star,
And yet her heart is ever near.

Great feelings hath she of her own,
Which lesser souls may never know;
God giveth them to her alone,
And sweet they are as any tone
Wherewith the wind may choose to blow.

Yet in herself she dwelleth not,
Although no home were half so fair;
No simplest duty is forgot,
Life hath no dim and lowly spot
That doth not in her sunshine share.

She doeth little kindnesses,
Which most leave undone, or despise:
For naught that sets one heart at ease,
And giveth happiness or peace,
Is low-esteemèd in her eyes.

She hath no scorn of common things,
And, though she seem of other birth,
Round us her heart intwines and clings,
And patiently she folds her wings
To tread the humble paths of earth.

Blessing she is: God made her so,
And deeds of week-day holiness
Fall from her noiseless as the snow,
Nor hath she ever chanced to know
That aught were easier than to bless.

She is most fair, and thereunto
Her life doth rightly harmonize;
Feeling or thought that was not true
Ne'er made less beautiful the blue
Unclouded heaven of her eyes.

She is a woman: one in whom
The spring-time of her childish years
Hath never lost its fresh perfume,
Though knowing well that life hath room
For many blights and many tears.

I love her with a love as still
As a broad river's peaceful might,
Which, by high tower and lowly mill,
Seems following its own wayward will,
And yet doth ever flow aright.

And, on its full, deep breast serene,
Like quiet isles my duties lie;
It flows around them and between,
And makes them fresh and fair and green,
Sweet homes wherein to live and die.

James Russell Lowell

The Blessed Damozel

The blessed damozel leaned out
  From the gold bar of Heaven;
Her eyes were deeper than the depth
  Of waters stilled at even;
She had three lilies in her hand,
  And the stars in her hair were seven.

Her robe, ungirt from clasp to hem,
  No wrought flowers did adorn,
But a white rose of Mary's gift,
  For service meetly worn;
Her hair that lay along her back
  Was yellow, like ripe corn.

Herseemed she scarce had been a day
  One of God's choristers;
The wonder was not yet quite gone
  From that still look of hers;
Albeit, to them she left, her day
  Had counted as ten years.

(To one, it is ten years of years.
  . . . Yet now, and in this place,
Surely she leaned o'er me — her hair
  Fell all about my face. . . .
Nothing: the autumn fall of leaves.
  The whole year sets apace.)

It was the rampart of God's house

That she was standing on;
By God built over the sheer depth
  The which is Space begun;
So high, that looking downward thence
  She scarce could see the sun.

It lies in Heaven, across the flood
  Of ether, as a bridge.
Beneath, the tides of day and night
  With flame and darkness ridge
The void, as low as where this earth
  Spins like a fretful midge.

Around her, lovers, newly met
  'Mid deathless love's acclaims,
Spoke evermore among themselves
  Their heart-remembered names;
And the souls mounting up to God
  Went by her like thin flames.

And still she bowed herself and stooped
  Out of the circling charm;
Until her bosom must have made
  The bar she leaned on warm,
And the lilies lay as if asleep
  Along her bended arm.

From the fixed place of Heaven she saw
  Time like a pulse shake fierce
Through all the worlds. Her gaze still strove
  Within the gulf to pierce
Its path; and now she spoke as when

The stars sang in their spheres.

The sun was gone now; the curled moon
   Was like a little feather
Fluttering far down the gulf; and now
   She spoke through the still weather.
Her voice was like the voice the stars
   Had when they sang together.

(Ah sweet! Even now, in that bird's song,
   Strove not her accents there,
Fain to be hearkened? When those bells
   Possessed the mid-day air,
Strove not her steps to reach my side
   Down all the echoing stair?)

"I wish that he were come to me,
   For he will come," she said.
"Have I not prayed in Heaven? — on earth,
   Lord, Lord, has he not pray'd?
Are not two prayers a perfect strength?
   And shall I feel afraid?

"When round his head the aureole clings,
   And he is clothed in white,
I'll take his hand and go with him
   To the deep wells of light;
As unto a stream we will step down,
   And bathe there in God's sight.

"We two will stand beside that shrine,
   Occult, withheld, untrod,

Whose lamps are stirred continually
    With prayer sent up to God;
And see our old prayers, granted, melt
    Each like a little cloud.

"We two will lie i' the shadow of
    That living mystic tree
Within whose secret growth the Dove
    Is sometimes felt to be,
While every leaf that His plumes touch
    Saith His Name audibly.

"And I myself will teach to him,
    I myself, lying so,
The songs I sing here; which his voice
    Shall pause in, hushed and slow,
And find some knowledge at each pause,
    Or some new thing to know."

(Alas! we two, we two, thou say'st!
    Yea, one wast thou with me
That once of old. But shall God lift
    To endless unity
The soul whose likeness with thy soul
    Was but its love for thee?)

"We two," she said, "will seek the groves
    Where the lady Mary is,
With her five handmaidens, whose names
    Are five sweet symphonies,
Cecily, Gertrude, Magdalen,
    Margaret and Rosalys.

"Circlewise sit they, with bound locks
  And foreheads garlanded;
Into the fine cloth white like flame
  Weaving the golden thread,
To fashion the birth-robes for them
  Who are just born, being dead.

"He shall fear, haply, and be dumb:
  Then will I lay my cheek
To his, and tell about our love,
  Not once abashed or weak:
And the dear Mother will approve
  My pride, and let me speak.

"Herself shall bring us, hand in hand,
  To Him round whom all souls
Kneel, the clear-ranged unnumbered heads
  Bowed with their aureoles:
And angels meeting us shall sing
  To their citherns and citoles.

"There will I ask of Christ the Lord
  This much for him and me: —
Only to live as once on earth
  With Love, — only to be,
As then awhile, for ever now
  Together, I and he."

She gazed and listened and then said,
  Less sad of speech than mild, —
"All this is when he comes." She ceased.

The light thrilled towards her, fill'd
With angels in strong level flight.
   Her eyes prayed, and she smil'd.

(I saw her smile.) But soon their path
   Was vague in distant spheres:
And then she cast her arms along
   The golden barriers,
And laid her face between her hands,
   And wept. (I heard her tears.)

               Dante Gabriel Rossetti

Mid-Rapture

Thou lovely and belovèd, thou my love;
Whose kiss seems still the first; whose
     summoning eyes,
Even now, as for our love-world's new
     sunrise,
Shed very dawn; whose voice, attuned above
All modulation of the deep-bowered dove,
Is like a hand laid softly on the soul;
Whose hand is like a sweet voice to control
Those worn tired brows it hath the keeping
     of: —
What word can answer to thy word, — what
     gaze
To thine, which now absorbs within its
     sphere
My worshipping face, till I am mirrored
     there

Light-circled in a heaven of deep-drawn
    rays?
  What clasp, what kiss mine inmost heart
    can prove,
  O lovely and belovèd, O my love?
Dante Gabriel Rossetti

A Birthday

My heart is like a singing bird
  Whose nest is in a watered shoot;
My heart is like an apple-tree
  Whose boughs are bent with thick-set
    fruit;
My heart is like a rainbow shell
  That paddles in a halcyon sea;
My heart is gladder than all these,
  Because my love is come to me.

Raise me a dais of silk and down;
  Hang it with vair and purple dyes;
Carve it in doves and pomegranates,
  And peacocks with a hundred eyes;
Work it in gold and silver grapes,
  In leaves and silver fleurs-de-lys;
Because the birthday of my life
  Is come, my love is come to me.
Christina Georgina Rossetti

The First Day

I wish I could remember the first day,
First hour, first moment of your meeting
  me,
If bright or dim the season, it might be
Summer or Winter for aught I can say;
So unrecorded did it slip away,
So blind was I to see and to foresee,
So dull to mark the budding of my tree
That would not blossom yet for many a
  May.
If only I could recollect it, such
A day of days! I let it come and go
As traceless as a thaw of bygone snow;
It seemed to mean so little, meant so much;
If only now I could recall that touch,
First touch of hand in hand — Did one but
  know!

Christina Georgina Rossetti

Rondel

Kissing her hair, I sat against her feet,
Wove and unwove it, wound and found it
  sweet;
Made fast therewith her hands, drew down
  her eyes,
Deep as deep flowers and dreamy like dim
  skies;

With her own tresses bound and found her
    fair,
        Kissing her hair.

Sleep were no sweeter than her face to me,
Sleep of cold sea-bloom under the cold sea;
What pain could get between my face and
    hers?
What new sweet thing would love not relish
    worse?
Unless, perhaps, white death had kissed me
    there,
        Kissing her hair.
                    Algernon Charles Swinburne

I Will Not Let Thee Go

    I will not let thee go.
Ends all our month-long love in this?
    Can it be summed up so,
    Quit in a single kiss?
    I will not let thee go.

    I will not let thee go.
If thy words' breath could scare thy deeds,
    As the soft south can blow
    And toss the feathered seeds,
    Then might I let thee go.

    I will not let thee go.
Had not the great sun seen, I might;

Or were he reckoned slow
To bring the false to light,
Then might I let thee go.

I will not let thee go.
The stars that crowd the summer skies
Have watched us so below
With all their million eyes,
I dare not let thee go.

I will not let thee go.
Have we not chid the changeful moon,
Now rising late, and now
Because she set too soon,
And shall I let thee go?

I will not let thee go.
Have not the young flowers been content,
Plucked ere their buds could blow,
To seal our sacrament?
I cannot let thee go.

I will not let thee go.
I hold thee by too many bands:
Thou sayest farewell, and lo!
I have thee by the hands,
And will not let thee go.

Robert Bridges

When She Comes Home

When she comes home again! A thousand
  ways
I fashion, to myself, the tenderness
Of my glad welcome: I shall tremble — yes;
And touch her, as when first in the old days
I touched her girlish hand, nor dared upraise
Mine eyes, such was my faint heart's sweet
  distress
Then silence: and the perfume of her dress:
The room will sway a little, and a haze
Cloy eyesight — soul-sight, even — for a
  space;
And tears — yes; and the ache here in the
  throat,
To know that I so ill deserve the place
Her arms make for me; and the sobbing note
I stay with kisses, ere the tearful face
Again is hidden in the old embrace.

James Whitcomb Riley

Romance

I will make you brooches and toys for your
  delight
Of bird-song at morning and star-shine at
  night.
I will make a palace fit for you and me,

Of green days in forests and blue days at
    sea.

I will make my kitchen, and you shall keep
    your room,
Where white flows the river and bright
    blows the broom,
And you shall wash your linen and keep
    your body white
In rainfall at morning and dewfall at night.

And this shall be for music when no one
    else is near,
The fine song for singing, the rare song to
    hear!
That only I remember, that only you admire,
Of the broad road that stretches and the
    roadside fire.

Robert Louis Stevenson

Kashmiri Song

Pale hands I love beside the Shalimar,
    Where are you now? Who lies beneath
    your spell?
Whom do you lead on Rapture's Roadway,
    far,
    Before you agonize them in farewell?

The lamplight seems to glimmer with a
    flicker of surprise,

As I turn it low — to rest me of the dazzle
        in my eyes,
And light my pipe in silence, save a sigh
        that seems to yoke
Its fate with my tobacco and to vanish with
        the smoke.

'Tis a *fragrant* retrospection, — for the
        loving thoughts that start
Into being are like perfume from the
        blossom of the heart;
And to dream the old dreams over is a
        luxury divine —
When my truant fancies wander with that old
        sweetheart of mine.

Though I hear beneath my study, like a
        fluttering of wings,
The voices of my children and the mother as
        she sings —
I feel no twinge of conscience to deny me
        any theme
When Care has cast her anchor in the harbor
        of a dream —

In fact, to speak in earnest, I believe it adds
        a charm
To spice the good a trifle with a little dust
        of harm, —
For I find an extra flavor in Memory's
        mellow wine

That makes me drink the deeper to that old
    sweetheart of mine.

O Childhood-days enchanted! O the magic
    of the Spring! —
With all green boughs to blossom white, and
    all bluebirds to sing!
When all the air, to toss and quaff, made
    life a jubilee
And changed the children's song and laugh
    to shrieks of ecstasy.

With eyes half closed in clouds that ooze
    from lips that taste, as well,
The peppermint and cinnamon, I hear the
    old school bell,
And from "Recess" romp in again from
    "Blackman's" broken line,
To smile, behind my "lesson", at that old
    sweetheart of mine.

A face of lily beauty, with a form of airy
    grace,
Float out of my tobacco as the Genii from
    the vase;
And I thrill beneath the glances of a pair of
    azure eyes
As glowing as the summer and as tender as
    the skies.

I can see the pink sunbonnet and the little
    checkered dress

She wore when first I kissed her and she
    answered the caress
With the written declaration that, ''as surely
    as the vine
Grew 'round the stump'' she loved me —
    that old sweetheart of mine.

Again I made her presents, in a really
    helpless way, —
The big ''Rhode Island Greening'' — I was
    hungry, too, that day! —
But I follow her from Spelling, with her
    hand behind her — so —
And I slip the apple in it — and the Teacher
    doesn't know!

Oh, pale dispensers of my Joys and Pains.
    Holding the doors of Heaven and of Hell,
How the hot blood rushed wildly through the
    veins
    Beneath your touch, until you waved
    farewell.

Pale hands, pink-tipped, like Lotus buds that
    float
    On those cool waters where we used to
    dwell,
I would have rather felt you round my throat
    Crushing our life than waving me
    farewell!

Laurence Hope

Light

The night has a thousand eyes,
   The day but one;
Yet the light of the bright world dies
   With the dying sun.

The mind has a thousand eyes,
   And the heart but one;
Yet the light of a whole life dies
   When its love is done.

Francis W. Bourdillon

Will You Love Me When I'm Old?

I would ask of you, my darling,
   A question soft and low,
That gives me many a heartache
   As the moments come and go.

Your love I know is truthful,
   But the truest love grows cold;
It is this that I would ask you:
   Will you love me when I'm old?

Life's morn will soon be waning,
   And its evening bells be tolled,
But my heart shall know no sadness,
   If you'll love me when I'm old.

Down the stream of life together
 We are sailing side by side,
Hoping some bright day to anchor
 Safe beyond the surging tide.
Today our sky is cloudless,
 But the night may clouds unfold;
But, though storms may gather round us,
 Will you love me when I'm old?

When my hair shall shade the snowdrift,
 And mine eyes shall dimmer grow,
I would lean upon some loved one,
 Through the valley as I go.
I would claim of you a promise,
 Worth to me a world of gold;
It is only this, my darling,
 That you'll love me when I'm old.

Unknown

New Friends and Old Friends

Make new friends, but keep the old;
Those are silver, these are gold.
New-made friendships, like new wine,
Age will mellow and refine.
Friendships that have stood the test —
Time and change — are surely best;
Brow may wrinkle, hair grow gray,
Friendship never knows decay.
For 'mid old friends, tried and true,
Once more we our youth renew.

But old friends, alas! may die,
New friends must their place supply.
Cherish friendship in your breast —
New is good, but old is best;
Make new friends, but keep the old;
Those are silver, these are gold.

Joseph Parry

Spring Night

The park is filled with night and fog,
   The veils are drawn about the world,
The drowsy lights along the paths
   Are dim and pearled.

Gold and gleaming the empty streets,
   Gold and gleaming the misty lake,
The mirrored lights like sunken swords,
   Glimmer and shake.

Oh, is it not enough to be
Here with this beauty over me?
My throat should ache with praise, and I
Should kneel in joy beneath the sky.
O beauty, are you not enough?
Why am I crying after love
With youth, a singing voice, and eyes
To take earth's wonder with surprise?
Why have I put off my pride,
Why am I unsatisfied, —
I, for whom the pensive night

Binds her cloudy hair with light, —
I, for whom all beauty burns
Like incense in a million urns?
O beauty, are you not enough?
Why am I crying after love?

Sara Teasdale

Love Song

Had I concealed my love
And you so loved me longer,
Since all the wise reprove
Confession of that hunger
In any human creature,
It had not been my nature.

I could not so insult
The beauty of that spirit
Who like a thunderbolt
Has broken me, or near it;
To love I have been candid,
Honest, and open-handed.

Although I love you well
And shall for ever love you,
I set that archangel
The depths of heaven above you;
And I shall love you, keeping
His word, and no more weeping.

Elinor Wylie

A Friend's Greeting

I'd like to be the sort of friend that you have
    been to me;
I'd like to be the help that you've been
    always glad to be;
I'd like to mean as much to you each minute
    of the day
As you have meant, old friend of mine, to
    me along the way.

I'd like to do the big things and the splendid
    things for you,
To brush the gray from out your skies and
    leave them only blue;
I'd like to say the kindly things that I so oft
    have heard,
And feel that I could rouse your soul the
    way that mine you've stirred.

I'd like to give you back the joy that you
    have given me,
Yet that were wishing you a need I hope
    will never be;
I'd like to make you feel as rich as I, who
    travel on
Undaunted in the darkest hours with you to
    lean upon.

I'm wishing at this Christmas time that I
    could but repay

A portion of the gladness that you've strewn
  along my way;
And could I have one wish this year, this
  only would it be:
I'd like to be the sort of friend that you have
  been to me.

Edgar A. Guest

Music I Heard

Music I heard with you was more than
  music,
And bread I broke with you was more than
  bread;
Now that I am without you, all is desolate;
All that was once so beautiful is dead.

Your hands once touched this table and this
  silver,
And I have seen your fingers hold this glass.
These things do not remember you, beloved,
And yet your touch upon them will not pass.

For it was in my heart you moved among
  them,
And blessed them with your hands and with
  your eyes;
And in my heart they will remember
  always, —
They knew you once, O beautiful and wise.

Conrad Aiken

Ashes of Life

Love has gone and left me, and the days are
    all alike.
  Eat I must, and sleep I will — and would
    that night were here!
But ah, to lie awake and hear the slow hours
    strike!
  Would that it were day again, with
    twilight near!

Love has gone and left me, and I don't
    know what to do;
  This or that or what you will is all the
    same to me;
But all the things that I begin I leave before
    I'm through —
  There's little use in anything as far as I
    can see.

Love has gone and left me, and the
    neighbors knock and borrow,
  And life goes on forever like the gnawing
    of a mouse.
And to-morrow and to-morrow and to-
    morrow and to-morrow
  There's this little street and this little
    house.

Edna St. Vincent Millay

My Grandmother's Love Letters

There are no stars tonight
But those of memory.
Yet how much room for memory there is
In the loose girdle of soft rain.

There is even room enough
For the letters of my mother's mother,
Elizabeth,
That have been pressed so long
Into a corner of the roof
That they are brown and soft,
And liable to melt as snow.

Over the greatness of such space
Steps must be gentle.
It is all hung by an invisible white hair.
It trembles as birch limbs webbing the air.

And I ask myself:

"Are your fingers long enough to play
Old keys that are but echoes:
Is the silence strong enough
To carry back the music to its source
And back to you again
As though to her?"

Yet I would lead my grandmother by the
  hand
Through much of what she would not
  understand;
And so I stumble. And the rain continues on
  the roof
With such a sound of gently pitying
  laughter.

                              Hart Crane

Nature and the Seasons

The Wild Honey Suckle

Fair flower, that dost so comely grow,
Hid in this silent, dull retreat,
Untouched thy honied blossoms blow,
Unseen thy little branches greet:
　　No roving foot shall crush thee here.
　　No busy hand provoke a tear.

By Nature's self in white arrayed,
She bade thee shun the vulgar eye,
And planted here the guardian shade,
And sent soft waters murmuring by;
　　Thus quietly thy summer goes.
　　Thy days declining to repose.

Smit with those charms, that must decay,
I grieve to see your future doom:
They died — nor were those flowers more
　　gay,
The flowers that did in Eden bloom;
　　Unpitying frosts, and Autumn's power
　　Shall leave no vestige of this flower.

From morning suns and evening dews
At first thy little being came:

If nothing once, you nothing lose,
For when you die you are the same;
   The space between, is but an hour,
   The frail duration of a flower.

Philip Freneau

To Spring

O Thou with dewy locks, who lookest down
Through the clear windows of the morning,
   turn
Thine angel eyes upon our western isle,
Which in full choir hails thy approach, O
   Spring!

The hills tell one another, and the listening
Valleys hear; all our longing eyes are turned
Up to thy bright pavilions: issue forth
And let thy holy feet visit our clime!

Come o'er the eastern hills, and let our
   winds
Kiss thy perfumed garments; let us taste
Thy morn and evening breath; scatter thy
   pearls
Upon our lovesick land that mourns for thee.

O deck her forth with thy fair fingers; pour
Thy soft kisses on her bosom; and put

Thy golden crown upon her languished head,
Whose modest tresses are bound up for thee!
William Blake

Flow Gently, Sweet Afton

Flow gently, sweet Afton, among thy green
  braes!
Flow gently, I'll sing thee a song in thy
  praise!
My Mary's asleep by thy murmuring
  stream —
Flow gently, sweet Afton, disturb not her
  dream!

Thou stock dove whose echo resounds
  through the glen,
Ye wild whistling blackbirds in yon thorny
  den,
Thou green-crested lapwing, thy screaming
  forbear —
I charge you, disturb not my slumbering
  fair!

How lofty, sweet Afton, thy neighboring
  hills,
Far marked with the courses of clear
  winding rills!
There daily I wander, as noon rises high,
My flocks and my Mary's sweet cot in my
  eye.

How pleasant thy banks and green valleys
  below,
Where wild in the woodlands the primroses
  blow;
There oft, as mild Evening weeps over the
  lea,
The sweet-scented birk shades my Mary and
  me.

Thy crystal stream, Afton, how lovely it
  glides,
And winds by the cot where my Mary
  resides!
How wanton thy waters her snowy feet lave,
As, gathering sweet flowerets, she stems thy
  clear wave!

Flow gently, sweet Afton, among thy green
  braes!
Flow gently, sweet river, the theme of my
  lays!
My Mary's asleep by thy murmuring
  stream —
Flow gently, sweet Afton, disturb not her
  dream!

Robert Burns

It Is a Beauteous Evening, Calm and Free

It is a beauteous evening, calm and free;
The holy time is quiet as a Nun
Breathless with adoration; the broad sun
Is sinking down in his tranquility;
The gentleness of heaven broods o'er the
   Sea;
Listen! the mighty Being is awake,
And doth with his eternal motion make
A sound like thunder — everlastingly.
Dear Child! dear Girl! that walkest with me
   here,
If thou appear untouched by solemn thought,
Thy nature is not therefore less divine:
Thou liest in Abraham's bosom all the year,
And worship'st at the Temple's inner shrine,
God being with thee when we know it not.

                         William Wordsworth

Composed Upon Westminster Bridge

Earth has not anything to show more fair:
Dull would he be of soul who could pass by
A sight so touching in its majesty:
This city now doth like a garment wear
The beauty of the morning; silent, bare,
Ships, towers, domes, theaters, and temples
   lie

Open unto the fields, and to the sky;
All bright and glittering in the smokeless
   air.

Never did sun more beautifully steep
In his first splendor valley, rock, or hill;
Ne'er saw I, never felt, a calm so deep!
The river glideth at his own sweet will:
Dear God! the very houses seem asleep;
And all that mighty heart is lying still!
                    William Wordsworth

Tintern Abbey

Five years have past; five summers, with the
   length
Of five long winters! and again I hear
These waters, rolling from their mountain-
   springs
With a soft inland murmur. — Once again
Do I behold these steep and lofty cliffs,
That on a wild secluded scene impress
Thoughts of more deep seclusion, and
   connect
The landscape with the quiet of the sky.
The day is come when I again repose
Here, under this dark sycamore, and view
These plots of cottage-ground, these
   orchard-tufts,
Which at this season, with their unripe
   fruits,

Are clad in one green hue, and lose
themselves
'Mid groves and copses. Once again I see
These hedge-rows, hardly hedge-rows, little
lines
Of sportive wood run wild: these pastoral
farms,
Green to the very door; and wreaths of
smoke
Sent up, in silence, from among the trees!
With some uncertain notice, as might seem
Of vagrant dwellers in the houseless woods,
Or of some Hermit's cave, where by his fire
The Hermit sits alone.
These beauteous forms,
Through a long absence, have not been to
me
As is a landscape to a blind man's eye:
But oft, in lonely rooms, and 'mid the din
Of towns and cities, I have owed to them
In hours of weariness, sensations sweet,
Felt in the blood, and felt along the heart;
And passing even into my purer mind,
With tranquil restoration: — feelings too
Of unremembered pleasure: such, perhaps,
As have no slight or trivial influence
On that best portion of a good man's life,
His little, nameless, unremembered acts
Of kindness and of love. Nor less, I trust,
To them I may have owed another gift,
Of aspect more sublime; that blessed mood,
In which the burden of the mystery,

In which the heavy and the weary weight
Of all this unintelligible world,
Is lightened: — that serene and blessed
  mood,
In which the affections gently lead us on, —
Until, the breath of this corporeal frame
And even the motion of our human blood
Almost suspended, we are laid asleep
In body, and become a living soul:
While with an eye made quiet by the power
Of harmony, and the deep power of joy,
We see into the life of things.
                                    If this
Be but a vain belief, yet, oh! how oft —
In darkness and amid the many shapes
Of joyless daylight; when the fretful stir
Unprofitable, and the fever of the world,
Have hung upon the beatings of my heart —
How oft, in spirit, have I turned to thee,
O sylvan Wye! thou wanderer thro' the
  woods,
How often has my spirit turned to thee!
  And now, with gleams of half
  extinguished thought,
With many recognitions dim and faint,
And somewhat of a sad perplexity,
The picture of the mind revives again:
While here I stand, not only with the sense
Of present pleasure, but with pleasing
  thoughts
That in this moment there is life and food
For future years. And so I dare to hope,

Though changed, no doubt, from what I was
    when first
I came among these hills; when like a roe
I bounded o'er the mountains, by the sides
Of the deep rivers, and the lonely streams,
Wherever nature led: more like a man
Flying from something that he dreads, than
    one
Who sought the thing he loved. For nature
    then
(The coarser pleasures of my boyish days,
And their glad animal movements all gone
    by)
To me was all in all. — I cannot paint
What then I was. The sounding cataract
Haunted me like a passion: the tall rock,
The mountain, and the deep and gloomy
    wood,
Their colours and their forms, were then to
    me
An appetite; a feeling and a love,
That had no need of a remoter charm,
By thought supplied, nor any interest
Unborrowed from the eye. — That time is
    past,
And all its aching joys are now no more,
And all its dizzy raptures. Not for this
Faint I, nor mourn nor murmur; other gifts
Have followed; for such loss, I would
    believe,
Abundant recompense. For I have learned
To look on nature, not as in the hour

Of thoughtless youth: but hearing oftentimes
The still, sad music of humanity,
Nor harsh nor grating, though of ample
   power
To chasten and subdue. And I have felt
A presence that disturbs me with the joy
Of elevated thoughts; a sense sublime
Of something far more deeply interfused,
Whose dwelling is the light of setting suns,
And the round ocean, and the living air,
And the blue sky, and in the mind of man;
A motion and a spirit, that impels
All thinking things, all objects of all
   thought,
And rolls through all things. Therefore am I
   still
A lover of the meadows and the woods,
And mountains; and of all that we behold
From this green earth; of all the mighty
   world
Of eye, and ear, — both what they half
   create,
And what perceive; well pleased to
   recognize
In nature and the language of the sense,
The anchor of my purest thoughts, the
   nurse,
The guide, the guardian of my heart, and
   soul
Of all my moral being.
                              Nor perchance,
If I were not thus taught, should I the more

Suffer my genial spirits to decay:
For thou art with me here upon the banks
Of this fair river; thou my dearest Friend,
My dear, dear Friend; and in thy voice I
  catch
The language of my former heart, and read
My former pleasures in the shooting lights
Of thy wild eyes. Oh! yet a little while
May I behold in thee what I was once,
My dear, dear Sister! and this prayer I
  make,
Knowing that Nature never did betray
The heart that loved her; 'tis her privilege,
Through all the years of this our life, to lead
From joy to joy: for she can so inform
The mind that is within us, so impress
With quietness and beauty, and so feed
With lofty thoughts, that neither evil
  tongues,
Rash judgments, nor the sneers of selfish
  men,
Nor greetings where no kindness is, nor all
The dreary intercourse of daily life,
Shall e'er prevail against us, or disturb
Our cheerful faith that all which we behold
Is full of blessings. Therefore let the moon
Shine on thee in thy solitary walk;
And let the misty mountain-winds be free
To blow against thee: and, in after years,
When these wild ecstasies shall be matured
Into a sober pleasure; when thy mind
Shall be a mansion for all lovely forms,

Thy memory be as a dwelling-place
For all sweet sounds and harmonies; oh!
    then,
If solitude, or fear, or pain, or grief,
Should be thy portion, with what healing
    thoughts
Of tender joy wilt thou remember me,
And these my exhortations! Nor,
    perchance —
If I should be where I no more can hear
Thy voice, nor catch from thy wild eyes
    these gleams
Of past existence — wilt thou then forget
That on the banks of this delightful stream
We stood together; and that I, so long
A worshipper of Nature, hither came
Unwearied in that service: rather say
With warmer love — oh! with far deeper
    zeal
Of holier love. Nor wilt thou then forget,
That after many wanderings, many years
Of absence, these steep woods and lofty
    cliffs,
And this green pastoral landscape, were to
    me
More dear, both for themselves and for thy
    sake!

William Wordsworth

The Sea

There is a pleasure in the pathless woods,
There is a rapture on the lonely shore,
There is society where none intrudes
By the deep sea, and music in its roar:
I love not man the less, but nature more,
From these our interviews, in which I
    steal
From all I may be, or have been before,
To mingle with the universe, and feel
What I can ne'er express, yet cannot all
    conceal.

Roll on, thou deep and dark blue Ocean,
    — roll!
Ten thousand fleets sweep over thee in
    vain;
Man marks the earth with ruin, — his
    control
Stops with the shore; — upon the watery
    plain
The wrecks are all thy deed, nor doth
    remain
A shadow of man's ravage, save his own,
When, for a moment, like a drop of rain,
He sinks into thy depths with bubbling
    groan,
Without a grave, unknelled, uncoffined, and
    unknown.

His steps are not upon thy paths, — thy
    fields
Are not a spoil for him, — thou dost arise
And shake him from thee; the vile
    strength he wields
For earth's destruction thou dost all
    despise,
Spurning him from thy bosom to the
    skies,
And send'st him, shivering in thy playful
    spray
And howling, to his gods, where haply
    lies
His petty hope in some near port or bay,
And dashest him again to earth: — there let
    him lay.

The armaments which thunderstrike the
    walls
Of rock-built cities, bidding nations quake
And monarchs tremble in their capitals,
The oak leviathans, whose huge ribs make
Their clay creator the vain title take
Of lord of thee and arbiter of war, —
These are thy toys, and, as the snowy
    flake,
They melt into thy yeast of waves, which
    mar
Alike the Armada's pride or spoils of
    Trafalgar.

Thy shores are empires, changed in all
  save thee;
Assyria, Greece, Rome, Carthage, what
  are they?
Thy waters wasted them while they were
  free,
And many a tyrant since; their shores
  obey
The stranger, slave, or savage; their decay
Has dried up realms to deserts: not so
  thou;
Unchangeable save to thy wild waves'
  play,
Time writes no wrinkles on thine azure
  brow;
Such as creation's dawn beheld, thou rollest
  now.

Thou glorious mirror, where the
  Almighty's form
Glasses itself in tempests; in all time,
Calm or convulsed, — in breeze, or gale,
  or storm,
Icing the pole, or in the torrid clime
Dark-heaving; boundless, endless, and
  sublime,
The image of Eternity, — the throne
Of the Invisible! even from out thy slime
The monsters of the deep are made; each
  zone
Obeys thee; thou goest forth, dread,
  fathomless, alone.

And I have loved thee, Ocean! and my joy
Of youthful sports was on thy breast to be
Borne, like thy bubbles, onward; from a
   boy
I wantoned with thy breakers, — they to
   me
Were a delight; and if the freshening sea
Made them a terror, 'twas a pleasing fear;
For I was as it were a child of thee,
And trusted to thy billows far and near,
And laid my land upon thy mane, — as I do
   here.

George Gordon, Lord Byron

The Cloud

I bring fresh showers for the thirsting
   flowers,
   From the seas and the streams;
I bear light shade for the leaves when laid
   In their noonday dreams.
From my wings are shaken the dews that
   waken
   The sweet buds every one,
When rocked to rest on their mother's
   breast,
   As she dances about the sun.
I wield the flail of the lashing hail,
   And whiten the green plains under,

And then again I dissolve it in rain,
   And laugh as I pass in thunder.

I sift the snow on the mountains below,
   And their great pines groan aghast,
And all the night 'tis my pillow white,
   While I sleep in the arms of the blast.
Sublime on the towers of my skiey bowers,
   Lightning, my pilot, sits,
In a cavern under is fettered the thunder,
   It struggles and howls at fits;
Over earth and ocean, with gentle motion,
   This pilot is guiding me,
Lured by the love of the genii that move
   In the depths of the purple sea;
Over the rills, and the crags, and the hills,
   Over the lakes and the plains,
Wherever he dream, under mountain or
     stream,
   The Spirit he loves remains;
And I all the while bask in heaven's blue
     smile,
   Whilst he is dissolving in rains.

The sanguine sunrise, with his meteor eyes,
   And his burning plumes outspread,
Leaps on the back of my sailing rack,
   When the morning star shines dead,
As on the jag of a mountain crag,
   Which an earthquake rocks and swings,
An eagle alit one moment may sit
   In the light of its golden wings.

And when sunset may breathe, from the lit
    sea beneath,
  Its ardours of rest and of love,
And the crimson pall of eve may fall
  From the depth of heaven above,
With wings folded I rest, on mine airy nest,
  As still as a brooding dove.

That orbèd maiden with white fire laden,
  Whom mortals call the moon,
Glides glimmering o'er my fleece-like floor,
  By the midnight breezes strewn:
And wherever the beat of her unseen feet,
  Which only the angels hear,
May have broken the woof of my tent's thin
    roof,
  The stars peep behind her and peer;
And I laugh to see them whirl and flee,
  Like a swarm of golden bees,
When I widen the rent in my wind-built tent,
  Till the calm rivers, lakes, and seas,
Like strips of the sky fallen through me on
    high,
  Are each paved with the moon and these.

I bind the sun's throne with a burning zone,
  And the moon's with a girdle of pearl;
The volcanoes are dim, and the stars reel
    and swim,
  When the whirlwinds my banner unfurl.
From cape to cape, with a bridge-like shape,
  Over a torrent sea,

Sunbeam-proof, I hang like a roof,
  The mountains its columns be.
The triumphal arch through which I march
  With hurricane, fire, and snow,
When the powers of the air are chained to
    my chair,
  Is the million-coloured bow;
The sphere-fire above its soft colours wove,
  While the moist earth was laughing
    below.

I am the daughter of earth and water,
  And the nursling of the sky;
I pass through the pores of the ocean and
    shores;
  I change, but I cannot die.
For after the rain, when with never a stain
  The pavilion of heaven is bare,
And the winds and sunbeams, with their
    convex gleams,
  Build up the blue dome of air,
I silently laugh at my own cenotaph,
  And out of the caverns of rain,
Like a child from the womb, like a ghost
    from the tomb,
  I arise and unbuild it again.

Percy Bysshe Shelley

The Yellow Violet

When beechen buds begin to swell,
  And woods the blue-bird's warble know,
The yellow violet's modest bell
  Peeps from the last year's leaves below.

Ere russet fields their green resume,
  Sweet flower, I love, in forest bare,
To meet thee, when thy faint perfume
  Alone is in the virgin air.

Of all her train, the hands of Spring
  First plant thee in the watery mould,
And I have seen thee blossoming
  Beside the snow-bank's edges cold.

Thy parent sun, who bade thee view
  Pale skies, and chilling moisture sip,
Has bathed thee in his own bright hue,
  And streaked with jet thy glowing lip.

Yet slight thy form, and low thy seat,
  And earthward bent thy gentle eye,
Unapt the passing view to meet
  When loftier flowers are flaunting nigh.

Oft, in the sunless April day,
  Thy early smile has stayed my walk;
But midst the gorgeous blooms of May,
  I passed thee on thy humble stalk.

So they, who climb to wealth, forget
    The friends in darker fortunes tried.
I copied them — but I regret
    That I should ape the ways of pride.

And when again the genial hour
    Awakes the painted tribes of light,
I'll not o'erlook the modest flower
    That made the woods of April bright.
                William Cullen Bryant

Ode to a Nightingale

My heart aches, and a drowsy numbness
        pains
    My sense, as though of hemlock I had
        drunk,
Or emptied some dull opiate to the drains
    One minute past, and Lethe-wards had
        sunk:
'Tis not through envy of thy happy lot,
    But being too happy in thine happiness —
        That thou, light-wingèd Dryad of the
        trees,
        In some melodious plot
    Of beechen green, and shadows
        numberless,
        Singest of summer in full-throated ease.

O for a draught of vintage! that hath been
  Cooled a long age in the deep delvèd
     earth,
Tasting of Flora and the country green,
  Dance, and Provençal song, and sunburnt
     mirth!
O for a beaker full of the warm South,
  Full of the true, the blushful Hippocrene,
    With beaded bubbles winking at the
     brim,
     And purple-stainèd mouth;
That I might drink, and leave the world
     unseen,
    And with thee fade away into the forest
     dim:

Fade away, dissolve, and quite forget
  What thou among the leaves hast never
     known,
The weariness, the fever, and the fret
  Here, where men sit and hear each other
     groan;
Where palsy shakes a few, sad, last gray
     hairs,
  Where youth grows pale, and specter-thin,
     and dies;
    Where but to think is to be full of
     sorrow
     And leaden-eyed despairs,
Where Beauty cannot keep her lustrous
     eyes,

Or new Love pine at them beyond to-
morrow.

Away! away! for I will fly to thee,
  Not charioted by Bacchus and his pards,
But on the viewless wings of Poesy,
  Though the dull brain perplexes and
    retards:
Already with thee! tender is the night,
  And haply the Queen-Moon is on her
    throne,
    Clustered around by all her starry Fays;
    But here there is no light,
Save what from heaven is with the breezes
  blown
    Through verdurous glooms and winding
    mossy ways.

I cannot see what flowers are at my feet,
  Nor what soft incense hangs upon the
    boughs,
But, in embalmèd darkness, guess each
  sweet
Wherewith the seasonable month endows
The grass, the thicket, and the fruit-tree
  wild;
  White hawthorn, and the pastoral
    eglantine;
    Fast-fading violets covered up in leaves;
    And mid-May's eldest child,
The coming musk-rose, full of dewy
  wine,

The murmurous haunt of flies on
summer eves.

Darkling I listen; and for many a time
I have been half in love with easeful
Death,
Called him soft names in many a musèd
rhyme,
To take into the air my quiet breath;
Now more than ever seems it rich to die,
To cease upon the midnight with no pain,
While thou art pouring forth thy soul
abroad
In such an ecstasy!
Still wouldst thou sing, and I have ears in
vain —
To thy high requiem become a sod.

Thou wast not born for death, immortal
Bird!
No hungry generations tread thee down;
The voice I hear this passing night was
heard
In ancient days by emperor and clown:
Perhaps the self-same song that found a path
Through the sad heart of Ruth, when, sick
for home,
She stood in tears amid the alien corn;
The same that oft-times hath
Charmed magic casements, opening on the
foam
Of perilous seas, in faery lands forlorn.

Forlorn! the very word is like a bell
   To toll me back from thee to my sole self!
Adieu! the fancy cannot cheat so well
   As she is famed to do, deceiving elf.
Adieu! adieu! thy plaintive anthem fades
   Past the near meadows, over the still
        stream,
      Up the hill-side; and now 'tis buried
        deep
   In the next valley-glades:
Was it a vision, or a waking dream?
      Fled is that music: — Do I wake or
        sleep?

John Keats

Autumn

I saw old Autumn in the misty morn
Stand shadowless like Silence, listening
To silence, for no lonely bird would sing
Into his hollow ear from woods forlorn,
Nor lowly hedge nor solitary thorn; —
Shaking his languid locks all dewy bright
With tangled gossamer that fell by night,
   Pearling his coronet of golden corn.

Where are the songs of Summer? — With
        the sun,
Oping the dusky eyelids of the South,

Till shade and silence waken up as one,
And Morning sings with a warm odorous
      mouth.
Where are the merry birds? — Away, away,
On panting wings through the inclement
      skies,
   Lest owls should prey
   Undazzled at noonday,
And tear with horny beak their lustrous
      eyes.

Where are the blooms of Summer? — In the
      West,
Blushing their last to the last sunny hours,
When the mild Eve by sudden Night is prest
Like tearful Proserpine, snatch'd from her
      flow'rs
   To a most gloomy breast.
Where is the pride of Summer, — the green
      prime, —
The many, many leaves all twinkling? —
      Three
On the moss'd elm; three on the naked lime
Trembling, — and one upon the old oak-
      tree!
   Where is the Dryad's immortality? —
Gone into mournful cypress and dark yew,
Or wearing the long gloomy Winter through
   In the smooth holly's green eternity.

The squirrel gloats on his accomplish'd
      hoard,

The ants have brimm'd their garners with
      ripe grain,
    And honey bees have stored
  The sweets of Summer in their luscious
      cells;
  The swallows all have wing'd across the
      main;
  But here the autumn Melancholy dwells,
    And sighs her tearful spells
  Amongst the sunless shadows of the plain.
    Alone, alone,
    Upon a mossy stone,
She sits and reckons up the dead and gone
With the last leaves for a love-rosary,
Whilst all the wither'd world looks drearily,
Like a dim picture of the drownèd past
In the hush'd mind's mysterious far away,
Doubtful what ghostly thing will steal the
      last
Into that distance, grey upon the grey.

O go and sit with her, and be o'ershaded
Under the languid downfall of her hair!
She wears a coronal of flowers faded
Upon her forehead, and a face of care; —
There is enough of wither'd everywhere
To make her bower, — and enough of
      gloom;
There is enough of sadness to invite,
If only for the rose that died, whose doom
Is Beauty's, — she that with the living
      bloom

Of conscious cheeks most beautifies the
        light:
There is enough of sorrowing, and quite
Enough of bitter fruits the earth doth
        bear, —
Enough of chilly droppings for her bowl;
Enough of fear and shadowy despair,
To frame her cloudy prison for the soul!

Thomas Hood

The Snow-Storm

Announced by all the trumpets of the sky,
Arrives the snow, and, driving o'er the
        fields,
Seems nowhere to alight: the whited air
Hides hills and woods, the river, and the
        heaven,
And veils the farm-house at the garden's
        end.
The sled and traveller stopped, the courier's
        feet
Delayed, all friends shut out, the housemates
        sit
Around the radiant fireplace, enclosed
In a tumultuous privacy of storm.

    Come see the north wind's masonry.
Out of an unseen quarry evermore
Furnished with tile, the fierce artificer

Curves his white bastions with projected
    roof
Round every windward stake, or tree, or
    door.
Speeding, the myriad-handed, his wild work
So fanciful, so savage, naught cares he
For number or proportion. Mockingly,
On coop or kennel he hangs Parian wreaths;
A swan-like form invests the hidden thorn;
Fills up the farmer's lane from wall to wall,
Maugre the farmer's sighs; and at the gate
A tapering turret overtops the work.
And when his hours are numbered, and the
    world
Is all his own, retiring, as he were not,
Leaves, when the sun appears, astonished
    Art
To mimic in slow structures, stone by stone,
Built in an age, the mad wind's night-work,
The frolic architecture of the snow.

Ralph Waldo Emerson

Fable

The mountain and the squirrel
Had a quarrel;
And the former called the latter "Little
    Prig."
Bun replied,
"You are doubtless very big;

But all sorts of things and weather
Must be taken in together
To make up a year
And a sphere.
And I think it's no disgrace
To occupy my place.
If I'm not so large as you,
You are not so small as I,
And not half so spry.
I'll not deny you make
A very pretty squirrel track;
Talents differ: all is well and wisely put;
If I cannot carry forests on my back,
Neither can you crack a nut.''

Ralph Waldo Emerson

Hymn to the Night

I heard the trailing garments of the Night
   Sweep through her marble halls!
I saw her sable skirts all fringed with light
   From the celestial walls!

I felt her presence, by its spell of might,
   Stoop o'er me from above;
The calm, majestic presence of the Night,
   As of the one I love.

I heard the sounds of sorrow and delight,
   The manifold, soft chimes,

That fill the haunted chambers of the Night,
  Like some old poet's rhymes.

From the cool cisterns of the midnight air
  My spirit drank repose;
The fountain of perpetual peace flows
    there, —
  From those deep cisterns flows.

O holy Night! from thee I learn to bear
  What man has borne before!
Thou layest thy finger on the lips of Care,
  And they complain no more.

Peace! Peace! Orestes-like I breathe this
    prayer!
  Descend with broad-winged flight,
The welcome, the thrice-prayed for, the
    most fair,
  The best-loved Night!
                    Henry Wadsworth Longfellow

The Fire of Drift-Wood

We sat within the farm-house old,
  Whose windows, looking o'er the bay,
Gave to the sea-breeze damp and cold,
  An easy entrance, night and day.

Not far away we saw the port,

The strange, old-fashioned, silent town,
The lighthouse, the dismantled fort,
   The wooden houses, quaint and brown.

We sat and talked until the night,
   Descending, filled the little room;
Our faces faded from the sight,
   Our voices only broke the gloom.

We spake of many a vanished scene,
   Of what we once had thought and said,
Of what had been, and might have been,
   And who was changed, and who was
      dead.

And all that fills the hearts of friends,
   When first they feel, with secret pain,
Their lives thenceforth have separate ends,
   And never can be one again;

The first slight swerving of the heart,
   That words are powerless to express,
And leave it still unsaid in part,
   Or say it in too great excess.

The very tones in which we spake
   Had something strange, I could but mark;
The leaves of memory seemed to make
   A mournful rustling in the dark.

Oft died the words upon our lips,
   As suddenly, from out the fire

Built of the wreck of stranded ships,
  The flames would leap and then expire.

And, as their splendor flashed and failed,
  We thought of wrecks upon the main,
Of ships dismasted, that were hailed
  And sent no answer back again.

The windows, rattling in their frames,
  The ocean, roaring up the beach,
The gusty blast, the bickering flames,
  All mingled vaguely in our speech;

Until they made themselves a part
  Of fancies floating through the brain,
The long-lost ventures of the heart,
  That send no answers back again.

O flames that glowed! O hearts that yearned!
  They were indeed too much akin,
The drift-wood fire without that burned,
  The thoughts that burned and glowed
    within.
                    Henry Wadsworth Longfellow

The Tide Rises, the Tide Falls

The tide rises, the tide falls,
The twilight darkens, the curlew calls;
Along the sea-sands damp and brown

The traveller hastens toward the town,
  And the tide rises, the tide falls.

Darkness settles on roofs and walls,
But the sea, the sea in the darkness calls;
The little waves, with their soft, white
    hands,
Efface the footprints in the sands,
  And the tide rises, the tide falls.

The morning breaks; the steeds in their stalls
Stamp and neigh, as the hostler calls;
The day returns, but nevermore
Returns the traveller to the shore,
  And the tide rises, the tide falls.
                    Henry Wadsworth Longfellow

Blow, Bugle, Blow

The splendour falls on castle walls
  And snowy summits old in story:
The long light shakes across the lakes,
  And the wild cataract leaps in glory.
Blow, bugle, blow, set the wild echoes
    flying,
Blow, bugle; answer, echoes, dying, dying,
    dying.

  O hark, O hear! how thin and clear,
    And thinner, clearer, farther going!

O sweet and far from cliff and scar
      The horns of Elfland faintly blowing!
Blow, let us hear the purple glens replying:
Blow, bugle; answer, echoes, dying, dying,
    dying.

O love, they die in yon rich sky,
      They faint on hill or field or river:
Our echoes roll from soul to soul,
      And grow for ever and for ever.
Blow, bugle, blow, set the wild echoes
    flying,
And answer, echoes, answer, dying, dying,
    dying.

                    Alfred, Lord Tennyson

Break, Break, Break

Break, break, break,
    On thy cold grey stones, O Sea!
And I would that my tongue could utter
    The thoughts that arise in me.

O well for the fisherman's boy,
    That he shouts with his sister at play!
O well for the sailor lad,
    That he sings in his boat on the bay!

And the stately ships go on
    To their haven under the hill;
But O for the touch of a vanished hand,

And the sound of a voice that is still!

Break, break, break,
  At the foot of thy crags, O Sea!
But the tender grace of a day that is dead
  Will never come back to me.

Alfred, Lord Tennyson

Pippa's Song

The year's at the spring,
And day's at the morn;
Morning's at seven;
The hill-side's dew-pearl'd;
The lark's on the wing;
The snail's on the thorn;
God's in His heaven —
All's right with the world!

Robert Browning

Nature

O nature! I do not aspire
To be the highest in thy choir, —
To be a meteor in thy sky,
Or comet that may range on high;
Only a zephyr that may blow
Among the reeds by the river low;
Give me thy most privy place
Where to run my airy race.

In some withdrawn, unpublic mead
Let me sigh upon a reed,
Or in the woods, with leafy din,
Whisper the still evening in:
Some still work give me to do, —
Only — be it near to you!

For I'd rather be thy child
And pupil, in the forest wild,
Than be the king of men elsewhere,
And most sovereign slave of care;
To have one moment of thy dawn,
Than share the city's year forlorn.

Henry David Thoreau

The Blue-Bird

Beneath yon Larkspur's azure bells
That sun their bees in balmy air
In mould no more the Blue-Bird dwells
Though late he found interment there.

All stiff he lay beneath the Fir
When shrill the March piped overhead,
And Pity gave him sepulchre
Within the Garden's sheltered bed.

And soft she sighed — Too soon he came;
On wings of hope he met the knell;
His heavenly tint the dust shall tame;

Ah, some misgiving had been well!

But, look, the clear etherial hue
In June it makes the Larkspur's dower;
It is the self-same welkin-blue —
The Bird's transfigured in the Flower.
Herman Melville

What Is So Rare As a Day in June

And what is so rare as a day in June?
    Then, if ever, come perfect days;
Then Heaven tries the earth if it be in tune,
    And over it softly her warm ear lays:
Whether we look, or whether we listen,
We hear life murmur, or see it glisten;
Every clod feels a stir of might,
    An instinct within it that reaches and
        towers,
And, groping blindly above it for light,
    Climbs to a soul in grass and flowers;
The flush of life may well be seen
    Thrilling back over hills and valleys;
The cowslip startles in meadows green,
    The buttercup catches the sun in its
        chalice,
And there's never a leaf nor a blade too
        mean
    To be some happy creature's palace;
The little bird sits at his door in the sun,

Atilt like a blossom among the leaves,
And lets his illumined being o'errun
  With the deluge of summer it receives;
His mate feels the eggs beneath her wings,
And the heart in her dumb breast flutters and
      sings;
He sings to the wide world, and she to her
      nest, —
In the nice ear of Nature which song is the
      best?

Now is the high tide of the year,
  And whatever of life hath ebbed away
Comes flooding back, with a ripply cheer,
  Into every bare inlet and creek and bay;
Now the heart is so full that a drop overfills
      it,
We are happy now because God wills it;
No matter how barren the past may have
      been,
'T is enough for us now that the leaves are
      green;
We sit in the warm shade and feel right well
How the sap creeps up and the blossoms
      swell;
We may shut our eyes, but we cannot help
      knowing
That skies are clear and grass is growing;
The breeze comes whispering in our ear,
That dandelions are blossoming near,
That maize has sprouted, that streams are
      flowing,

That the river is bluer than the sky,
That the robin is plastering his house hard
    by;
And if the breeze kept the good news back,
For other couriers we should not lack;
    We could guess it all by yon heifer's
      lowing,
And hark! how clear bold chanticleer,
Warmed with the new wine of the year,
    Tells all in his lusty crowing!
                James Russell Lowell

A Noiseless Patient Spider

A noiseless patient spider,
I mark'd where on a little promontory it
    stood isolated,
Mark'd how to explore the vacant vast
    surrounding,
It launch'd forth filament, filament,
    filament, out of itself.
Ever unreeling them, ever tirelessly speeding
    them.

And you O my soul where you stand,
Surrounded, detached, in measureless oceans
    of space,
Ceaselessly musing, venturing, throwing,
    seeking the spheres to connect them.
Till the bridge you will need be form'd, till
    the ductile anchor hold,

Till the gossamer thread you fling catch
    somewhere, O my soul.

Grass

A child said *What is the grass?* fetching it to
    me with full hands;
How could I answer the child? I do not
    know what it is any more than he.

I guess it must be the flag of my disposition,
    out of hopeful green stuff woven.
Or I guess it is the handkerchief of the Lord,
A scented gift and remembrancer designedly
    dropt,
Bearing the owner's name some way in the
    corners, that we may see and remark, and
    say *Whose?*
Or I guess the grass is itself a child, the
    produced babe of the vegetation.

Or I guess it is a uniform hieroglyphic,
And it means, Sprouting alike in broad
    zones and narrow zones,
Growing among black folks as among white,
Kanuck, Tuckahoe, Congressman, Cuff, I
    give them the same, I receive them the
    same.
And now it seems to me the beautiful uncut
    hair of graves.

Tenderly will I use you curling grass,
It may be you transpire from the breasts of
    young men,
It may be if I had known them I would have
    loved them,
It may be you are from old people, or from
    offspring taken soon out of their mothers'
    laps,
And here you are the mothers' laps.

This grass is very dark to be from the white
    heads of old mothers,
Darker than the colorless beards of old men,
Dark to come from under the faint red roofs
    of mouths.

O I perceive after all so many uttering
    tongues,
And I perceive they do not come from the
    roofs of mouths for nothing.
I wish I could translate the hints about the
    dead young men and women,
And the hints about old men and mothers,
    and the off-spring taken soon out of their
    laps.

What do you think has become of the young
    and old men?
And what do you think has become of the
    women and children?

They are alive and well somewhere,
The smallest sprout shows there is really no
   death,
And if ever there was it led forward life,
   and does not wait at the end to arrest it,
And ceas'd the moment life appear'd.
All goes onward and outward, nothing
   collapses,
And to die is different from what any one
   supposed, and luckier.

From *Song of Myself*
Walt Whitman

A Bird Came Down the Walk

A Bird came down the Walk —
He did not know I saw —
He bit an Angleworm in halves
And ate the fellow, raw,

And then he drank a Dew
From a convenient Grass —
And then hopped sidewise to the Wall
To let a Beetle pass —

He glanced with rapid eyes
That hurried all around —
They looked like frightened Beads, I
   thought —
He stirred his Velvet Head

Like one in danger, Cautious,
I offered him a Crumb
And he unrolled his feathers
And rowed him softer home —

Than Oars divide the Ocean,
Too silver for a seam —
Or Butterflies, off Banks of Noon
Leap, plashless as they swim.

Emily Dickinson

The Wind

Who has seen the wind?
　　Neither I nor you.
But when the leaves hang trembling,
　　The wind is passing through.

Who has seen the wind?
　　Neither you nor I.
But when the trees bow down their heads,
　　The wind is passing by.

Christina Georgina Rossetti

October's Bright Blue Weather

O suns and skies and clouds of June,
　　And flowers of June together,
Ye cannot rival for one hour
　　October's bright blue weather.

When loud the humblebee makes haste,
  Belated, thriftless vagrant,
And Golden Rod is dying fast,
  And lanes with grapes are fragrant;

When Gentians roll their fringes tight,
  To save them for the morning,
And chestnuts fall from satin burrs
  Without a sound of warning;

When on the ground red apples lie
  In piles like jewels shining,
And redder still on old stone walls
  Are leaves of woodbine twining;

When all the lovely wayside things
  Their white-winged seeds are sowing,
And in the fields, still green and fair,
  Late aftermaths are growing;

When springs run low, and on the brooks,
  In idle golden freighting,
Bright leaves sink noiseless in the hush
  Of woods, for winter waiting;

When comrades seek sweet country haunts,
  By twos and twos together,
And count like misers, hour by hour,
  October's bright blue weather.

O suns and skies and flowers of June,
    Count all your boasts together,
Love loveth best of all the year
    October's bright blue weather.

Helen Hunt Jackson

My Garden

A garden is a lovesome thing, God wot!
Rose plot,
Fringed pool,
Ferned grot —
The veriest school
Of peace; and yet the fool
Contends that God is not —
Not God! in gardens! when the eve is cool?
Nay, but I have a sign;
'Tis very sure God walks in mine.

Thomas Edward Brown

Inversnaid

This darksome burn, horseback brown,
His rollrock highroad roaring down,
In coop and in comb the fleece of his foam
Flutes and low to the lake falls home.

A windpuff-bonnet of fawn-froth
Turns and twindles over the broth

Of a pool so pitchblack, fell-frowning,
It rounds and rounds Despair to drowning.

Degged with dew, dappled with dew
Are the groins of the braes that the brook
   treads through,
Wiry heathpacks, flitches of fern,
And the beadbonny ash that sits over the
   burn.

What would the world be, once bereft
Of wet and of wildness? Let them be left,
O let them be left, wildness and wet;
Long live the weeds and the wilderness yet.
                    Gerard Manley Hopkins

Loveliest of Trees

Loveliest of trees, the cherry now
Is hung with blooms along the bough,
And stands about the woodland ride
Wearing white for Eastertide.

Now, of my threescore years and ten,
Twenty will not come again,
And take from seventy springs a score,
It only leaves me fifty more.

And since to look at things in bloom
Fifty springs are little room,

About the woodlands I will go
To see the cherry hung with snow.
                                        A. E. Housman

Lilacs

Lilacs,
False blue,
White,
Purple,
Colour of lilac,
Your great puffs of flowers
Are everywhere in this my New England.
Among your heart-shaped leaves
Orange orioles hop like music-box birds and
     sing
Their little weak soft songs;
In the crooks of your branches
The bright eyes of song sparrows sitting on
     spotted eggs
Peer restlessly through the light and shadow
Of all Springs.
Lilacs in dooryards
Holding quiet conversations with an early
     moon;
Lilacs watching a deserted house
Settling sideways into the grass of an old
     road;
Lilacs, wind-beaten, staggering under a
     lopsided shock of bloom

Above a cellar dug into a hill.
You are everywhere.
You were everywhere.
You tapped the window when the preacher
    preached his sermon,
And ran along the road beside the boy going
    to school.
You stood by pasture-bars to give the cows
    good milking,
You persuaded the housewife that her dish
    pan was of silver
And her husband an image of pure gold.
You flaunted the fragrance of your blossoms
Through the wide doors of Custom
    Houses —
You, and sandal-wood, and tea,
Charging the noses of quill-driving clerks
When a ship was in from China.
You called to them: ''Goose-quill men,
    goose-quill men,
May is a month for flitting,''
Until they writhed on their high stools
And wrote poetry on their letter-sheets
    behind the propped-up ledgers.
Paradoxical New England clerks,
Writing inventories in ledgers, reading the
    ''Song of Solomon'' at night,
So many verses before bed-time,
Because it was the Bible.
The dead fed you
Amid the slant stones of graveyards.
Pale ghosts who planted you

Came in the night-time
And let their thin hair blow through your
   clustered stems.
You are of the green sea,
And of the stone hills which reach a long
   distance.
You are of elm-shaded streets with little
   shops where they sell kites and marbles,
You are of great parks where everyone
   walks and nobody is at home.
You cover the blind sides of greenhouses
And lean over the top to say a hurry-word
   through the glass
To your friends, the grapes, inside.

Lilacs,
False blue,
White,
Purple,
Colour of lilac,
You have forgotten your Eastern origin,
The veiled women with eyes like panthers,
The swollen, aggressive turbans of jewelled
   Pashas.
Now you are a very decent flower,
A reticent flower,
A curiously clear-cut, candid flower,
Standing beside clean doorways,
Friendly to a house-cat and a pair of
   spectacles,
Making poetry out of a bit of moonlight
And a hundred or two sharp blossoms.

Maine knows you,
Has for years and years;
New Hampshire knows you,
And Massachusetts
And Vermont.
Cape Cod starts you along the beaches to
    Rhode Island;
Connecticut takes you from a river to the
    sea.
You are brighter than apples,
Sweeter than tulips,
You are the great flood of our souls
Bursting above the leaf-shapes of our hearts,
You are the smell of all Summers,
The love of wives and children,
The recollection of the gardens of little
    children,
You are State Houses and Charters
And the familiar treading of the foot to and
    fro on a road it knows.
May is lilac here in New England,
May is a thrush singing "Sun up!" on a tip-
    top ash-tree,
May is white clouds behind pine-trees
Puffed out and marching upon a blue sky.
May is a green as no other,
May is much sun through small leaves,
May is soft earth,
And apple-blossoms,
And windows open to a South wind.
May is a full light wind of lilac
From Canada to Narragansett Bay.

Lilacs,
False blue,
White,
Purple,
Colour of lilac,
Heart-leaves of lilac all over New England,
Roots of lilac under all the soil of New
  England,
Lilac in me because I am New England,
Because my roots are in it,
Because my leaves are of it,
Because my flowers are for it,
Because it is my country
And I speak to it of itself
And sing of it with my own voice
Since certainly it is mine.

Amy Lowell

The Pasture

I'm going out to clean the pasture spring;
I'll only stop to rake the leaves away
(And wait to watch the water clear, I may):
I shan't be gone long. — You come too.

I'm going out to fetch the little calf
That's standing by the mother. It's so young
It totters when she licks it with her tongue.
I shan't be gone long. — You come too.

Robert Frost

Mowing

There was never a sound beside the wood
  but one,
And that was my long scythe whispering to
  the ground.
What was it it whispered? I knew not well
  myself;
Perhaps it was something about the heat of
  the sun,
Something, perhaps, about the lack of
  sound —
And that was why it whispered and did not
  speak.
It was no dream of the gift of idle hours,
Or easy gold at the hand of fay or elf:
Anything more than the truth would have
  seemed too weak
To the earnest love that laid the swale in
  rows,
Not without feeble-pointed spikes of flowers
(Pale orchises), and scared a bright green
  snake.
The fact is the sweetest dream that labor
  knows.
My long scythe whispered and left the hay
  to make.

Robert Frost

Tree at My Window

Tree at my window, window tree,
My sash is lowered when night comes on;
But let there never be curtain drawn
Between you and me.

Vague dream-head lifted out of the ground,
And thing next most diffuse to cloud,
Not all your light tongues talking aloud
Could be profound.

But tree, I have seen you taken and tossed,
And if you have seen me when I slept,
You have seen me when I was taken and
    swept
And all but lost.

That day she put our heads together,
Fate had her imagination about her —
Your head so much concerned with outer,
Mine with inner, weather.

Robert Frost

My November Guest

My Sorrow, when she's here with me,
    Thinks these dark days of autumn rain
    Are beautiful as days can be;

She loves the bare, the withered tree;
   She walks the sodden pasture lane.

Her pleasure will not let me stay.
   She talks and I am fain to list:
She's glad the birds are gone away,
She's glad her simple worsted grey
   Is silver now with clinging mist.

The desolate, deserted trees,
   The faded earth, the heavy sky,
The beauties she so truly sees,
She thinks I have no eye for these,
   And vexes me for reason why.

Not yesterday I learned to know
   The love of bare November days
Before the coming of the snow,
But it were vain to tell her so,
   And they are better for her praise.

Robert Frost

Thirteen Ways of Looking at a Blackbird

I

Among twenty snowy mountains,
The only moving thing
Was the eye of the blackbird.

II

I was of three minds,
Like a tree
In which there are three blackbirds.

III

The blackbird whirled in the autumn winds.
It was a small part of the pantomime.

IV

A man and a woman
Are one.
A man and a woman and a blackbird
Are one.

V

I do not know which to prefer,
The beauty of inflections
Or the beauty of innuendoes,
The blackbird whistling
Or just after.

VI

Icicles filled the long window
With barbaric glass.
The shadow of the blackbird
Crossed it, to and fro.
The mood
Traced in the shadow
An indecipherable cause.

VII

O thin men of Haddam,
Why do you imagine golden birds?
Do you not see how the blackbird
Walks around the feet
Of the women about you?

VIII

I know noble accents
And lucid, inescapable rhythms;
But I know, too,
That the blackbird is involved
In what I know.

IX

When the blackbird flew out of sight,
It marked the edge
Of one of many circles.

X

At the sight of blackbirds
Flying in a green light,
Even the bawds of euphony
Would cry out sharply.

XI

He rode over Connecticut
In a glass coach.
Once, a fear pierced him,
In that he mistook
The shadow of his equipage
For blackbirds.

XII

The river is moving.
The blackbird must be flying.

XIII

It was evening all afternoon.
It was snowing
And it was going to snow.
The blackbird sat
In the cedar-limbs.

Wallace Stevens

Queen-Ann's Lace

Her body is not so white as
anemone petals nor so smooth — nor
so remote a thing. It is a field
of the wild carrot taking
the field by force: the grass
does not raise above it.
Here is no question of whiteness,
white as can be, with a purple mole
at the center of each flower.

Each flower is a hand's span
of her whiteness. Wherever
his hand has lain there is
a tiny purple blemish. Each part
is a blossom under his touch

220

to which the fibres of her being
stem one by one, each of its end,
until the whole field is a
white desire, empty, a single stem;
a cluster, flower by flower,
a pious wish to whiteness gone over —
or nothing.
                    William Carlos Williams

God's World

O world, I cannot hold thee close enough!
    Thy winds, thy wide grey skies!
    Thy mists, that roll and rise!
Thy woods, this autumn day, that ache and
        sag
And all but cry with colour! That gaunt crag
To crush! To lift the lean of that black bluff!
World, World, I cannot get thee close
        enough!

Long have I known a glory in it all,
    But never knew I this;
    Here such a passion is
As stretcheth me apart, — Lord, I do fear
Thou'st made the world too beautiful this
        year;
My soul is all but out of me, — let fall
No burning leaf; prithee, let no bird call.
                    Edna St. Vincent Millay

Home and Family

A Thanksgiving to God for His House

Lord, thou hast given me a cell
    Wherein to dwell,
A little house, whose humble roof
    Is weather-proof,
Under the spars of which I lie
    Both soft and dry;
Where thou, my chamber for to ward,
    Hast set a guard
Of harmless thoughts to watch and keep
    Me, while I sleep.
Low is my porch, as is my fate,
    Both void of state;
And yet the threshold of my door
    Is worn by th' poor,
Who thither come and freely get
    Good words, or meat.
Like as my parlor, so my hall
    And kitchen's small;
A little buttery, and therein
    A little bin,
Which keeps my little loaf of bread
    Unchipped, unflead;
Some brittle sticks of thorn or briar
    Make me a fire,

Close by whose living coal I sit,
    And glow like it.
Lord, I confess, too, when I dine,
    The pulse is thine,
And all.those other bits that be
    There placed by thee;
The worts, the purslain, and the mess
    Of water-cress,
Which of thy kindness thou hast sent;
    And my content
Makes those, and my belovèd beet,
    To be more sweet.
'T is thou that crown'st my glittering hearth
    With guiltless mirth,
And giv'st me wassail bowls to drink,
    Spiced to the brink.
Lord, 'tis thy plenty-dropping hand
    That soils my land,
And giv'st me, for my bushel sown,
    Twice ten for one;
Thou mak'st my teeming hen to lay
    Her egg each day;
Besides my healthful ewes to bear
    Me twins each year;
The while the conduits of my kine
    Run cream, for wine.

All these, and better thou dost send
    Me, to this end,
That I should render, for my part,
    A thankful heart,
Which, fired with incense, I resign,

As wholly thine;
But the acceptance, that must be,
My Christ, by thee.

Robert Herrick

Old Age

The seas are quiet when the winds give o'er;
So calm are we when passions are no more.
For then we know how vain it was to boast
Of fleeting things, so certain to be lost.
Clouds of affection from our younger eyes
Conceal that emptiness which age descries.

The soul's dark cottage, battered and
    decayed,
Lets in new light through chinks that Time
    has made:
Stronger by weakness, wiser men become
As they draw near to their eternal home.
Leaving the old, both worlds at once they
    view
That stand upon the threshold of the new.

Edmund Waller

Nurse's Song

When the voices of children are heard on the
    green
And laughing is heard on the hill,

227

My heart is at rest within my breast,
  And everything else is still.

"Then come home, my children, the sun is
    gone down,
  And the dews of the night arise;
Come, come, leave off play, and let us away
  Till the morning appears in the skies."

"No, no, let us play, for it is yet day,
  And we cannot go to sleep;
Besides in the sky the little birds fly,
  And the hills are all covered with sheep."

"Well, well, go and play till the light fades
    away,
  And then go home to bed."
The little ones leaped and shouted and
    laughed;
  And all the hills echoèd.

                              William Blake

We Are Seven

        A simple child,
    That lightly draws its breath,
And feels its life in every limb,
    What should it know of death?

I met a little cottage girl:
  She was eight years old, she said;

Her hair was thick with many a curl
    That clustered round her head.

She had a rustic, woodland air,
    And she was wildly clad;
Her eyes were fair, and very fair; —
    Her beauty made me glad.

"Sisters and brothers, little maid,
    How many may you be?"
"How many? Seven in all," she said,
    And wondering looked at me.

"And where are they? I pray you tell."
    She answered, "Seven are we;
And two of us at Conway dwell,
    And two are gone to sea;
"Two of us in the churchyard lie,
    My sister and my brother;
And in the churchyard cottage I
    Dwell near them with my mother."

"You say that two at Conway dwell,
    And two are gone to sea,
Yet ye are seven! I pray you tell,
    Sweet maid, how this may be?"

Then did the little maid reply:
    "Seven boys and girls are we;
Two of us in the churchyard lie,
    Beneath the churchyard tree."

"You run about, my little maid,
    Your limbs they are alive;
If two are in the churchyard laid,
    Then ye are only five."

"Their graves are green, they may be
        seen,"
    The little maid replied,
"Twelve steps or more from my mother's
        door,
    And they are side by side.

"My stockings there I often knit,
    My kerchief there I hem;
And there upon the ground I sit —
    I sit and sing to them.

"And often after sunset, sir,
    When it is light and fair,
I take my little porringer,
    And eat my supper there.

"The first that died was little Jane;
    In bed she moaning lay,
Till God released her of her pain;
    And then she went away.

"So in the churchyard she was laid;
    And when the grass was dry,
Together round her grave we play'd,
    My brother John and I.

"And when the ground was white with
    snow,
  And I could run and slide,
My brother John was forced to go,
  And he lies by her side."

"How many are you, then," said I,
  "If they two are in Heaven?"
The little maiden did reply,
  "Oh, master, we are seven!"

"But they are dead — those two are dead,
  Their spirits are in Heaven!"
'Twas throwing words away, for still
The little maid would have her will,
  And said, "Nay, we are seven!"
                    William Wordsworth

On His Seventy-Fifth Birthday

I strove with none; for none was worth my
    strife.
  Nature I loved, and next to Nature, Art;
I warmed both hands before the fire of life;
  It sinks, and I am ready to depart.
                  Walter Savage Landor

Youth and Age

Verse, a breeze 'mid blossoms straying,
Where Hope clung feeding like a bee, —
Both were mine! Life went a-maying
With Nature, Hope, and Poesy
                   When I was young!
When I was young? — Ah, woful When!
Ah, for the change 'twixt Now and Then!
This breathing house not built with hands,
This body that does me grievous wrong,
O'er aery cliffs and glittering sands,
How lightly *then* it flashed along: —
Like those trim skiffs, unknown of yore,
On winding lakes and rivers wide,
That ask no aid of sail or oar,
That fear no spite of wind or tide!
Naught cared this body for wind or weather
When Youth and I lived in't together.
Flowers are lovely; Love is flower-like;
Friendship is a sheltering tree;
Oh! the joys that came down shower-like,
Of Friendship, Love, and Liberty
                   Ere I was old!
Ere I was old? Ah, woful Ere,
Which tells me, Youth's no longer here!
O Youth! for years so many and sweet,
'Tis known that Thou and I were one.
I'll think it but a fond conceit —
It cannot be that Thou art gone!
Thy vesper-bell hath not yet tolled: —

And thou wert aye a masker bold!
What strange disguise hast now put on
To make believe that thou art gone?
I see these locks in silvery slips,
This drooping gait, this altered size:
But Springtide blossoms on thy lips,
And tears take sunshine from thine eyes!
Life is but thought: so think I will
That Youth and I are house-mates still.

Dewdrops are the gems of morning,
But the tears of mournful eve!
Where no hope is, life's a warning
That only serves to make us grieve
                        When we are old:
That only serves to make us grieve
With oft and tedious taking-leave,
Like some poor nigh-related guest,
That may not rudely be dismissed,
Yet hath outstayed his welcome while,
And tells the jest without the smile.
Samuel Taylor Coleridge

Long, Long Be My Heart with Such Memories Filled

Farewell! — but whenever you welcome the
   hour
That awakens the night-song of mirth in
   your bower,

Then think of the friend who once welcomed
    it too,
And forgot his own griefs, to be happy with
    you.
His griefs may return, — not a hope may
    remain
Of the few that have brightened his pathway
    of pain, —
But he ne'er will forget the short vision that
    threw
Its enchantment around him, while ling'ring
    with you!

And still on that evening, when Pleasure
    fills up
To the highest top sparkle each heart and
    each cup,
Where'er my path lies, be it gloomy or
    bright,
My soul, happy friends, shall be with you
    that night;
Shall join in your revels, your sports, and
    your wiles,
And return to me, beaming all o'er with
    your smiles, —
Too blest if it tell me that, 'mid the gay
    cheer,
Some kind voice had murmured, "I wish he
    were here!"

Let fate do her worst, there are relics of joy,

Bright dreams of the past, which she cannot
    destroy;
Which come, in the night-time of sorrow
    and care,
And bring back the features that joy used to
    wear.
Long, long be my heart with such memories
    filled!
Like the vase in which roses have once been
    distilled, —
You may break, you may shatter the vase, if
    you will,
But the scent of the roses will hang 'round it
    still.

Thomas Moore

Oft in the Stilly Night

Oft in the stilly night,
    Ere Slumber's chain has bound me,
Fond Memory brings the light
    Of other days around me;
        The smiles, the tears,
        Of boyhood's years,
    The words of love then spoken;
        The eyes that shone,
        Now dimmed and gone,
    The cheerful hearts now broken!
Thus in the stilly night,
    Ere Slumber's chain has bound me,

Sad Memory brings the light
  Of other days around me.

When I remember all
  The friends, so linked together,
I've seen around me fall,
  Like leaves in wintry weather;
    I feel like one
    Who treads alone
  Some banquet-hall deserted,
    Whose lights are fled,
    Whose garlands dead,
  And all but he departed!
Thus in the stilly night,
  Ere Slumber's chain has bound me,
Sad Memory brings the light
  Of other days around me.
                    Thomas Moore

Sweet and Low

Sweet and low, sweet and low,
  Wind of the western sea,
Low, low, breathe and blow,
  Wind of the western sea!
Over the rolling waters go,
Come from the dying moon, and blow,
  Blow him again to me;
While my little one, while my pretty one,
  sleeps.

Sleep and rest, sleep and rest,
  Father will come to thee soon;
Rest, rest, on mother's breast,
  ,Father will come to thee soon;
Father ,will come to his babe in the nest,
Silver sails all out of the west
  Under the silver moon:
Sleep, my little one, sleep, my pretty one,
    sleep.

Alfred, Lord Tennyson

The Old Man Dreams

Oh for one hour of youthful joy!
  Give back my twentieth spring!
I'd rather laugh, a bright-haired boy,
  Than reign, a gray-beard king.

Off with the spoils of wrinkled age!
  Away with Learning's crown!
Tear out life's Wisdom-written page,
  And dash its trophies down!

One moment let my life-blood stream
  From boyhood's fount of flame!
Give me one giddy, reeling dream
  Of life all love and fame!

My listening angel heard the prayer,
  And, calmly smiling, said,

"If I but touch thy silvered hair,
    Thy hasty wish hath sped.

"But is there nothing in thy track
    To bid thee fondly stay,
While the swift seasons hurry back
    To find the wished-for day?"

"Ah, truest soul of womankind!
    Without thee what were life?
One bliss I cannot leave behind:
    I'll take — my — precious — wife!"

The angel took a sapphire pen
    And wrote in rainbow dew,
The man would be a boy again,
    And be a husband, too!

"And is there nothing yet unsaid,
    Before the change appears?
Remember, all their gifts have fled
    With those dissolving years."

"Why, yes;" for memory would recall
    My fond paternal joys;
"I could not bear to leave them all —
    I'll take — my — girl — and — boys."

The smiling angel dropped his pen, —
    "Why, this will never do;
The man would be a boy again,
    And be a father, too!"

And so I laughed, — my laughter woke
The household with its noise, —
And wrote my dream, when morning broke,
To please the gray-haired boys.

Oliver Wendell Holmes

Young and Old

When all the world is young, lad,
And all the trees are green;
And every goose a swan, lad,
And every lass a queen;
Then hey for boot and horse, lad,
And round the world away;
Young blood must have its course, lad,
And every dog his day.

When all the world is old, lad,
And all the trees are brown;
And all the sport is stale, lad,
And all the wheels run down;
Creep home, and take your place there,
The spent and maimed among:
God grant you find one face there,
You loved when all was young.

Charles Kingsley

A Child's Laughter

All the bells of heaven may ring,
All the birds of heaven may sing,
All the wells on earth may spring,
All the winds on earth may bring
   All sweet sounds together;
Sweeter far than all things heard,
Hand of harper, tone of bird,
Sound of woods at sundawn stirred,
Welling water's winsome word,
   Wind in warm wan weather,

One thing yet there is, that none
Hearing ere its chime be done
Knows not well the sweetest one
Heard of man beneath the sun,
   Hoped in heaven hereafter;
Soft and strong and loud and light —
Very sound of very light
Heard from morning's rosiest height —
When the soul of all delight
   Fills a child's clear laughter.

Golden bells of welcome rolled
Never forth such notes, nor told
Hours so blithe in tones so bold,
As the radiant mouth of gold
   Here that rings forth heaven.
If the golden-crested wren
Were a nightingale — why, then,

Something seen and heard of men
Might be half as sweet as when
    Laughs a child of seven.
              Algernon Charles Swinburne

My Dog

I have no dog, but it must be
Somewhere there's one belongs to me —
A little chap with wagging tail,
And dark brown eyes that never quail,
But look you through, and through, and
through,
With love unspeakable and true.

Somewhere it must be, I opine,
There is a little dog of mine
With cold black nose that sniffs around
In search of what things may be found
In pocket or some nook hard by
Where I have hid them from his eye.

Somewhere my doggie pulls and tugs
The fringes of rebellious rugs,
Or with the mischief of the pup
Chews all my shoes and slippers up,
And when he's done it to the core,
With eyes all eager, pleads for more.

Somewhere upon his hinder legs
My little doggie sits and begs,

And in a wistful minor tone
Pleads for the pleasures of the bone —
I pray it be his owner's whim
To yield, and grant the same to him.

Somewhere a little dog doth wait;
It may be by some garden gate.
With eyes alert and tail attent —
You know the kind of tail that's meant —
With stores of yelps of glad delight
To bid me welcome home at night.

Somewhere a little dog is seen,
His nose two shaggy paws between,
Flat on his stomach, one eye shut
Held fast in dreamy slumber, but
The other open, ready for
His master coming through the door.

John Kenrick Bangs

The Power of the Dog

There is sorrow enough in the natural way
From men and women to fill our day;
And when we are certain of sorrow in store,
Why do we always arrange for more?
Brothers and Sisters, I bid you beware
Of giving your heart to a dog to tear.

Buy a pup and your money will buy
Love unflinching that cannot lie —
Perfect passion and worship fed
By a kick in the ribs or a pat on the head.
Nevertheless it is hardly fair
To risk your heart for a dog to tear.

When the fourteen years which Nature
   permits
Are closing in asthma, or tumour, or fits,
And the vet's unspoken prescription runs
To lethal chambers or loaded guns,
Then you will find — it's your own affair —
But . . . you've given your heart to a dog
   to tear.

When the body that lived at your single will,
With its whimper of welcome, is stilled
   (how still!);
When the spirit that answered your every
   mood
Is gone — wherever it goes — for good,
You will discover how much you care,
And will give your heart to a dog to tear.

We've sorrow enough in the natural way,
When it comes to burying Christian clay.
Our loves are not given, but only lent,
At compound interest of cent per cent.
Though it is not always the case, I believe,
That the longer we've kept 'em, the more do
   we grieve:

For, when debts are payable, right or wrong,
A short-time loan is as bad as a long —
So why in — Heaven (before we are there)
Should we give our hearts to a dog to tear?

Rudyard Kipling

A Prayer for My Daughter

Once more the storm is howling, and half
  hid
Under this cradle-hood and coverlid
My child sleeps on. There is no obstacle
But Gregory's wood and one bare hill
Whereby the haystack and roof levelling
  wind,
Bred on the Atlantic, can be stayed;
And for an hour I have walked and prayed
Because of the great gloom that is in my
  mind.

I have walked and prayed for this young
  child an hour
And heard the sea-wind scream upon the
  tower,
And under the arches of the bridge, and
  scream
In the elms above the flooded stream;
Imagining in excited reverie
That in the future years had come,
Dancing to a frenzied drum,
Out of the murderous innocence of the sea.

May she be granted beauty and yet not
Beauty to make a stranger's eye distraught,
Or hers before a looking-glass, for such,
Being made beautiful overmuch,
Consider beauty a sufficient end,
Lose natural kindness and maybe
The heart-revealing intimacy
That chooses right, and never finds a friend.

Helen being chosen found life flat and dull
And later had much trouble from a fool,
While that great Queen, that rose out of the
    spray,
Being fatherless could have her way,
Yet chose a bandy-legged smith for man.
It's certain that fine women eat
A crazy salad with their meat,
Whereby the Horn of Plenty is undone.

In courtesy I'd have her chiefly learned,
Hearts are not had as a gift, but hearts are
    earned
By those that are not entirely beautiful;
Yet many, that have played the fool
For beauty's very self, has charm made
    wise,
And many a poor man that has roved,
Loved and thought himself beloved,
From a glad kindness cannot take his eyes.

May she become a flourishing hidden tree
That all her thoughts may like the linnet be
And have no business but dispensing round
Their magnanimities of sound,
Nor but in merriment begin a chase,
Nor but in merriment a quarrel.
Oh, may she live like some green laurel
Rooted in one dear perpetual place.

My mind, because the minds that I have
     loved,
The sort of beauty that I have approved,
Prosper but little, has dried up of late,
Yet knows that to be choked with hate
May well be of all evil chances chief.
If there's no hatred in a mind
Assault and battery of the wind
Can never tear the linnet from the leaf.

An intellectual hatred is the worst,
So let her think opinions are accursed.
Have I not seen the loveliest woman born
Out of the mouth of Plenty's horn,
Because of her opinionated mind
Barter that horn and every good
By quiet natures understood
For an old bellows full of angry wind?

Considering that, all hatred driven hence,
The soul recovers radical innocence
And learns at last that it is self-delighting,
Self-appeasing, self-affrighting,

And that its own sweet will is heaven's will;
She can, though every face should scowl
And every windy quarter howl
Or every bellows burst, be happy still.

And may her bridegroom bring her to a
    house
Where all's accustomed, ceremonious;
For arrogance and hatred are the wares
Peddled in the thoroughfares.
How but in custom and in ceremony
Are innocence and beauty born?
Ceremony's a name for the rich horn,
And custom for the spreading laurel tree.

William Butler Yeats

Home

It takes a heap o' livin' in a house t' make it
    home,
A heap o' sun an' shadder, an' ye
    sometimes have t' roam
Afore ye really 'preciate the things ye lef'
    behind,
An' hunger fer 'em somehow, with 'em
    allus on yer mind.
It don't make any differunce how rich ye get
    t' be,
How much yer chairs an' tables cost, how
    great yer luxury;

It ain't home t' ye, though it be the palace
   of a king,
Until somehow yer soul is sort o' wrapped
   round everything.

Home ain't a place that gold can buy or get
   up in a minute;
Afore it's home there's got t' be a heap o'
   livin' in it;
Within the walls there's got t' be some
   babies born, and then
Right there ye've got t' bring 'em up t'
   women good, an' men;
And gradjerly, as time goes on, ye find ye
   wouldn't part
With anything they ever used — they've
   grown into yer heart;
The old high chairs, the playthings, too, the
   little shoes they wore
Ye hoard; an' if ye could ye'd keep the
   thumb-marks on the door.

Ye've got t' weep t' make it home, ye've
   got t' sit an' sigh
An' watch beside a loved one's bed, an'
   know that Death is nigh;
An' in the stillness o' the night t' see
   Death's angel come,
An' close the eyes o' her that smiled, an'
   leave her sweet voice dumb.
For these are scenes that grip the heart, an'
   when yer tears are dried,

Ye find the home is dearer than it was, an'
    sanctified;
An' tuggin' at ye always are the pleasant
    memories
O' her that was an' is no more — ye can't
    escape from these.

Ye've got to sing an' dance fer years, ye've
    got t' romp an' play,
An' learn t' love the things ye have by usin'
    'em each day;
Even the roses round the porch must
    blossom year by year
Afore they 'come a part o' ye, suggestin'
    someone dear
Who used t' love 'em long ago, and trained
    'em just t' run
The way they do, so's they would get the
    early mornin' sun;
Ye've got to love each brick an' stone from
    cellar up t' dome:
It takes a heap o' livin' in a house t' make it
    home.

Edgar A. Guest

Becoming a Dad

Old women say that men don't know
The pain through which all mothers go,
And maybe that is true, and yet
I vow I never shall forget

The night he came. I suffered, too,
Those bleak and dreary long hours through;
I paced the floor and mopped my brow
And waited for his glad wee-ow!
I went upstairs and then came down,
Because I saw the doctor frown
And knew beyond the slightest doubt
He wished to goodness I'd clear out.

I walked into the yard for air
And back again to hear her there,
And met the nurse, as calm as though
My world was not in deepest woe,
And when I questioned, seeking speech
Of consolation that would reach
Into my soul and strengthen me
For dreary hours that were to be:
''Progressing nicely!'' that was all
She said and tip-toed down the hall;
''Progressing nicely!'' nothing more,
And left me there to pace the floor.

And once the nurse came out in haste
For something that had been misplaced,
And I that had been growing bold
Then felt my blood grow icy cold;
And fear's stern chill swept over me.
I stood and watched and tried to see
Just what it was she came to get.
I haven't learned that secret yet.
I half-believe that nurse in white

Was adding fuel to my fright
And taking an unholy glee,
From time to time, in torturing me.

Then silence! To her room I crept
And was informed the doctor slept!
The doctor slept! Oh, vicious thought,
While she at death's door bravely fought
And suffered untold anguish deep,
The doctor lulled himself to sleep.
I looked and saw him stretched out flat
And could have killed the man for that.
Then morning broke, and oh, the joy:
With dawn there came to us our boy.
And in a glorious little while
I went in there and saw her smile!

I must have looked a human wreck,
My collar wilted at my neck,
My hair awry, my features drawn
With all the suffering I had borne.
She looked at me and softly said,
"If I were you, I'd go to bed."
Her's was the bitterer part, I know;
She traveled through the vale of woe.
But now when women folks recall
The pain and anguish of it all
I answer them in manner sad:
"It's no cinch to become a dad."

Edgar A. Guest

Piano

Softly, in the dusk, a woman is singing to
    me;
Taking me back down the vista of years, till
    I see
A child sitting under the piano, in the boom
    of the tingling strings
And pressing the small, poised feet of a
    mother who smiles as she sings.

In spite of myself, the insidious mastery of
    song
Betrays me back, till the heart of me weeps
    to belong
To the old Sunday evenings at home, with
    winter outside
And hymns in the cosy parlour, the tinkling
    piano our guide.

So now it is vain for the singer to burst into
    clamour
With the great black piano appassionato.
    The glamour
Of childish days is upon me, my manhood is
    cast
Down in the flood of remembrance, I weep
    like a child for the past.

D. H. Lawrence

Prayer for This House

May nothing evil cross this door,
And may ill fortune never pry
About these windows; may the roar
　And rain go by.

Strengthened by faith, these rafters will
Withstand the batt'ring of the storm;
This hearth, though all the world grow chill,
　Will keep us warm.

Peace shall walk softly through these rooms,
Touching our lips with holy wine,
Till ev'ry casual corner blooms
　Into a shrine.

Laughter shall drown the raucous shout;
And, though these shelt'ring walls are thin,
May they be strong to keep hate out
　And hold love in.

Louis Untermeyer

The Hand That Rocks the Cradle Is the Hand That Rules the World

Blessing on the hand of women!
　Angels guard its strength and grace,
In the palace, cottage, hovel,
　Oh, no matter where the place;

Would that never storms assailed it,
    Rainbows ever gently curled;
For the hand that rocks the cradle
    Is the hand that rules the world.

Infancy's the tender fountain,
    Power may with beauty flow,
Mother's first to guide the streamlets,
    From them souls unresting grow —
Grow on for the good or evil,
    Sunshine streamed or evil hurled;
For the hand that rocks the cradle
    Is the hand that rules the world.

Woman, how divine your mission
    Here upon our natal sod!
Keep, oh, keep the young heart open
    Always to the breath of God!
All true trophies of the ages
    Are from mother-love impearled;
For the hand that rocks the cradle
    Is the hand that rules the world.

Blessings on the hand of women!
    Fathers, sons, and daughters cry,
And the sacred song is mingled
    With the worship in the sky —
Mingles where no tempest darkens,
    Rainbows evermore are hurled;
For the hand that rocks the cradle
    Is the hand that rules the world.
                            William Ross Wallace

Roofs

(For Amelia Josephine Burr)

The road is wide and the stars are out and
    the breath of the night is sweet,
And this is the time when wanderlust should
    seize upon my feet.
But I'm glad to turn from the open road and
    the starlight on my face,
And leave the splendor of out-of-doors for a
    human dwelling place.

I never have seen a vagabond who really
    liked to roam
All up and down the streets of the world and
    not to have a home:
The tramp who slept in your barn last night
    and left at break of day
Will wander only until he finds another
    place to stay.

A gypsy-man will sleep in his cart with
    canvas overhead;
Or else he'll go into his tent when it is time
    for bed.
He'll sit on the grass and take his ease so
    long as the sun is high,
But when it is dark he wants a roof to keep
    away the sky.

If you call a gypsy a vagabond, I think you
    do him wrong,
For he never goes a-travelling but he takes
    his home along.
And the only reason a road is good, as every
    wanderer knows,
Is just because of the homes, the homes, the
    homes to which it goes.

They say that life is a highway and its
    milestones are the years,
And now and then there's a toll-gate where
    you buy your way with tears.
It's a rough road and a steep road and it
    stretches broad and far,
But it leads at last to a golden Town where
    golden Houses are.

Joyce Kilmer

My Mother

Who fed me from her gentle breast
And hushed me in her arms to rest,
And on my cheek sweet kisses prest?
    My mother.

When sleep forsook my open eye,
Who was it sung sweet lullaby
And rocked me that I should not cry?
    My mother.

Who sat and watched my infant head
When sleeping in my cradle bed,
And tears of sweet affection shed?
    My mother.

When pain and sickness made me cry,
Who gazed upon my heavy eye
And wept, for fear that I should die?
    My mother.

Who ran to help me when I fell
And would some pretty story tell,
Or kiss the part to make it well?
    My mother.

Who taught my infant lips to pray,
To love God's holy word and day,
And walk in wisdom's pleasant way?
    My mother.

And can I ever cease to be
Affectionate and kind to thee
Who wast so very kind to me, —
    My mother.

Oh no, the thought I cannot bear;
And if God please my life to spare
I hope I shall reward thy care,
    My mother.

When thou art feeble, old and gray,
My healthy arm shall be thy stay,

And I will soothe thy pains away,
        My mother.

And when I see thee hang thy head,
'Twill be my turn to watch thy bed,
And tears of sweet affection shed, —
        My mother.
                            Jane Taylor

Rock Me to Sleep

Backward, turn backward, O time, in your
    flight,
Make me a child again just for to-night!
Mother, come back from the echoless shore,
Take me again to your heart as of yore;
Kiss from my forehead the furrows of care,
Smooth the few silver threads out of my
    hair;
Over my slumbers your loving watch
    keep; —
Rock me to sleep, Mother — rock me to
    sleep!

Backward, flow backward, oh, tide of the
    years!
I am so weary of toil and of tears —
Toil without recompense, tears all in vain —
Take them, and give me my childhood
    again!

I have grown weary of dust and decay —
Weary of flinging my soul-wealth away;
Weary of sowing for others to reap; —
Rock me to sleep, Mother — rock me to
　　sleep!

Tired of the hollow, the base, the untrue,
Mother, O Mother, my heart calls for you!
Many a summer the grass has grown green,
Blossomed and faded, our faces between:
Yet, with strong yearning and passionate
　　pain,
Long I to-night for your presence again.
Come from the silence so long and so deep;
　　—
Rock me to sleep, Mother — rock me to
　　sleep!

Over my heart, in the days that are flown,
No love like mother-love ever has shone;
No other worship abides and endures —
Faithful, unselfish, and patient like yours:
None like a mother can charm away pain
From the sick soul and the world-weary
　　brain.
Slumber's soft calms o'er my heavy lids
　　creep; —
Rock me to sleep, Mother — rock me to
　　sleep!

Come, let your brown hair, just lighted with
　　gold,

259

Fall on your shoulders again as of old;
Let it drop over my forehead to-night,
Shading my faint eyes away from the light;
For with its sunny-edged shadows once more
Haply will throng the sweet visions of yore;
Lovingly, softly, its bright billows
    sweep: —
Rock me to sleep, Mother — rock me to
    sleep!

Mother, dear Mother, the years have been
    long
Since I last listened your lullaby song:
Sing, then, and unto my soul it shall seem
Womanhood's years have been only a
    dream.
Clasped to your heart in a loving embrace,
With your light lashes just sweeping my
    face,
Never hereafter to wake or to weep; —
Rock me to sleep, Mother — rock me to
    sleep!

Elizabeth Akers Allen

Home Is Where There Is One
to Love Us

Home's not merely four square walls,
Though with pictures hung and gilded;
Home is where Affection calls —

Filled with shrines the Hearth had builded!
Home! Go watch the faithful dove,
Sailing 'neath the heaven above us.
Home is where there's one to love!
Home is where there's one to love us.

Home's not merely roof and room,
It needs something to endear it;
Home is where the heart can bloom,
Where there's some kind lip to cheer it!
What is home with none to meet,
None to welcome, none to greet us?
Home is sweet, and only sweet,
Where there's one we love to meet us!

Charles Swain

Suppose

Suppose, my little lady,
   Your doll should break her head;
Could you make it whole by crying
   Till your eyes and nose were red?
And wouldn't it be pleasanter
   To treat it as a joke,
And say you're glad 'twas dolly's
   And not your own that broke?

Suppose you're dressed for walking,
   And the rain comes pouring down;
Will it clear off any sooner
   Because you scold and frown?

And wouldn't it be nicer
  For you to smile than pout,
And so make sunshine in the house
  When there is none without?

Suppose your task, my little man,
  Is very hard to get;
Will it make it any easier
  For you to sit and fret?
And wouldn't it be wiser,
  Than waiting like a dunce,
To go to work in earnest
  And learn the thing at once?

Suppose that some boys have a horse,
  And some a coach and pair;
Will it tire you less while walking
  To say, ''It isn't fair''?
And wouldn't it be nobler
  To keep your temper sweet,
And in your heart be thankful
  You can walk upon your feet?

Suppose the world don't please you.
  Nor the way some people do;
Do you think the whole creation
  Will be altered just for you?
And isn't it, my boy or girl,
  The wisest, bravest plan,
Whatever comes, or doesn't come,
  To do the best you can?

                              Phoebe Cary

My Mother's Garden

Her heart is like her garden,
Old-fashioned, quaint and sweet,
With here a wealth of blossoms,
And there a still retreat.
Sweet violets are hiding,
We know as we pass by,
And lilies, pure as angel thoughts,
Are opening somewhere nigh.

Forget-me-nots there linger,
To full perfection brought,
And there bloom purple pansies
In many a tender thought.
There love's own roses blossom,
As from enchanted ground,
And lavish perfume exquisite
The whole glad year around.

And in that quiet garden —
The garden of her heart —
Songbirds are always singing
Their songs of cheer apart.
And from it floats forever,
O'ercoming sin and strife,
Sweet as the breath of roses blown,
The fragrance of her life.

Alice E. Allen

Grief and Death

Even Such Is Time

Even such is Time, which takes in trust
  Our youth, and joys, and all we have;
And pays us but with age and dust,
  Which, in the dark and silent grave,
When we have wandered all our ways,
Shuts up the story of our days:
  And from which earth and grave and dust
  The Lord shall raise me up, I trust.
                  Sir Walter Raleigh

Death the Leveller

The glories of our blood and state
  Are shadows, not substantial things;
There is no armour against Fate;
  Death lays his icy hand on kings:
      Sceptre and crown
      Must tumble down,
And in the dust be equal made
With the poor crookèd scythe and spade.

Some men with swords may reap the field,
  And plant fresh laurels where they kill;

But their strong nerves at last must yield;
　They tame but one another still:
　　　Early or late
　　　They stoop to fate,
And must give up their murmuring breath
When they, pale captives, creep to death.

The garlands wither on your brow;
　Then boast no more your mighty deeds!
Upon Death's purple altar now
　See where the victor-victim bleeds.
　　　Your heads must come
　　　To the cold tomb:
Only the actions of the just
Smell sweet and blossom in their dust.

James Shirley

They Are All Gone

They are all gone into the world of light!
　And I alone sit lingering here;
Their very memory is fair and bright,
　　And my sad thoughts doth clear.

It glows and glitters in my cloudy breast,
　Like stars upon some gloomy grove,
Or those faint beams in which this hill is
　　dressed,
　　After the sun's remove.

I see them walking in an air of glory,
  Whose light doth trample on my days;
My days, which are at best but dull and
    hoary,
      Mere glimmering and decays.

O holy Hope! and high Humility!
  High as the heavens above!
These are your walks, and you have showed
    them me,
      To kindle my cold love.

Dear beauteous Death! the jewel of the just,
  Shining nowhere but in the dark;
What mysteries do lie beyond thy dust,
      Could man outlook that mark!

He that hath found some fledged bird's nest
    may know
  At first sight if the bird be flown;
But what fair well or grove he sings in now,
      That is to him unknown.

And yet, as angels in some brighter dreams
  Call to the soul when man doth sleep,
So some strange thoughts transcend our
    wonted themes,
      And into glory peep.

If a star were confined into a tomb,
  Her captive flames must needs burn there;

But when the hand that locked her up gives
    room,
        She'll shine through all the sphere.

O Father of eternal life, and all
    Created glories under Thee!
Resume Thy spirit from this world of thrall
        Into true liberty.

Either disperse these mists, which blot and
    fill
    My perspective still as they pass;
Or else remove me hence unto that hill
        Where I shall need no glass.
                   Henry Vaughan

On His Deceased Wife

Methought I saw my late espousèd Saint
Brought to me like Alcestis from the grave,
Whom Jove's great Son to her glad Husband
    gave,
Rescued from death by force though pale
    and faint,
Mine as whom washed from spot of child-
    bed taint,
Purification in the old Law did save,
And such, as yet once more I trust to have
Full sight of her in Heaven without restraint,
Came vested all in white, pure as her mind:

Her face was veiled, yet to my fancied
   sight,
Love, sweetness, goodness, in her person
   shined
So clear, as in no face with more delight.
But O as to embrace me she inclined
I waked, she fled, and day brought back my
   night.

John Milton

Vital Spark of Heavenly Flame

Vital spark of heavenly flame!
Quit, O quit this mortal frame:
   Trembling, hoping, lingering, flying,
   O the pain, the bliss of dying!
Cease, fond Nature, cease thy strife,
And let me languish into life.

   Hark! they whisper; angels say,
   Sister Spirit, come away!
   What is this absorbs me quite?
   Steals my senses, shuts my sight,
Drowns my spirits, draws my breath?
Tell me, my soul, can this be death?

The world recedes; it disappears!
Heav'n opens on my eyes! my ears
   With sounds seraphic ring!
Lend, lend your wings! I mount! I fly!

O Grave! where is thy victory?
O Death! where is thy sting?
Alexander Pope

A Slumber Did My Spirit Seal

A slumber did my spirit seal;
  I had no human fears;
She seemed a thing that could not feel
  The touch of earthly years.

No motion has she now, no force;
  She neither hears nor sees;
Rolled round in earth's diurnal course,
  With rocks, and stones, and trees.
William Wordsworth

Desideria

Surprised by joy — impatient as the Wind
  I turned to share the transport — O! with
    whom
But thee, deep buried in the silent tomb,
That spot which no vicissitude can find?
Love, faithful love, recall'd thee to my
    mind —
  But how could I forget thee? Through
    what power,
Even for the least division of an hour,

Have I been so beguiled as to be blind
To my most grievous loss? — That
      thought's return
   Was the worst pang that sorrow ever bore,
Save one, one only, when I stood forlorn,
   Knowing my heart's best treasure was no
      more;
That neither present time, nor years unborn
   Could to my sight that heavenly face
      restore.

                              William Wordsworth

Prospice

Fear death? — to feel the fog in my throat,
   The mist in my face,
When the snows begin, and the blasts denote
   I am nearing the place,
The power of the night, the press of the
      storm,
   The post of the foe;
Where he stands, the Arch Fear in a visible
      form,
   Yet the strong man must go;

For the journey is done and the summit
      attained,
   And the barriers fall,
Though a battle's to fight ere the guerdon be
      gained,

The reward of it all.
I was ever a fighter, so — one fight more,
   The best and the last!
I would hate that death bandaged my eyes,
      and forebore,
   And bade me creep past.
No! let me taste the whole of it, fare like my
      peers
   The heroes of old,
Bear the brunt, in a minute pay glad life's
      arrears
   Of pain, darkness and cold.
For sudden the worst turns the best to the
      brave,
   The black minute's at end,
And the elements' rage, the fiend-voices that
      rave,
   Shall dwindle, shall blend,
Shall change, shall become first a peace out
      of pain,
   Then a light, then thy breast,
O thou soul of my soul! I shall clasp thee
      again,
   And with God be the rest!

                              Robert Browning

Remembrance

Cold in the earth, and the deep snow piled
   above thee!
Far, far removed, cold in the dreary grave!

Have I forgot, my Only Love, to love thee,
Severed at last by Time's all-wearing wave?

Now, when alone, do my thoughts no longer
   hover
Over the mountains on Angora's shore;
Resting their wings where heath and fern-
   leaves cover
That noble heart for ever, ever more?

Cold in the earth, and fifteen wild
   Decembers
From those brown hills have melted into
   spring —
Faithful indeed is the spirit that remembers
After such years of change and suffering!

Sweet Love of youth, forgive if I forget thee
While the World's tide is bearing me along:
Sterner desires and darker hopes beset me,
Hopes which obscure but cannot do thee
   wrong.

No other Sun has lightened up my heaven;
No other Star has ever shone for me:
All my life's bliss from thy dear life was
   given —
All my life's bliss is in the grave with thee.

But when the days of golden dreams had
   perished
And even Despair was powerless to destroy,

Then did I learn how existence could be
  cherished,
Strengthened and fed without the aid of joy;

Then did I check the tears of useless
  passion,
Weaned my young soul from yearning after
  thine:
Sternly denied its burning wish to hasten
Down to that tomb already more than mine!

And even yet, I dare not let it languish,
Dare not indulge in Memory's rapturous
  pain;
Once drinking deep of that divinest anguish,
How could I seek the empty world again?

Emily Brontë

The Death of the Flowers

The melancholy days are come, the saddest
  of the year,
Of wailing winds, and naked woods, and
  meadows brown and sere.
Heaped in the hollows of the grove, the
  autumn leaves die dead;
They rustle to the eddying gust, and to the
  rabbit's tread;
The robin and the wren are flown, and from
  the shrubs the jay,

And from the wood-top calls the crow
  through all the gloomy day.

Where are the flowers, the fair young
  flowers, that lately sprang and stood
In brighter light and softer airs, a beauteous
  sisterhood?
Alas! they all are in their graves, the gentle
  race of flowers
Are lying in their lowly beds, with the fair
  and good of ours.
The rain is falling where they lie, but the
  cold November rain
Calls not from out the gloomy earth the
  lovely ones again.

The wind-flower and the violet, they
  perished long ago,
And the brier-rose and the orchis died amid
  the summer glow;
But on the hill the golden-rod, and the aster
  in the wood,
And the yellow sun-flower by the brook, in
  autumn beauty stood,
Till fell the frost from the clear cold heaven,
  as falls the plague on men,
And the brightness of their smile was gone,
  from upland, glade, and glen.

And now, when comes the calm mild day,
  as still such days will come,

To call the squirrel and the bee from out
   their winter home;
When the sound of dropping nuts is heard,
   though all the trees are still,
And twinkle in the smoky light the waters of
   the rill,
The south wind searches for the flowers
   whose fragrance late he bore,
And sighs to find them in the wood and by
   the stream no more.

And then I think of one who in her youthful
   beauty died,
The fair meek blossom that grew up and
   faded by my side.
In the cold moist earth we laid her, when the
   forest cast the leaf,
And we wept that one so lovely should have
   a life so brief:
Yet not unmeet it was that one like that
   young friend of ours,
So gentle and so beautiful, should perish
   with the flowers.

William Cullen Bryant

Along the Road

I walked a mile with Pleasure;
   She chattered all the way,
But left me none the wiser
   For all she had to say.

I walked a mile with Sorrow
    And ne'er a word said she;
But oh, the things I learned from her
    When Sorrow walked with me!
        Robert Browning Hamilton

Telling the Bees

Here is the place; right over the hill
    Runs the path I took;
You can see the gap in the old wall still,
    And the stepping-stones in the shallow
        brook.

There is the house, with the gate red-barred,
    And the poplars tall;
And the barn's brown length, and the cattle-
        yard,
    And the white horns tossing above the
        wall.

There are the beehives ranged in the sun;
    And down by the brink
Of the brook are her poor flowers, weed-
        o'errun,
    Pansy and daffodil, rose and pink.

A year has gone, as the tortoise goes,
    Heavy and slow;

And the same rose blows, and the same sun
     glows,
  And the same brook sings of a year ago.

There's the same sweet clover-smell in the
     breeze;
  And the June sun warm
Tangles his wings of fire in the trees,
  Setting, as then, over Fernside farm.

I mind me how with a lover's care
  From my Sunday coat
I brushed off the burrs, and smoothed my
     hair,
  And cooled at the brookside my brow and
     throat.

Since we parted, a month had passed, —
  To love, a year;
Down through the beeches I looked at last
  On the little red gate and the well-sweep
     near.

I can see it all now, — the slantwise rain
  Of light through the leaves.
The sundown's blaze on her window-pane,
  The bloom of her roses under the eaves.

Just the same as a month before, —
  The house and the trees,

The barn's brown gable, the vine by the
      door, —
  Nothing changed but the hives of bees.

Before them, under the garden wall,
  Forward and back,
Went drearily singing the chore-girl small,
  Draping each hive with a shred of black.

Trembling, I listened: the summer sun
  Had the chill of snow:
For I knew she was telling the bees of one
  Gone on the journey we all must go!

Then I said to myself, "My Mary weeps
  For the dead to-day:
Haply her blind old grandsire sleeps
  The fret and the pain of his age away."

But her dog whined low: on the doorway
      sill,
  With his cane to his chin,
The old man sat; and the chore-girl still
  Sang to the bees stealing out and in.

And the song she was singing ever since
  In my ear sounds on: —
"Stay at home, pretty bees, fly not hence!
  Mistress Mary is dead and gone!"
              John Greenleaf Whittier

Verses Written in 1872

Though he that, ever kind and true,
Kept stoutly step by step with you,
Your whole long, gusty lifetime through,
  Be gone a while before —
Be now a moment gone before —
Yet doubt not; soon the season shall restore
  Your friend to you.
He has but turned the corner — still
He pushes on with right good will
Through mire and marsh, by heugh and hill
  That selfsame arduous way —
That selfsame, upland, hopeful way,
That you and he, through many a doubtful
    day
  Attempted still.

He is not dead — this friend — not dead,
But in the path we mortals tread
Got some few trifling steps ahead,
  And nearer to the end;
So that you, too, once past the bend,
Shall meet again, as face to face, this friend
  You fancy dead.

Push gaily on, brave heart, the while
You travel forward mile by mile,
He loiters, with a backward smile,
  Till you can overtake;
And strains his eyes to search his wake,

Or, whistling as he sees you through the
    brake,
    Waits on a stile.
                            Robert Louis Stevenson

Not Thou But I

It must have been for one of us, my own,
To drink this cup and eat this bitter bread,
Had not my tears upon thy face been shed,
Thy tears had dropped on mine; if I alone
Did not walk now, thy spirit would have
    known
My loneliness, and did my feet not tread
This weary path and steep, thy feet had bled
For mine, and thy mouth had for mine made
    moan;
And so it comforts me, yea, not in vain
To think of thy eternity of sleep,
To know thine eyes are tearless though mine
    weep;
And when this cup's last bitterness I drain,
One thought shall still its primal sweetness
    keep —
Thou hadst the peace and I the undying
    pain.
                            Philip Bourke Marston

So Might It Be

Death, when you come to me, tread with a
    footstep
  Light as the moon's on the grasses asleep,
So that I know not the moment of darkness,
  Know not the drag and the draw of the
    deep.

Death, when you come to me, let there be
    sunlight,
  Dogs and dear creatures about me at play,
Flowers in the fields and the song of the
    blackbird —
  Spring in the world when you fetch me
    away!

John Galsworthy

To an Athlete Dying Young

The time you won your town the race
We chaired you through the market-place;
Man and boy stood cheering by,
And home we brought you shoulder-high.

To-day, the road all runners come,
Shoulder-high we bring you home,
And set you at your threshold down,
Townsman of a stiller town.

Smart lad, to slip betimes away
From fields where glory does not stay
And early though the laurel grows
It withers quicker than the rose.

Eyes the shady night has shut
Cannot see the record cut,
And silence sounds no worse than cheers
After earth has stopped the ears:

Now you will not swell the rout
Of lads that wore their honours out,
Runners whom renown outran
And the name died before the man.

So set, before its echoes fade,
The fleet foot on the sill of shade,
And hold to the low lintel up
The still-defended challenge-cup.

And round that early-laurelled head
Will flock to gaze the strengthless dead,
And find unwithered on its curls
The garland briefer than a girl's.

A. E. Housman

The House with Nobody in It

Whenever I walk to Suffern along the Erie
    track
I go by a poor old farmhouse with its
    shingles broken and black.
I suppose I've passed it a hundred times, but
    I always stop for a minute
And look at the house, the tragic house, the
    house with nobody in it.

I never have seen a haunted house, but I
    hear there are such things;
That they hold the talk of spirits, their mirth
    and sorrowings.
I know this house isn't haunted, and I wish
    it were, I do;
For it wouldn't be so lonely if it had a ghost
    or two.

This house on the road to Suffern needs a
    dozen panes of glass,
And somebody ought to weed the walk and
    take a scythe to the grass.
It needs new paint and shingles, and the
    vines should be trimmed and tied;
But what it needs the most of all is some
    people living inside.

If I had a lot of money and all my debts
    were paid,

I'd put a gang of men to work with brush
    and saw and spade.
I'd buy that place and fix it up the way it
    used to be,
And I'd find some people who wanted a
    home and give it to them free.

Now a new house standing empty, with
    staring window and door,
Looks idle, perhaps, and foolish, like a hat
    on its block in the store.
But there's nothing mournful about it; it
    cannot be sad and lone
For the lack of something within it that it
    has never known.

But a house that has done what a house
    should do, a house that has sheltered life,
That has put its loving wooden arms around
    a man and his wife,
A house that has echoed a baby's laugh and
    held up his stumbling feet,
Is the saddest sight, when it's left alone,
    that ever your eyes could meet.

So whenever I go to Suffern along the Erie
    track
I never go by the empty house without
    stopping and looking back;
Yet it hurts me to look at the crumbling roof
    and the shutters fallen apart,

For I can't help thinking the poor old house
  is a house with a broken heart.
Joyce Kilmer

Should You Go First

Should you go first and I remain
  To walk the road alone,
I'll live in memory's garden, dear,
  With happy days we've known.
In Spring I'll wait for roses red,
  When fades the lilac blue,
In early Fall, when brown leaves call
  I'll catch a glimpse of you.

Should you go first and I remain
  For battles to be fought,
Each thing you've touched along the way
  Will be a hallowed spot.
I'll hear your voice, I'll see your smile,
  Though blindly I may grope,
The memory of your helping hand
  Will buoy me on with hope.

Should you go first and I remain
  To finish with the scroll,
No length'ning shadows shall creep in
  To make this life seem droll.
We've known so much of happiness,
  We've had our cup of joy,

And memory is one gift of God
    That death cannot destroy.

Should you go first and I remain,
    One thing I'd have you do:
Walk slowly down that long, lone path,
    For soon I'll follow you.
I'll want to know each step you take
    That I may walk the same,
For some day down that lonely road
    You'll hear me call your name.

                A. K. Rowswell

Tract

I will teach you my townspeople
how to perform a funeral
for you have it over a troop
of artists —
unless one should scour the world —
you have the ground sense necessary.

See! the hearse leads.
I begin with a design for a hearse.
For Christ's sake not black —
nor white either — and not polished!
Let it be weathered — like a farm wagon —
with gilt wheels (this could be
applied fresh at small expense)
or no wheels at all:
a rough dray to drag over the ground.

Knock the glass out!
My God — glass, my townspeople!
For what purpose? Is it for the dead
to look out or for us to see
how well he is housed or to see
the flowers or the lack of them —
or what?
To keep the rain and snow from him?
He will have a heavier rain soon:
pebbles and dirt and what not.
Let there be no glass —
and no upholstery, phew!
and no little brass rollers
and small easy wheels on the bottom —
my townspeople what are you thinking of?

A rough plain hearse then
with gilt wheels and no top at all.
On this the coffin lies
by its own weight.

                No wreaths please —
especially no hot house flowers.
Some common memento is better,
something he prized and is known by:
his old clothes — a few books perhaps —
God knows what! You realize
how we are about these things
my townspeople —
something will be found — anything
even flowers if he had come to that.

So much for the hearse.

For heaven's sake though see to the driver!
Take off the silk hat! In fact
that's no place at all for him —
up there unceremoniously
dragging our friend out to his own dignity!
Bring him down — bring him down!
Low and inconspicuous! I'd not have him
   ride
on the wagon at all — damn him —
the undertaker's understrapper!
Let him hold the reins
and walk at the side
and inconspicuously too!

Then briefly as to yourselves:
Walk behind — as they do in France,
seventh class, or if you ride
Hell take curtains! Go with some show
of inconvenience; sit openly —
to the weather as to grief.

Or do you think you can shut grief in?
What — from us? We who have perhaps
nothing to lose? Share with us
share with us — it will be money
in your pockets.

        Go now
I think you are ready.
         William Carlos Williams

A Refusal to Mourn the Death, by Fire, of a Child in London

Never until the mankind making
Bird beast and flower
Fathering and all humbling darkness
Tells with silence the last light breaking
And the still hour
Is come of the sea tumbling in harness

And I must enter again the round
Zion of the water bead
And the synagogue of the ear of corn
Shall I let pray the shadow of a sound
Or sow my salt seed
In the least valley of sackcloth to mourn

The majesty and burning of the child's
　　death.
I shall not murder
The mankind of her going with a grave truth
Nor blaspheme down the stations of the
　　breath
With any further
Elegy of innocence and youth

Deep with the first dead lies London's
　　daughter,
Robed in the long friends,
The grains beyond age, the dark veins of her
　　mother

Secret by the unmourning water
Of the riding Thames.
After the first death, there is no other.

Dylan Thomas

Patriotism and War

The Harp that Once Through Tara's Halls

The harp that once through Tara's halls
   The soul of music shed,
Now hangs as mute on Tara's walls
   As if that soul were fled.
So sleeps the pride of former days,
   So glory's thrill is o'er,
And hearts that once beat high for praise
   Now feel that pulse no more!
No more to chiefs and ladies bright
   The harp of Tara swells;
The chord alone that breaks at night
   Its tale of ruin tells.
Thus Freedom now so seldom wakes,
   The only throb she gives
Is when some heart indignant breaks,
   To show that still she lives.

Thomas Moore

Concord Hymn

*At the completion of the Concord Monument,
April 19, 1836*

By the rude bridge that arched the flood,
　　Their flag to April's breeze unfurled,
Here once the embattled farmers stood,
　　And fired the shot heard round the world.

The foe long since in silence slept;
　　Alike the conqueror silent sleeps;
And Time the ruined bridge has swept
　　Down the dark stream which seaward
　　　creeps.

On this green bank, by this soft stream,
　　We set to-day a votive stone;
That memory may their deed redeem,
　　When, like our sires, our sons are gone.

Spirit, that made those heroes dare
　　To die, and leave their children free,
Bid Time and Nature gently spare
　　The shaft we raise to them and thee.

Ralph Waldo Emerson

Emily Geiger

'Twas in the days of the Revolution, —
   Dark days were they and drear, —
And by Carolina firesides
   The women sat in fear;
For the men were away at the fighting,
   And sad was the news that came,
That the battle was lost; and the death-list
   Held many a loved one's name.

When as heart-sore they sat round the camp-
     fires,
   "What, ho! Who'll volunteer
To carry a message to Sumter?"
   A voice rang loud and clear.
There was a sudden silence,
   But not a man replied;
They knew too well of the peril
   Of one who dared that ride.

Outspoke then Emily Geiger
   With a rich flush on her cheek, —
"Give me the message to be sent;
   I am the one you seek.
For I am a Southern woman;
   And I'd rather do and dare
Than sit by a lonely fireside,
   My heart gnawed through with care."

They gave her the precious missive;

And on her own good steed
She rode away, 'mid the cheers of the men,
    Upon her daring deed.
And away through the lonely forests,
    Steadily galloping on,
She saw the sun sink low in the sky,
    And in the west go down.

"Halt! — or I fire!" On a sudden
    A rifle clicked close by.
"Let you pass? Not we, till we know you
        are
    No messenger or spy."
"She's a Whig, — from her face, — I will
        wager,"
    Swore the officer of the day.
"To the guard-house, and send for a woman
    To search her without delay."

No time did she lose in bewailing;
    As the bolt creaked in the lock,
She quickly drew the precious note
    That was hidden in her frock.
And she read it through with hurried care,
    Then ate it piece by piece,
And calmly sat her down to wait
    Till time should bring release.

They brought her out in a little,
    And set her on her steed,
With many a rude apology,
    For his discourteous deed.

On, on, once more through the forest black,
  The good horse panting strains,
Till the sentry's challenge: "Who comes
    there?"
  Tells that the end she gains.

Ere an hour, in the camp of Sumter
  There was hurrying to and fro.
"Saddle and mount, saddle and mount,"
  The bugles shrilly blow.
"Forward trot!" and the long ranks wheel,
  And into the darkness glides:
Long shall the British rue that march
  And Emily Geiger's ride.

Unknown

The March into Virginia

Ending in the First Manassas
(July 1861)

Did all the lets and bars appear
  To every just or larger end,
Whence should come the trust and cheer?
  Youth must its ignorant impulse lend —
Age finds place in the rear.
  All wars are boyish, and are fought by
    boys,
The champions and enthusiasts of the state:
  Turbid ardours and vain joys
    Not barrenly abate —

Stimulants to the power mature,
    Preparatives of fate.

Who here forecasteth the event?
What heart but spurns at precedent
And warnings of the wise,
Contemned foreclosures of surprise?
The banners play, the bugles call,
The air is blue and prodigal.
    No berrying party, pleasure-wooed,
No picnic party in the May,
Ever went less loth than they
    Into that leafy neighborhood.
In Bacchic glee they file toward Fate,
Moloch's uninitiate;
Expectancy, and glad surmise
Of battle's unknown mysteries.

All they feel is this: 'tis glory,
A rapture sharp, though transitory,
Yet lasting in belaurelled story.
So they gaily go to fight,
Chatting left and laughing right.

But some who this blithe mood present,
    As on in lightsome files they fare,
Shall die experienced ere three days are
        spent —
    Perish, enlightened by the volleyed glare;
Or shame survive, and, like to adamant,
    The throe of Second Manassas share.

                    Herman Melville

302

The Blue and the Gray

By the flow of the inland river,
  Whence the fleets of iron have fled,
Where the blades of the grave grass quiver,
  Asleep are the ranks of the dead; —
    Under the sod and the dew,
      Waiting the judgment day; —
    Under the one, the Blue;
      Under the other, the Gray.

These in the robings of glory,
  Those in the gloom of defeat,
All with the battle blood gory,
  In the dusk of eternity meet; —
    Under the sod and the dew,
      Waiting the judgment day; —
    Under the laurel, the Blue;
      Under the willow, the Gray.

From the silence of sorrowful hours
  The desolate mourners go,
Lovingly laden with flowers
  Alike for the friend and the foe, —
    Under the sod and the dew,
      Waiting the judgment day; —
    Under the roses, the Blue;
      Under the lilies, the Gray.

So with an equal splendor
  The morning sun rays fall,
With a touch, impartially tender,
  On the blossoms blooming for all; —
    Under the sod and the dew,
      Waiting the judgment day; —
    'Broidered with gold, the Blue;
      Mellowed with gold, the Gray.

So, when the summer calleth,
  On forest and field of grain
With an equal murmur falleth
  The cooling drip of the rain; —
    Under the sod and the dew,
      Waiting the judgment day; —
    Wet with the rain, the Blue;
      Wet with the rain, the Gray.

Sadly, but not with upbraiding,
  The generous deed was done;
In the storm of the years that are fading,
  No braver battle was won; —
    Under the sod and the dew,
      Waiting the judgment day; —
    Under the blossoms, the Blue;
      Under the garlands, the Gray.

No more shall the war cry sever,
  Or the winding rivers be red;
They banish our anger forever
  When they laurel the graves of our dead!
    Under the sod and the dew,

Waiting the judgment day; —
Love and tears for the Blue,
Tears and love for the Gray.
                    Frances Miles Finch

The Fighting Race

"Read out the names!" and Burke sat back,
    And Kelly drooped his head,
While Shea — they called him Scholar
    Jack —
    Went down the list of the dead.
Officers, seamen, gunners, marines,
    The crews of the gig and yawl,
The bearded man and the lad in his teens,
    Carpenters, coal passers — all.
Then, knocking the ashes from out his pipe,
    Said Burke in an offhand way:
"We're all in that dead man's list, by cripe!
    Kelly and Burke and Shea."
"Well, here's to the Maine, and I'm sorry
    for Spain,"
    Said Kelly and Burke and Shea.

"Wherever there's Kellys there's trouble,"
    said Burke.
    "Wherever fighting's the game,
Or a spice of danger in grown man's work,"
    Said Kelly, "you'll find my name."
"And do we fall short," said Burke, getting
    mad,

305

"When it's touch and go for life?"
Said Shea, "It's thirty-odd years, bedad,
    Since I charged to drum and fife
Up Marye's Heights, and my old canteen
    Stopped a rebel ball on its way;
There were blossoms of blood on our sprigs
        of green —
    Kelly and Burke and Shea —
And the dead didn't brag." "Well, here's to
        the flag!"
    Said Kelly and Burke and Shea.

"I wish 'twas in Ireland, for there's the
        place,"
    Said Burke, "that we'd die by right,
In the cradle of our soldier race,
    After one good stand-up fight.
My grandfather fell on Vinegar Hill,
    And fighting was not his trade;
But his rusty pike's in the cabin still,
    With Hessian blood on the blade."
"Aye, aye," said Kelly, "the pikes were
        great
    When the word was 'clear the way!'
We were thick on the roll in ninety-eight —
    Kelly and Burke and Shea."
"Well, here's to the pike and the sword and
        the like!"
    Said Kelly and Burke and Shea.

And Shea, the scholar, with rising joy,
    Said, "We were at Ramillies;

306

We left our bones at Fontenoy
  And up in the Pyrenees;
Before Dunkirk, on Landen's plain,
  Cremona, Lille, and Ghent;
We're all over Austria, France and Spain,
  Wherever they pitched a tent.
We've died for England from Waterloo
  To Egypt and Dargai;
And still there's enough for a corps or crew,
  Kelly and Burke and Shea.''
''Well, here's to good honest fighting
    blood!''
  Said Kelly and Burke and Shea.

''Oh, the fighting races don't die out,
  If they seldom die in bed,
For love is first in their hearts, no doubt,''
  Said Burke; then Kelly said:
''When Michael, the Irish Archangel,
    stands,
  The Angel with the sword,
And the battle dead from a hundred lands
  Are ranged in one big horde,
Our line, that for Gabriel's trumpet waits,
  Will stretch three deep that day,
From Jehoshaphat to the Golden Gates —
  Kelly and Burke and Shea.''
''Well, here's thank God for the race and
    the sod!''
  Said Kelly and Burke and Shea.
                    Joseph I. C. Clarke

England, My England

What have I done for you,
  England, my England?
What is there I would not do,
  England, my own?
With your glorious eyes austere,
As the Lord were walking near,
Whispering terrible things and dear
    As the Song on your bugles blown,
      England —
    Round the world on your bugles blown!

Where shall the watchful Sun,
  England, my England,
Match the master-work you've done,
  England, my own?
When shall he rejoice agen
Such a breed of mighty men
As come forward, one to ten,
    To the Song on your bugles blown,
      England —
    Down the years on your bugles blown?

Ever the faith endures,
  England, my England: —
''Take and break us: we are yours,
  England, my own!
Life is good, and joy runs high
Between English earth and sky:
Death is death; but we shall die

To the Song on your bugles blown,
    England —
To the stars on your bugles blown!''

They call you proud and hard,
    England, my England:
You with worlds to watch and ward,
    England, my own!
You whose mailed hand keeps the keys
Of such teeming destinies,
You could know nor dread nor ease
    Were the Song on your bugles blown,
      England,
    Round the Pit on your bugles blown!

Mother of Ships whose might
    England, my England,
Is the fierce old Sea's delight,
    England, my own,
Chosen daughter of the Lord,
Spouse-in-Chief of the ancient Sword,
There's the menace of the Word
    In the Song on your bugles blown,
      England —
    Out of heaven on your bugles blown!
              William Ernest Henley

America for Me

'Tis fine to see the Old World, and travel up
and down
Among the famous palaces and cities of
renown,
To admire the crumbly castles and the
statues of the kings, —
But now I think I've had enough of
antiquated things.

So it's home again, and home again,
America for me!
My heart is turning home again, and there
I long to be
In the land of youth and freedom beyond
the ocean bars,
Where the air is full of sunlight and the
flag is full of stars.

Oh, London is a man's town, there's power
in the air;
And Paris is a woman's town, with flowers
in her hair;
And it's sweet to dream in Venice, and it's
great to study Rome,
But when it comes to living, there is no
place like home.

I like the German fir-woods, in green
battalions drilled;

I like the gardens of Versailles with flashing
  fountains filled;
But, oh, to take your hand, my dear, and
  ramble for a day
In the friendly western woodland where
  Nature has her way!

I know that Europe's wonderful, yet
  something seems to lack!
The Past is too much with her, and the
  people looking back.
But the glory of the Present is to make the
  Future free, —
We love our land for what she is and what
  she is to be.

  Oh, it's home again, and home again,
    America for me!
  I want a ship that's westward bound to
    plough the rolling sea
  To the blessed Land of Room Enough
    beyond the ocean bars,
  Where the air is full of sunlight and the
    flag is full of stars.

Henry Van Dyke

I Have Loved England

I have loved England, dearly and deeply,
Since the first morning, shining and pure,
The white cliffs, of Dover, I saw rising
    steeply,
Out of the sea that once made her secure.

I had no thought then of husband or lover,
I was a traveler, the guest of a week;
Yet when they pointed "the white cliffs of
    Dover"
Startled I found there were tears on my
    cheek.

I have loved England, and still as a stranger,
Here is my home, and I still am alone.
Now in her hour of trial and danger,
Only the English are really her own.

From *The White Cliffs*
Alice Duer Miller

Grass

Pile the bodies high at Austerlitz and
    Waterloo.
Shovel them under and let me work —
    I am the grass; I cover all.

And pile them high at Gettysburg

And pile them high at Ypres and Verdun.
Shovel them under and let me work.
Two years, ten years, and passengers ask the
    conductor:
  What place is this?
  Where are we now?

  I am the grass.
  Let me work.

Carl Sandburg

Faith and Inspiration

The Lord Is My Shepherd

The Lord is my shepherd; I shall not want.

He maketh me to lie down in green pastures: he leadeth me beside the still waters.

He restoreth my soul: he leadeth me in the paths of righteousness for his name's sake.

Yea, though I walk through the valley of the shadow of death, I will fear no evil: for thou art with me; thy rod and thy staff they comfort me.

Thou preparest a table before me in the presence of mine enemies: thou anointest my head with oil; my cup runneth over.

Surely goodness and mercy shall follow me all the days of my life: and I will dwell in the house of the Lord forever.

Psalm 23

Batter My Heart

Batter my heart, three personed God; for
   you
As yet but knock, breathe, shine, and seek
   to mend;
That I may rise and stand, o'erthrow me and
   bend
Your force to break, blow, burn and make
   me new.
I, like an usurped town, to another due,
Labour to admit you, but Oh, to no end;
Reason, your viceroy in me, me should
   defend,
But is captived and proves weak or untrue.

Yet dearly I love you and would be loved
   fain,
But am betrothed unto your enemy:
Divorce me, untie or break that knot again,
Take me to you, imprison me, for I
Except you enthrall me, never shall be free,
Nor ever chaste, except you ravish me.

John Donne

At the Round Earth's Imagined Corners

At the round earth's imagined corners, blow
Your trumpets, angels, and arise, arise
From death, you numberless infinities
Of souls, and to your scattered bodies go;

All whom the flood did, and fire shall
    o'erthrow;
All whom war, dearth, age, agues,
    tyrannies,
Despair, law, chance, hath slain, and you
    whose eyes
Shall behold God, and never taste death's
    woe.

But let them sleep, Lord, and me mourn a
    space,
For, if above all these, my sins abound,
'Tis late to ask abundance of Thy grace,
When we are there; here on this lowly
    ground,
Teach me how to repent; for that's as good
As if Thou hadst sealed my pardon with Thy
    blood.

John Donne

His Litany to the Holy Spirit

In the hour of my distress,
When temptations me oppress,
And when I my sins confess,
    Sweet Spirit, comfort me!

When I lie within my bed,
Sick in heart and sick in head,
And with doubts discomforted,
    Sweet Spirit, comfort me!

When the house doth sigh and weep,
And the world is drowned in sleep,
Yet mine eyes the watch do keep,
  Sweet Spirit, comfort me!

When the artless doctor sees
No one hope, but of his fees,
And his skill runs on the lees,
  Sweet Spirit, comfort me!

When his potion and his pill,
His, or none, or little skill,
Meet for nothing, but to kill,
  Sweet Spirit, comfort me!

When the passing-bell doth toll,
And the furies in a shoal
Come to fright a parting soul,
  Sweet Spirit, comfort me!

When the tapers now burn blue,
And the comforters are few,
And that number more than true,
  Sweet Spirit, comfort me!

When the priest his last hath prayed,
And I nod to what is said
'Cause my speech is now decayed,
  Sweet Spirit, comfort me!

When, God knows, I'm tossed about
Either with despair or doubt,
Yet, before the glass be out,
  Sweet Spirit, comfort me!

When the tempter me pursu'th
With the sins of all my youth,
And half damns me with untruth,
  Sweet Spirit, comfort me!

When the flames and hellish cries
Fright mine ears and fright mine eyes,
And all terrors me surprise,
  Sweet Spirit, comfort me!

When the Judgment is revealed,
And that opened which was sealed,
When to Thee I have appealed,
  Sweet Spirit, comfort me!

Robert Herrick

The Collar

I struck the board, and cried, "No more;
  I will abroad!
What, shall I ever sigh and pine?
My lines and life are free; free as the road,
  Loose as the wind, as large as store.
    Shall I be still in suit?
Have I no harvest but a thorn

To let me blood, and not restore
What I have lost with cordial fruit?
    Sure there was wine
  Before my sighs did dry it; there was corn
    Before my tears did drown it;
  Is the year only lost to me?
  Have I no bays to crown it,
No flowers, no garlands gay? all blasted,
    All wasted?
  Not so, my heart; but there is fruit,
    And thou hast hands.
  Recover all thy sigh-blown age
On double pleasures; leave thy cold dispute
Of what is fit and not; forsake thy cage,
    Thy rope of sands
Which petty thoughts have made; and made
    to thee
  Good cable, to enforce and draw,
    And be thy law,
While thou didst wink and wouldst not
    see.
    Away! take heed;
    I will abroad.
Call in thy death's head there, tie up thy
    fears:
    He that forbears
  To suit and serve his need
    Deserves his load.''
But as I raved, and grew more fierce and
    wild
    At every word,

Methought I heard one calling, "Child";
And I replied, "My Lord."

George Herbert

Prayer

Prayer, the Church's banquet, Angels' age,
    God's breath in man returning to his birth,
The soul in paraphrase, heart in pilgrimage,
    The Christian plummet, sounding heaven
        and earth;
Engine against the Almighty, sinner's tower,
    Reversèd thunder, Christ-side-piercing
        spear,
The six-days' world transposing in an hour,
    A kind of tune, which all things hear and
        fear;
Softness, and peace, and joy, and love, and
        bliss,
    Exalted manna, gladness of the best,
    Heaven in ordinary, man well drest,
The milky way, the bird of Paradise,
    Church-bells beyond the stars heard, the
        soul's blood,
    The land of spices; something
        understood.

George Herbert

Wise Men and Shepherds

Lord, when the wise men came from far,
Led to thy cradle by a star,
Then did the shepherds too rejoice,
Instructed by thy angel's voice.
Blest were the wise men in their skill,
And shepherds in their harmless will.

Wise men, in tracing Nature's laws,
Ascend unto the highest cause;
Shepherds with humble fearfulness
Walk safely, though their light be less.
Though wise men better know the way,
It seems no honest heart can stray.

There is no merit in the wise
But love, the shepherds' sacrifice.
Wise men, all ways of knowledge passed,
To the shepherds' wonder come at last.
To know can only wonder breed,
And not to know is wonder's seed.

A wise man at the altar bows,
And offers up his studied vows,
And is received. May not the tears,
Which spring too from a shepherd's fears,
And sighs upon his frailty spent,
Though not distinct, be eloquent?

'Tis true, the object sanctifies

All passions which within us rise,
But since no creature comprehends
The cause of causes, end of ends,
He who himself vouchsafes to know
Best pleases his creator so.

When then our sorrows we apply
To our own wants and poverty,
When we look up in all distress,
And our own misery confess,
Sending both thanks and prayers above,
Then, though we do not know, we love.

Sidney Godolphin

The Retreat

Happy those early days, when I
Shin'd in my Angel-infancy!
Before I understood this place
Appointed for my second race,
Or taught my soul to fancy aught
But a white celestial thought:
When yet I had not walk'd above
A mile or two from my first Love,
And looking back — at that short space —
Could see a glimpse of His bright face:
When on some gilded cloud, or flow'r,
My gazing soul would dwell an hour,
And in those weaker glories spy
Some shadows of eternity:
Before I taught my tongue to wound

My Conscience with a sinful sound,
Or had the black art to dispense
A several sin to ev'ry sense,
But felt through all this fleshly dress
Bright shoots of everlastingness.
   O how I long to travel back,
And tread again that ancient track!
That I might once more reach that plain
Where first I left my glorious train;
From whence th' enlightened spirit sees
That shady City of Palm-trees.
But ah! my soul with too much stay
Is drunk, and staggers in the way!
Some men a forward motion love,
But I by backward steps would move;
And when this dust falls to the urn,
In that state I came, return.

Henry Vaughan

My Spirit Longeth for Thee

My spirit longeth for thee
   Within my troubled breast,
Although I be unworthy
   Of so divine a guest.

Of so divine a guest
   Unworthy though I be,
Yet has my heart no rest
   Unless it come from thee.

Unless it come from thee,
In vain I look around;
In all that I can see,
No rest is to be found.

No rest is to be found
But in thy blessed Love;
O! let my wish be crowned,
And send it from above!

John Byrom

The Lamb

Little Lamb, who made thee?
Dost thou know who made thee?
Gave thee life, and bid thee feed,
By the stream and o'er the mead;
Gave thee clothing of delight,
Softest clothing, woolly, bright;
Gave thee such a tender voice,
Making all the vales rejoice?
Little Lamb, who made thee?
Dost thou know who made thee?

Little Lamb, I'll tell thee,
Little Lamb, I'll tell thee:
He is callèd by thy name,
For He calls Himself a Lamb.
He is meek, and He is mild;
He became a little child.
I a child, and thou a lamb,

We are callèd by His name.
  Little Lamb, God bless thee!
  Little Lamb, God bless thee!
                    William Blake

Auguries of Innocence

To see a World in a grain of sand,
And a Heaven in a wild flower,
Hold Infinity in the palm of your hand,
And Eternity in an hour.
A robin redbreast in a cage
Puts all Heaven in a rage.
A dove-house fill'd with doves and pigeons
Shudders Hell thro' all its regions.
A dog starv'd at his master's gate
Predicts the ruin of the State.
A horse misus'd upon the road
Calls to Heaven for human blood.
Each outcry of the hunted hare
A fibre from the brain does tear.
A skylark wounded in the wing,
A cherubim does cease to sing.
The game-cock clipt and arm'd for fight
Does the rising sun affright.

Every wolf's and lion's howl
Raises from Hell a Human soul.
The wild deer, wandering here and there,
Keeps the Human soul from care.
The lamb musus'd breeds public strife,

And yet forgives the butcher's knife.
The bat the flits at close of eve
Has left the brain that won't believe.
The owl that calls upon the night
Speaks the unbeliever's fright.
He who shall hurt the little wren
Shall never be belov'd by men.
He who the ox to wrath has mov'd
Shall never be by woman lov'd.
The wanton boy that kills the fly
Shall feel the spider's enmity.
He who torments the chafer's sprite
Weaves a bower in endless night.
The caterpillar on the leaf
Repeats to thee thy mother's grief.
Kill not the moth nor butterfly,
For the Last Judgment draweth nigh.
He who shall train the horse to war
Shall never pass the polar bar.
The beggar's dog and widow's cat,
Feed them, and thou wilt grow fat.
The gnat that sings his summer's song
Poison gets from Slander's tongue.
The poison of the snake and newt
Is the sweat of Envy's foot.
The poison of the honey-bee
Is the artist's jealousy.
The prince's robes and beggar's rags
Are toadstools on the miser's bags.
A truth that's told with bad intent
Beats all the lies you can invent.
It is right it should be so;

Man was made for joy and woe;
He who replies to words of Doubt
Doth put the light of knowledge out.
The strongest poison ever known
Came from Caesar's laurel crown.
Nought can deform the human race
Like to the armour's iron brace.
When gold and gems adorn the plough
To peaceful arts shall Envy bow.
A riddle, or the cricket's cry,
Is to Doubt a fit reply.
The emmet's inch and eagle's mile
Make lame Philosophy to smile.
He who doubts from what he sees
Will ne'er believe, do what you please.
If the Sun and Moon should doubt,
They'd immediately go out.
To be in a passion you good may do,
But no good if a passion is in you.
The whore and gambler, by the state
Licensed, build that nation's fate.
The harlot's cry from street to street
Shall weave Old England's winding-sheet.
The winner's shout, the loser's curse,
Dance before dead England's hearse.
Every night and every morn
Some to misery are born.
Every morn and every night
Some are born to sweet delight.
Some are born to sweet delight,
Some are born to endless night.
We are led to believe a lie

When we see not thro' the eye,
Which was born in a night, to perish in a
   night,
When the Soul slept in beams of light.
God appears, and God is Light,
To those poor souls who dwell in Night;
But does a Human Form display
To those who dwell in realms of Day.

William Blake

To a Waterfowl

Whither, midst falling dew,
While glow the heavens with the last steps
   of day,
Far, through their rosy depths, dost thou
   pursue
  Thy solitary way?

Vainly the fowler's eye
Might mark thy distant flight to do thee
   wrong,
As, darkly seen against the crimson sky,
  Thy figure floats along.

Seek'st thou the plashy brink
Of weedy lake, or marge of river wide,
Or where the rocking billows rise and sink
  On the chafed ocean-side?

There is a Power whose care
Teaches thy way along that pathless coast —
The desert and illimitable air —
  Lone wandering, but not lost.

All day thy wings have fanned,
At that far height, the cold, thin atmosphere,
Yet stoop not, weary, to the welcome land,
  Though the dark night is near.

And soon that toil shall end;
Soon shalt thou find a summer home, and
    rest,
And scream among thy fellows; reeds shall
    bend,
  Soon, o'er thy sheltered nest.

Thou'rt gone, the abyss of heaven
Hath swallowed up thy form; yet, on my
    heart
Deeply has sunk the lesson thou hast given,
  And shall not soon depart.

He who, from zone to zone,
Guides through the boundless sky thy certain
    flight,
In the long way that I must tread alone,
  Will lead my steps aright.
                    William Cullen Bryant

Lead, Kindly Light

Lead, kindly Light, amid the encircling
       gloom,
       Lead thou me on!
The night is dark, and I am far from home,
       Lead thou me on!
Keep thou my feet! I do not ask to see
The distant scene; one step enough for me.

I was not ever thus, nor prayed that thou
       Shouldst lead me on;
I loved to choose and see my path; but now
       Lead thou me on!
I loved the garish day; and, spite of fears,
Pride ruled my will: remember not past
       years.

So long thy power hath blest me, sure it still
       Will lead me on
O'er moon and fen, o'er crag and torrent,
       till
       The night is gone;
And with the morn those angel faces smile,
Which I have loved long since, and lost
       awhile.

John Henry Newman

Inspiration

If with light head erect I sing
Though all the Muses lend their force,
From my poor love of anything,
The verse is weak and shallow as its source.

But if with bended neck I grope
Listening behind me for my wit,
With faith superior to hope,
More anxious to keep back than forward
    it, —

Making my soul accomplice there
Unto the flame my heart hath lit,
Then will the verse forever wear, —
Time cannot bend the line which God has
    writ.

I hearing get, who had but ears,
And sight, who had but eyes before;
I moments live, who lived but years,
And truth discern, who knew but learning's
    lore.

Now chiefly is my natal hour,
And only now my prime of life;
Of manhood's strength it is the flower,
'Tis peace's end, and war's beginning strife.

It comes in summer's broadest noon,

By a gray wall, or some chance place,
Unseasoning time, insulting June,
And vexing day with its presuming face.

I will not doubt the love untold
Which not my worth nor want hath bought,
Which wooed me young, and wooes me old,
And to this evening hath me brought.
Henry David Thoreau

There Is No God

'There is no God,' the wicked saith,
    'And truly it's a blessing,
For what he might have done with us
    It's better only guessing.'

'There is no God,' a youngster thinks,
    'Or really, if there may be,
He surely didn't mean a man
    Always to be a baby.'

'There is no God, or if there is,'
    The tradesman thinks, ' 'twere funny
If he should take it ill in me
    To make a little money.'

'Whether there be,' the rich man says,
    'It matters very little,
For I and mine, thank somebody,
    Are not in want of victual.'

Some others, also, to themselves
  Who scarce so much as doubt it,
Think there is none, when they are well,
  And do not think about it.

But country folks who live beneath
  The shadow of the steeple;
The parson and the parson's wife,
  And mostly married people;

Youths green and happy in first love,
  So thankful for illusion;
And men caught out in what the world
  Calls guilt, in first confusion;

And almost everyone when age,
  Disease, or sorrows strike him,
Inclines to think there is a God,
  Or something very like him.
                    Arthur Hugh Clough

Evening Contemplation

Softly now the light of day
Fades upon my sight away;
Free from care, from labor free,
Lord, I would commune with Thee.

Thou, whose all-pervading eye
  Naught escapes, without, within!

Pardon each infirmity,
Open fault, and secret sin.

Soon for me the light of day
Shall for ever pass away;
Then, from sin and sorrow free,
Take me, Lord, to dwell with Thee.

Thou who, sinless, yet hast known
All of man's infirmity!
Then, from Thine eternal throne,
Jesus, look with pitying eye.
George Washington Doane

God's Grandeur

The world is charged with the grandeur of
God.
It will flame out, like shining from shook
foil;
It gathers to a greatness, like the ooze of oil
Crushed. Why do men then now not reck his
rod?

Generations have trod, have trod, have trod;
And all is seared with trade; bleared,
smeared with toil;
And wears man's smudge and shares man's
smell: the soil
Is bare now, nor can foot feel, being shod.

And for all this, nature is never spent;
There lives the dearest freshness deep down
   things;
And though the last lights off the black West
   went
Oh, morning, at the brown brink eastward,
   springs —
Because the Holy Ghost over the bent
World broods with warm breast and with ah!
   bright wings.

Gerard Manley Hopkins

Optimism

Talk happiness. The world is sad enough
Without your woes. No path is wholly
   rough;
Look for the places that are smooth and
   clear,
And speak of those, to rest the weary ear
Of Earth, so hurt by one continuous strain
Of human discontent and grief and pain.

Talk faith. The world is better off without
Your uttered ignorance and morbid doubt.
If you have faith in God, or man, or self,
Say so. If not, push back upon the shelf
Of silence all your thoughts, till faith shall
   come;

No one will grieve because your lips are
  dumb.

Talk health. The dreary, never-changing tale
Of mortal maladies is worn and stale.
You cannot charm, or interest, or please
By harping on that minor chord, disease.
Say you are well, or all is well with you,
And God shall hear your words and make
  them true.

Ella Wheeler Wilcox

How the Great Guest Came

Before the cathedral in grandeur rose
At Ingelburg where the Danube goes;
Before its forest of silver spires
Went airily up to the clouds and fires;
Before the oak had ready a beam,
While yet the arch was stone and dream —
There where the altar was later laid,
Conrad, the cobbler, plied his trade.

*   *   *

It happened one day at the year's white
  end —
Two neighbors called on their old-time
  friend;
And they found the shop, so meager and
  mean,

339

Made gay with a hundred boughs of green.
Conrad was stitching with face ashine,
But suddenly stopped as he twitched a
    twine:
"Old friends, good news! At dawn today,
As the cocks were scaring the night away,
The Lord appeared in a dream to me,
And said, 'I am coming your Guest to be!'
So I've been busy with feet astir,
Strewing the floor with branches of fir.
The wall is washed and the shelf is shined,
And over the rafter the holly twined.
He comes today, and the table is spread
With milk and honey and wheaten bread."

His friends went home; and his face grew
    still
As he watched for the shadow across the
    sill.
He lived all the moments o'er and o'er,
When the Lord should enter the lowly
    door —
The knock, the call, the latch pulled up,
The lighted face, the offered cup.
He would wash the feet where the spikes
    had been,
He would kiss the hands where the nails
    went in,
And then at the last would sit with Him
And break the bread as the day grew dim.

While the cobbler mused there passed his
    pane
A beggar drenched by the driving rain.
He called him in from the stony street
And gave him shoes for his bruisèd feet.
The beggar went and there came a crone,
Her face with wrinkles of sorrow sown.
A bundle of fagots bowed her back,
And she was spent with the wrench and
    rack.
He gave her his loaf and steadied her load
As she took her way on the weary road.
Then to his door came a little child,
Lost and afraid in the world so wild,
In the big, dark world. Catching it up,
He gave it the milk in the waiting cup,
And led it home to its mother's arms,
Out of the reach of the world's alarms.

The day went down in the crimson west
And with it the hope of the blessed Guest,
And Conrad sighed as the world turned gray:
"Why is it, Lord, that your feet delay?
Did You forget that this was the day?"
Then soft in the silence a Voice he heard:
"Lift up your heart, for I kept my word.
Three times I came to your friendly door;
Three times my shadow was on your floor.
I was the beggar with bruisèd feet;
I was the woman you gave to eat;
I was the child on the homeless street!"
                                    Edwin Markham

A Creed

There is a destiny that makes us brothers;
    None goes his way alone:
All that we send into the lives of others
    Comes back into our own.

I care not what his temples or his creeds,
    One thing holds firm and fast —
That into his fateful heap of days and deeds
    The soul of man is cast.

Edwin Markham

The Hound of Heaven

I fled Him, down the nights and down the
                 days;
    I fled Him, down the arches of the years;
I fled Him, down the labyrinthine ways
    Of my own mind; and in the mist of tears
I hid from Him, and under running laughter.
        Up vistaed hopes I sped;
        And shot, precipitated,
Adown Titanic glooms of chasmèd fears,
    From those strong Feet that followed,
              followed after.
        But with unhurrying chase,
        And unperturbèd pace,
    Deliberate speed, majestic instancy,
        They beat — and a Voice beat

More instant than the Feet —
"All things betray thee, who betrayest
Me."
I pleaded, outlaw-wise,
By many a hearted casement, curtained red,
  Trellised with intertwining charities;
(For, though I knew His love Who followèd,
    Yet was I sore adread
Lest, having Him, I must have naught
    beside);
But, if one little casement parted wide,
  The gust of His approach would clash it
    to.
Fear wist not to evade, as Love wist to
    pursue.
Across the margent of the world I fled,
  And troubled the gold gateways of the
    stars,
  Smiting for shelter on their clangèd bars;
    Fretted to dulcet jars
And silvern chatter the pale ports o' the
    moon.
I said to Dawn: Be sudden — to Eve: Be
    soon;
  With thy young skiey blossoms heap me
    over
    From this tremendous Lover —
Float thy vague veil about me, lest He see!
  I tempted all His servitors, but to find
My own betrayal in their constancy,
In faith to Him their fickleness to me,

Their traitorous trueness, and their loyal
    deceit.
To all swift things for swiftness did I sue;
    Clung to the whistling mane of every
        wind.
    But whether they swept, smoothly
        fleet,
    The long savannahs of the blue;
        Or whether, Thunder-driven,
    They clanged his chariot 'thwart a
        heaven
Plashy with flying lightnings round the spurn
    o' their feet: —
Fear wist not to evade as Love wist to
    pursue.
    Still with unhurrying chase,
    And unperturbèd pace,
Deliberate speed, majestic instancy,
    Came on the following Feet,
    And a Voice above their beat —
"Naught shelters thee, who wilt not
    shelter Me."

I sought no more that after which I strayed
    In face of man or maid;
But still within the little children's eyes
    Seems something, something that
        replies,
They at least are for me, surely for me!
I turned me to them very wistfully;
But just as their young eyes grew sudden
    fair

With dawning answers there,
Their angel plucked them from me by the
hair.
''Come then, ye other children, Nature's —
share
With me'' (said I) ''your delicate
fellowship;
Let me greet you lip to lip,
Let me twine with you caresses,
Wantoning
With our Lady-Mother's vagrant
tresses,
Banqueting
With her in her wind-walled
palace,
Underneath her azured daïs,
Quaffing, as your taintless way is,
From a chalice
Lucent-weeping out of the dayspring.
So it was done:
I in their delicate fellowship was one —
Drew the bolt of Nature's secrecies.
I knew all the swift importings
On the willful face of skies;
I knew how the clouds arise
Spumèd of the wild sea-snortings;
All that's born or dies
Rose and drooped with; made them
shapers
Of mine own moods, or wailful or divine;
With them joyed and was
bereaven.

I was heavy with the even,
When she lit her glimmering tapers
Round the day's dead sanctities.
I laughed in the morning's eyes.
I triumphed and I saddened with all weather,
Heaven and I wept together,
And its sweet tears were salt with mortal
mine.
Against the red throb of its sunset-heart
I laid my own to beat,
And share commingling heat;
But not by that, by that, was eased my
human smart.
In vain my tears were wet on Heaven's grey
cheek.
For ah! we know not what each other says,
These things and I; in sound *I*
speak —
Their sound is but their stir, they speak by
silences.
Nature, poor stepdame, cannot slake my
drouth;
Let her, if she would owe me,
Drop yon blue bosom-veil of sky, and show
me
The breasts o' her tenderness:
Never did any milk of hers once bless
My thirsting mouth.
Nigh and nigh draws the chase,
With unperturbèd pace,
Deliberate speed, majestic instancy;
And past those noisèd Feet

A Voice comes yet more fleet —
"Lo! naught contents thee, who
content'st not Me."
Naked I wait Thy love's uplifted stroke!
My harness piece by piece Thou hast hewn
from me,
And smitten me to my knee;
I am defenceless utterly.
I slept, methinks, and woke,
And, slowly gazing, find me stripped in
sleep.
In the rash lustihead of my young powers,
I shook the pillaring hours
And pulled my life upon me; grimed with
smears,
I stand amid the dust o' the mounded
years —
My mangled youth lies dead beneath the
heap,
My days have crackled and gone up in
smoke,
Have puffed and burst as sun-starts on a
stream.

Yea, faileth now even dream
The dreamer, and the lute the lutanist;
Even the linked fantasies, in whose
blossomy twist
I swung the earth a trinket at my wrist,
Are yielding; cords of all too weak account
For earth with heavy griefs so overplussed.
Ah! is Thy love indeed

A weed, albeit an amaranthine weed,
Suffering no flowers except its own to
   mount?
  Ah! must —
  Designer infinite! —
Ah! must Thou char the wood ere Thou
   canst limn with it?
My freshness spent its wavering shower i'
   the dust;
And now my heart is as a broken fount,
Wherein tear-drippings stagnate, spilt down
   ever
  From the dank thoughts that shiver
Upon the sighful branches of my mind.
  Such is; what is to be?
The pulp so bitter, how shall taste the rind?
I dimly guess what Time in mists confounds;
Yet ever and anon a trumpet sounds
From the hid battlements of Eternity;
Those shaken mists a space unsettle, then
Round the half-glimpsed turrets slowly wash
   again.
  But not ere him who summoneth
  I first have seen, enwound
With glooming robes purpureal, cypress-
   crowned;
His name I know, and what his trumpet
   saith.
Whether man's heart or life it be which
   yields
  Thee harvest, must Thy harvest-fields
  Be dunged with rotten death?

Now of that long pursuit
Comes at hand the bruit;
That Voice is round me like a
bursting sea:
"And is thy earth so marred,
Shattered in shard on shard?
Lo, all things fly thee, for thou fliest
Me!
Strange, piteous, futile thing!
Wherefore should any set thee love apart?
Seeing none but I make much of naught"
(He said),
"And human love needs human meriting:
How hast thou merited —
Of all man's clotted clay the dingiest clot?
Alack, thou knowest not
How little worthy of any love thou art!
Whom wilt thou find to love ignoble thee
Save Me, save only Me?
All which I took from thee I did but take,
Not for thy harms,
But just that thou might'st seek it in My
arms.
All which thy child's mistake
Fancies as lost, I have stored for thee at
home:
Rise, clasp My hand, and come!"

Halts by me that footfall:
Is my gloom, after all,
Shade of His hand, outstretched caressingly?

"Ah, fondest, blindest, weakest,
I am He Whom thou seekest!
Thou dravest love from thee, who dravest
Me."

Francis Thompson

Recessional

God of our fathers, known of old —
Lord of our far-flung battle line —
Beneath Whose awful hand we hold
Dominion over palm and pine —
Lord God of Hosts, be with us yet,
Lest we forget — lest we forget!

The tumult and the shouting dies;
The captains and the kings depart:
Still stands Thine ancient Sacrifice,
An humble and a contrite heart.
Lord God of Hosts, be with us yet,
Lest we forget — lest we forget!

Far-called, our navies melt away;
On dune and headland sinks the fire:
Lo, all our pomp of yesterday
Is one with Nineveh and Tyre!
Judge of the Nations, spare us yet,
Lest we forget — lest we forget!

If, drunk with sight of power, we loose

Wild tongues that have not Thee in
  awe —
Such boasting as the Gentiles use
  Or lesser breeds without the Law —
Lord God of Hosts, be with us yet,
  Lest we forget — lest we forget!

For heathen heart that puts her trust
  In recking tube and iron shard —
All valiant dust that builds on dust,
  And guarding, calls not Thee to guard —
For frantic boast and foolish word,
  Thy mercy on Thy people, Lord!
Amen.

Rudyard Kipling

Pray Without Ceasing

Unanswered yet the prayer your lips have
    pleaded
  In agony of heart these many years?
Does faith begin to fail, is hope declining,
  And think you all in vain those falling
    tears?
Say not the Father has not heard your
    prayer;
You shall have your desire, sometime,
    somewhere.

Unanswered yet? tho' when you first
    presented

This one petition at the Father's throne,
It seemed you could not wait the time of
    asking,
  So anxious was your heart to have it done;
If years have passed since then, do not
    despair,
For God will answer you sometime,
    somewhere.

Unanswered yet? But you are not unheeded;
  The promises of God forever stand;
To Him our days and years alike are equal;
  Have faith in God! It is your Lord's
    command.
Hold on to Jacob's angel, and your prayer
Shall bring a blessing down sometime,
    somewhere.

Unanswered yet? Nay, do not say
    unanswered,
  Perhaps your part is not yet wholly done,
The work began when first your prayer was
    uttered,
  And God will finish what He has begun.
Keep incense burning at the shrine of
    prayer,
And glory shall descend sometime,
    somewhere.

Unanswered yet? Faith cannot be
    unanswered;
  Her feet are firmly planted on the Rock;

Amid the wildest storms she stands
    undaunted,
  Nor quails before the loudest thunder
    shock.
She knows Omnipotence has heard her
    prayer,
And cries, "It shall be done sometime,
    somewhere."
                    Ophelia Guyon Browning

Rocked in the Cradle of the Deep

Rocked in the cradle of the deep
I lay me down in peace to sleep;
Secure I rest upon the wave,
For thou, O Lord, hast power to save.
I know thou wilt not slight my call,
For thou dost mark the sparrow's fall;
And calm and peaceful shall I sleep,
Rocked in the cradle of the deep.

When in the dead of night I lie
And gaze upon the trackless sky,
The star-bespangled heavenly scroll,
The boundless waters as they roll, —
I feel thy wondrous power to save
From perils of the stormy wave:
Rocked in the cradle of the deep
I calmly rest and soundly sleep.

And such the trust that still were mine,

Though stormy winds swept o'er the brine,
Or though the tempest's fiery breath
Roused me from sleep to wreck and death.
In ocean cave still safe with Thee
The gem of immortality!
And calm and peaceful shall I sleep
Rocked in the cradle of the deep.

Emma Willard

Opportunity

They do me wrong who say I come no more
    When once I knock and fail to find you
    in,
For every day I stand outside your door
    And bid you wake, and rise to fight and
    win.

Wail not for precious chances passed away,
    Weep not for golden ages on the wane!
Each night I burn the records of the day;
    At sunrise every soul is born again.

Laugh like a boy at splendors that have
    sped,
    To vanished joys be blind and deaf and
    dumb;
My judgments seal the dead past with its
    dead,
    But never bind a moment yet to come.

Tho' deep in mire, wring not your hands and
 weep;
 I lend my arm to all who say, ''I can!''
No shamefaced outcast ever sank so deep
 But yet might rise and be again a man.

Dost thou behold thy lost youth all aghast?
 Dost reel from righteous retribution's
 blow?
Then turn from blotted archives of the past
 And find the future's pages white as
 snow.

Art thou a mourner? Rouse thee from thy
 spell;
 Art thou a sinner? Sins may be forgiven;
Each morning gives thee wings to flee from
 hell,
 Each night a star to guide thy feet to
 Heaven.

Walter Malone

The House by the Side of the Road

*''He was a friend to man, and lived in a
house by the side of the road''* — *Homer*.

There are hermit souls that live withdrawn
 In the peace of their self-content;
There are souls, like stars, that dwell apart,

In a fellowless firmament;
There are pioneer souls that blaze their paths
　　Where highways never ran;
But let me live by the side of the road
　　And be a friend to man.

Let me live in a house by the side of the
　　road,
　　Where the race of men go by —
The men who are good and the men who are
　　bad,
　　As good and as bad as I.
I would not sit in the scorner's seat,
　　Or hurl the cynic's ban;
Let me live in a house by the side of the
　　road
　　And be a friend to man.

I see from my house by the side of the road,
　　By the side of the highway of life,
The men who press with the ardor of hope,
　　The men who are faint with the strife.
But I turn not away from their smiles nor
　　their tears —
　　Both parts of an infinite plan;
Let me live in my house by the side of the
　　road
　　And be a friend to man.

I know there are brook-gladdened meadows
　　ahead,
　　And mountains of wearisome height,

That the road passes on through the long
    afternoon
  And stretches away to the night.
But still I rejoice when the travelers rejoice,
  And weep with the strangers that moan,
Nor live in my house by the side of the road
  Like a man who dwells alone.

Let me live in my house by the side of the
    road
  Where the race of men go by —
They are good, they are bad, they are weak,
    they are strong,
  Wise, foolish — so am I.
Then why should I sit in the scorner's seat
  Or hurl the cynic's ban? —
Let me live in my house by the side of the
    road
  And be a friend to man.

                              Sam Walter Foss

A Prayer

Let me do my work each day;
And if the darkened hours of despair
    overcome me,
May I not forget the strength that comforted
    me
In the desolation of other times.
May I still remember the bright hours that
    found me

Walking over the silent hills of my
   childhood,
Or dreaming on the margin of the quiet
   river,
When a light glowed within me,
And I promised my early God to have
   courage
Amid the tempests of the changing years.
Spare me from bitterness
And from the sharp passions of unguarded
   moments.
May I not forget that poverty and riches are
   of the spirit.
Though the world know me not,
May my thoughts and actions be such
As shall keep me friendly with myself.
Lift my eyes from the earth,
And let me not forget the uses of the stars.
Forbid that I should judge others,
Lest I condemn myself.
Let me not follow the clamor of the world,
But walk calmly in my path.
Give me a few friends who will love me for
   what I am;
And keep ever burning before my vagrant
   steps
The kindly light of hope.
And though age and infirmity overtake me,
And I come not within sight of the castle of
   my dreams,
Teach me still to be thankful for life,

And for time's olden memories that are good
    and sweet;
And may the evening's twilight find me
    gentle still.

Max Ehrmann

Turn Again to Life

If I should die and leave you here a while,
Be not like others, sore undone, who keep
Long vigil by the silent dust and weep.
For my sake turn again to life and smile,
Nerving thy heart and trembling hand to do
That which will comfort other souls than
    thine;
Complete these dear unfinished tasks of
    mine,
And I, perchance, may therein comfort you.

Mary Lee Hall

Reflection and Contemplation

Reflection and Contemplation

Hyacinths to Feed Thy Soul

If of thy mortal goods thou art bereft,
And from thy slender store two loaves alone
  to thee are left,
Sell one, and with the dole
Buy hyacinths to feed thy soul.

Attributed to the Gulistan of
Moslih Eddin Saadi

My Mind to Me a Kingdom Is

My mind to me a kingdom is
  Such perfect joy therein I find,
That it excels all other bliss
That world affords or grows by kind.
  Though much I want which most would
    have,
  Yet still my mind forbids to crave.

No princely pomp, no wealthy store,
No force to win the victory,
No wily wit to salve a sore,
No shape to feed a loving eye;

To none of these I yield as thrall,
For why? my mind doth serve for all.

I see how plenty suffers oft,
And hasty climbers soon do fall;
I see that those which are aloft
Mishap doth threaten most of all;
   They get with toil, they keep with fear;
   Such cares my mind could never bear.

Sir Edward Dyer

They That Have Power to Hurt

They that have power to hurt, and will do
   none,
That do not do the thing they most do show,
Who, moving others, are themselves as
   stone,
Unmovèd, cold, and to temptation slow, —
They rightly do inherit heaven's graces,
And husband nature's riches from expense;
They are the lords and owners of their
   faces,
Others, but stewards of their excellence.

The summer's flower is to the summer sweet
Though to itself it only live and die;
But if that flower with base infection meet,
The basest weed outbraves his dignity:

364

For sweetest things turn sourest by their
    deeds;
Lilies that fester smell far worse than weeds.
                    William Shakespeare

When Forty Winters

When forty winters shall besiege thy brow
And dig deep trenches in thy beauty's field,
Thy youth's proud livery, so gazed on now,
Will be a tattered weed, of small worth held:
Then being asked where all thy beauty lies,
Where all the treasure of thy lusty days,
To say, within thine own deep-sunken eyes,
Were an ill-eating shame and thriftless
    praise.

How much more praise deserved thy
    beauty's use.
If thou couldst answer "This fair child of
    mine
Shall sum my count and make my old
    excuse,"
Proving his beauty by succession thine!
This were to be new made when thou art
    old,
And see thy blood warm when thou feel'st it
    cold.
                    William Shakespeare

On Time

Fly envious Time, till thou run out thy race,
Call on the lazy leaden-stepping hours,
Whose speed is but the heavy Plummet's
    pace;
And glut thy self with what thy womb
    devours,
Which is no more than what is false and
    vain,
And merely mortal dross;
So little is our loss,
So little is thy gain.
For when as each thing bad thou hast
    entomb'd,
And last of all, thy greedy self consum'd,
Then long Eternity shall greet our bliss
With an individual kiss;
And Joy shall overtake us as a flood,
When every thing that is sincerely good
And perfectly divine,
With Truth, and Peace, and Love shall ever
    shine
About the supreme Throne
Of him, t'whose happy-making sight alone,
When once our heav'nly-guided soul shall
    climb,
Then all this Earthy grossness quit,
Attir'd with Stars, we shall for ever sit,
Triumphing over Death, and Chance, and
    thee O Time.

John Milton

Know Then Thyself

Know then thyself, presume not God to
    scan,
The proper study of Mankind is Man.
Plac'd on this isthmus of a middle state,
A Being darkly wise, and rudely great:
With too much knowledge for the Sceptic
    side,
With too much weakness for the Stoic's
    pride,
He hangs between; in doubt to act, or rest;
In doubt to deem himself a God, or Beast;
In doubt his Mind or Body to prefer;
Born but to die, and reas'ning but to err;
Alike in ignorance, his reason such,
Whether he thinks too little, or too much:
Chaos of Thought and Passion, all confus'd;
Still my himself abus'd, or disabus'd;
Created half to rise, and half to fall;
Great lord of all things, yet a prey to all;
Sole judge of truth, in endless error hurl'd:
The glory, jest, and riddle of the world!

Self-love, the spring of motion, acts the
    soul;
Reason's comparing balance rules the whole.
Man, but for that, no action could attend,

And, but for this, were active to no end:
Fix'd like a plant on his peculiar spot,
To draw nutrition, propagate, and rot;
Or, meteor-like, flame lawless through the
    void,
Destroying others, by himself destroy'd.

  Most strength the moving principle
      requires;
Active its task, it prompts, impels, inspires.
Sedate and quiet the comparing lies,
Form'd but to check, delib'rate, and advise.
Self-love still stronger, as its objects nigh;
Reason's at distance, and in prospect lie:
That sees immediate good by present sense;
Reason, the future and the consequence.
Thicker than arguments, temptations throng,
At best more watchful this, but that more
      strong.
The action of the stronger to suspend
Reason still use, to reason still attend.
Attention, habit and experience gains;
Each strengthens reason, and self-love
      restrains.

  Vice is a monster of so frightful mien,
As, to be hated, needs but to be seen;
Yet seen too oft, familiar with her face,
We first endure, then pity, then embrace.
But where th' extreme of vice, was ne'er
      agreed:

Ask where's the north? at York, 'tis on the
     Tweed;
In Scotland, at the Orcades; and there,
At Greenland, Zembla, or the Lord knows
     where.
No creature owns it in the first degree,
But thinks his neighbour farther gone than
     he;
Ev'n those who dwell beneath its very zone,
Or never feel the rage, or never own;
What happier natures shrink at with affright,
The hard inhabitant contends is right.

    Honor and shame from no condition rise;
Act well your part, there all the honour lies.
Fortune in men has some small diff'rence
     made,
One flaunts in rags, one flutters in brocade;
The cobbler apron'd, and the parson
     gown'd,
The friar hooded, and the monarch crown'd.
'What differ more,' you cry, 'than crown
     and cowl?'
I'll tell you, friend! a wise man and a fool.
You'll find, if once the monarch acts the
     monk,
Or, cobbler-like, the parson will be drunk,
Worth makes the man, and want of it, the
     fellow;
The rest is all but leather or prunella.
                     Alexander Pope

Ode on a Distant Prospect of
Eton College

Ye distant spires, ye antique towers
   That crown the watery glade,
Where grateful Science still adores
   Her Henry's holy shade;
And ye, that from the stately brow
Of Windsor's heights th' expanse below
Of grove, of lawn, of mead survey,
Whose turf, whose shade, whose flowers
     among
Wanders the hoary Thames along
   His silver-winding way:

Ah happy hills! ah pleasing shade!
   Ah fields beloved in vain!
Where once my careless childhood stray'd,
   A stranger yet to pain!
I feel the gales that from ye blow
A momentary bliss bestow,
As waving fresh their gladsome wing
My weary soul they seem to soothe,
And, redolent of joy and youth,
   To breathe a second spring.

Say, Father Thames, for thou hast seen
   Full many a sprightly race
Disporting on thy margent green
   The paths of pleasure trace;
Who foremost now delight to cleave

With pliant arm, thy glassy wave?
The captive linnet which enthral?
What idle progeny succeed
To chase the rolling circle's speed,
   Or urge the flying ball?

While some on earnest business bent
   Their murmuring labours ply
'Gainst graver hours that bring constraint
   To sweeten liberty:
Some bold adventurers disdain
The limits of their little reign
And unknown regions dare descry:
Still as they run they look behind,
They hear a voice in every wind,
   And snatch a fearful joy.

Gay hope is theirs by fancy fed,
   Less pleasing when possest;
The tear forgot as soon as shed,
   The sunshine of the breast:
Theirs buxom health, of rosy hue,
Wild wit, invention ever new,
And lively cheer, of vigour born;
The thoughtless day, the easy night,
The spirits pure, the slumbers light
   That fly th' approach of morn.

Alas! regardless of their doom
   The little victims play;
No sense have they of ills to come,
   Nor care beyond to-day:

Yet see how all around 'em wait
The ministers of human fate
And black Misfortune's baleful train!
Ah show them where in ambush stand
To seize their prey, the murderous band!
 Ah, tell them they are men!

These shall the fury Passions tear
 The vultures of the mind,
Disdainful Anger, pallid Fear,
 And Shame that skulks behind;
Or pining Love shall waste their youth,
Or Jealousy with rankling tooth,
That inly gnaws the secret heart,
And Envy wan, and faded Care,
Grim-visaged comfortless Despair,
 And Sorrow's piercing dart.

Ambition this shall tempt to rise,
 Then whirl the wretch from high,
To bitter Scorn a sacrifice
 And grinning Infamy.
The stings of Falsehood those shall try
And hard Unkindness' alter'd eye,
That mocks the tear it forced to flow;
And keen Remorse with blood defiled,
And moody Madness laughing wild
 Amid severest woe.

Lo, in the vale of years beneath
 A griesly troop are seen,
The painful family of Death,

More hideous than their queen:
This racks the joints, this fires the veins,
That every labouring sinew strains,
Those in the deeper vitals rage:
Lo! Poverty, to fill the band,
That numbs the soul with icy hand,
 And slow-consuming Age.

To each his sufferings: all are men,
 Condemn'd alike to groan;
The tender for another's pain,
 Th' unfeeling for his own.
Yet, ah! why should they know their fate.
Since sorrow never comes too late,
And happiness too swiftly flies?
Thought would destroy their paradise.
No more; — where ignorance is bliss
 'Tis folly to be wise.

Thomas Gray

Night

The sun descending in the West,
The evening star does shine;
The birds are silent in their nest,
And I must seek for mine.

The moon, like a flower
In heaven's high bower,
With silent delight
Sits and smiles on the night.

Farewell, green fields and happy grove,
Where flocks have ta'en delight;
Where lambs have nibbled, silent move
The feet of angels bright:
    Unseen, they pour blessing,
    And joy without ceasing,
    On each bud and blossom,
    On each sleeping bosom.

They look in every thoughtless nest,
Where birds are covered warm;
They visit caves of every beast,
To keep them all from harm.
    If they see any weeping
    That should have been sleeping,
    They pour sleep on their head,
    And sit down by their bed.

When wolves and tigers howl for prey
They pitying stand and weep,
Seeking to drive their thirst away,
And keep them from the sheep.
    But, if they rush dreadful,
    The angels, most heedful,
    Receive each mild spirit
    New worlds to inherit.

And there the lion's ruddy eyes
Shall flow with tears of gold:
And pitying the tender cries,
And walking round the fold,

Saying: "Wrath by His meekness,
And by His health, sickness,
Are driven away
From our immortal day.

"And now beside thee, bleating lamb,
I can lie down and sleep.
Or think on Him who bore thy name,
Graze after thee, and weep.
  For, washed in life's river,
  My bright mane for ever
Shall shine like the gold,
As I guard o'er the fold."

William Blake

Ode

Intimations of Immortality from Recollections of Early Childhood

The Child is father of the Man;
And I could wish my days to be
Bound each to each by natural piety.

I

There was a time when meadow, grove, and
stream,
The earth, and every common sight,
To me did seem
Apparelled in celestial light,

375

The glory and the freshness of a dream.
It is not now as it hath been of yore; —
    Turn wheresoe'er I may,
    By night or day,
The things which I have seen I now can see
    no more.

II

    The Rainbow comes and goes,
    And lovely is the Rose,
    The Moon doth with delight
Look round her when the heavens are bare,
    Waters on a starry night
    Are beautiful and fair;
    The sunshine is a glorious birth;
    But yet I know, where'er I go,
That there hath past away a glory from the
    earth.

III

Now, while the birds thus sing a joyous
    song,
    And while the young lambs bound
    As to the tabor's sound,
To me alone there came a thought of grief:
A timely utterance gave that thought relief,
    And I again am strong:
The cataracts blow their trumpets from the
    steep;
No more shall grief of mine the season
    wrong;

I hear the Echoes through the mountains
throng,
The Winds come to me from the fields of
sleep,
And all the earth is gay;
Land and sea
Give themselves up to jollity,
And with the heart of May
Doth every beast keep holiday; —
Thou Child of Joy,
Shout round me, let me hear thy shouts,
thou happy Shepherdboy!

IV

Ye blessèd Creatures, I have heard the call
Ye to each other make; I see
The heavens laugh with you in your jubilee;
My heart is at your festival,
My head hath its coronal,
The fullness of your bliss, I feel — I feel it
all.
Oh evil day! if I were sullen
While Earth herself is adorning,
This sweet May-morning,
And the children are culling
On every side,
In a thousand valleys far and wide,
Fresh flowers; while the sun shines
warm,
And the Babe leaps up on his mother's
arm: —
I hear, I hear, with joy I hear!

— But there's a Tree, of many, one,
A single Field which I have looked upon,
Both of them speak of something that is
                    gone:
        The Pansy at my feet
        Doth the same tale repeat:
Whither is fled the visionary gleam?
Where is it now, the glory and the dream?

V

Our birth is but a sleep and a forgetting:
The Soul that rises with us, our life's Star,
        Hath had elsewhere its setting,
            And cometh from afar:
        Not in entire forgetfulness,
        And not in utter nakedness,
But trailing clouds of glory do we come
        From God, who is our home:
Heaven lies about us in our infancy!
Shades of the prison-house begin to close
        Upon the growing Boy,
But he beholds the light, and whence it
                    flows,
        He sees it in his joy;
The Youth, who daily farther from the east
        Must travel, still is Nature's priest,
        And by the vision splendid
        Is on his way attended;
At length the Man perceives it die away,
And fade into the light of common day.

VI

Earth fills her lap with pleasures of her own;
Yearnings she hath in her own natural kind,
And, even with something of a mother's
                    mind,
            And no unworthy aim,
        The homely nurse doth all she can
To make her Foster-child, her inmate
                    Man,
        Forget the glories he hath known,
And that imperial palace whence he came.

VII

Behold the Child among his new-born
                    blisses,
A six years' darling of a pigmy size!
See, where 'mid work of his own hand he
                    lies,
Fretted by sallies of his mother's kisses,
With light upon him from his father's eyes!
See, at his feet, some little plan or chart,
Some fragment from his dream of human
                    life,
Shaped by himself with newly-learnèd art;
            A wedding or a festival,
            A mourning or a funeral;
        And this hath now his heart,
        And unto this he frames his song:
            Then will he fit his tongue
To dialogues of business, love, or strife;
            But it will not be long
            Ere this be thrown aside,

And with new joy and pride
The little Actor cons another part;
Filling from time to time his 'humorous
stage'
With all the Persons, down to palsied Age,
That Life brings with her in her equipage;
As if his whole vocation
Were endless imitation.

VIII

Thou, whose exterior semblance doth belie
Thy soul's immensity;
Thou best philosopher, who yet dost keep
Thy heritage, thou eye among the blind,
That, deaf and silent, read'st the Eternal
Deep,
Haunted forever by the Eternal Mind, —
Mighty prophet! seer blest!
On whom those truths do rest,
Which we are toiling all our lives to find,
In darkness lost, the darkness of the grave;
Thou, over whom thy Immortality
Broods like the Day, a master o'er a slave,
A Presence which is not to be put by;
Thou little Child, yet glorious in the might
Of heaven-born freedom on thy being's
height,
Why with such earnest pains dost thou
provoke
The years to bring the inevitable yoke,
Thus blindly with thy blessedness at strife?

Full soon thy Soul shall have her earthly
                    freight,
And custom lie upon thee with a weight,
Heavy as frost, and deep almost as life!

IX

O joy! that in our embers
Is something that doth live,
That nature yet remembers
What was so fugitive!
The thought of our past years in me doth
                    breed
Perpetual benediction; not indeed
For that which is most worthy to be blest;
Delight and liberty, the simple creed
Of childhood, whether busy or at rest,
With new-fledged hope still fluttering in his
                    breast: —
Not for these I raise
The song of thanks and praise;
But for those obstinate questionings
Of sense and outward things,
Fallings from us, vanishings;
Blank misgivings of a Creature
Moving about in worlds not realized,
High instincts before which our mortal
                    nature
Did tremble like a guilty thing surprised:
But for those first affections,
Those shadowy recollections,
Which, be they what they may,
Are yet the fountain-light of all our day,

Are yet a master-light of all our seeing;
Uphold us, cherish, and have power to make
Our noisy years seem moments in the being
Of the Eternal Silence: truths that wake,
      To perish never:
Which neither listlessness, nor mad
              endeavor,
      Nor man nor boy,
Nor all that is at enmity with joy,
Can utterly abolish or destroy!
      Hence in a season of calm weather
      Though inland far we be,
Our souls have sight of that immortal sea
      Which brought us hither,
      Can in a moment travel thither,
And see the children sport upon the shore,
And hear the mighty waters rolling
          evermore.

X

Then sing, ye Birds, sing, sing a joyous
          song!
      And let the young Lambs bound
      As to the tabor's sound!
We in thought will join your throng,
      Ye that pipe and ye that play,
      Ye that through your hearts to-day
      Feel the gladness of the May!
What though the radiance which was once so
          bright
Be now forever taken from my sight,

Though nothing can bring back the
hour
Of splendor in the grass, of glory in the
flower;
We will grieve not, rather find
Strength in what remains behind;
In the primal sympathy
Which having been must ever be;
In the soothing thoughts that spring
Out of human suffering;
In the faith that looks through death,
In years that bring the philosophic mind.

XI

And O, ye Fountains, Meadows, Hills, and
Groves,
Forebode not any severing of our loves!
Yet in my heart of hearts I feel your might;
I only have relinquished one delight
To live beneath your more habitual sway.
I love the Brooks which down their channels
fret,
Even more than when I tripped lightly as
they;
The innocent brightness of a new-born Day
Is lovely yet;
The Clouds that gather round the setting sun
Do take a sober coloring from an eye
That hath kept watch o'er man's mortality;
Another race hath been, and other palms are
won.

Thanks to the human heart by which we
    live,
Thanks to its tenderness, its joys, and fears,
To me the meanest flower that blows can
    give
Thoughts that do often lie too deep for tears.
                William Wordsworth

Hymn to Intellectual Beauty

The awful shadow of some unseen Power
  Floats though unseen among us, —
    visiting
  This various world with as inconstant
    wing
As summer winds that creep from flower to
    flower;
Like moonbeams that behind some piny
    mountain shower,
    It visits with inconstant glance
    Each human heart and countenance;
Like hues and harmonies of evening, —
    Like clouds in starlight widely
      spread, —
    Like memory of music fled, —
    Like aught that for its grace may be
Dear, and yet dearer for its mystery.

Spirit of Beauty, that dost consecrate
  With thine own hues all thou dost shine
    upon

Of human thought or form, — where art
    thou gone?
Why dost thou pass away and leave our
    state,
This dim vast vale of tears, vacant and
    desolate?
    Ask why the sunlight not forever
    Weaves rainbows o'er yon mountain
      river,
Why aught should fail and fade that once is
    shown,
    Why fear and dream and death and birth
    Cast on the daylight of this earth
    Such gloom, — why man has such a
      scope
For love and hate, despondency and hope?

No voice from some sublimer world hath
    ever
    To sage or poet these responses given —
    Therefore the names of Daemon, Ghost,
      and Heaven,
Remain the records of their vain endeavor,
Frail spells — whose uttered charm might
    not avail to sever,
    From all we hear and all we see,
    Doubt, chance, and mutability.
Thy light alone — like mist o'er mountains
    driven,
    Or music by the night wind sent
    Through strings of some still
      instrument,

Or moonlight on a midnight stream,
Gives grace and truth to life's unquiet
    dream.

Love, Hope, and Self-esteem, like clouds
    depart
  And come, for some uncertain moments
      lent.
  Man were immortal, and omnipotent,
Didst thou, unknown and awful as thou art,
Keep with thy glorious train firm state
      within his heart.
    Thou messenger of sympathies,
    That wax and wane in lovers' eyes —
Thou — that to human thought art
      nourishment,
    Like darkness to a dying flame!
    Depart not as thy shadow came,
    Depart not — lest the grave should be,
Like life and fear, a dark reality.

While yet a boy I sought for ghosts, and
    sped
  Through many a listening chamber, cave
    and ruin,
  And starlight wood, with fearful steps
      pursuing
Hopes of high talk with the departed dead.
I called on poisonous names with which our
    youth is fed;
    I was not heard — I saw them not —
    When musing deeply on the lot

Of life, at that sweet time when winds are
          wooing
     All vital things that wake to bring
     News of birds and blossoming, —
     Sudden, thy shadow fell on me;
I shrieked, and clasped my hands in ecstasy!

I vowed that I would dedicate my powers
     To thee and thine — have I not kept the
          vow?
     With beating heart and streaming eyes,
          even now
I call the phantoms of a thousand hours
Each from his voiceless grave: they have in
          visioned bowers
     Of studious zeal or love's delight
     Outwatched with me the envious
          night —
They know that never joy illumed my brow
     Unlinked with hope that thou wouldst
          free
     This world from its dark slavery,
     That thou — O awful Loveliness,
Wouldst give whate'er these words cannot
          express.

The day becomes more solemn and serene
     When noon is past — there is a harmony
     In autumn, and a lustre in its sky,
Which through the summer is not heard or
          seen,
As if it could not be, as if it had not been!

Thus let thy power, which like the truth
  Of nature on thy passive youth
Descended, to my onward life supply
  Its calm — to one who worships thee,
  And every form containing thee,
  Whom, Spirit fair, thy spells did bind
To fear himself, and love all human kind.

Percy Bysshe Shelley

Thanatopsis

To him who in the love of Nature holds
Communion with her visible forms, she
    speaks
A various language; for his gayer hours
She has a voice of gladness, and a smile
And eloquence of beauty, and she glides
Into his darker musings, with a mild
And healing sympathy, that steals away
Their sharpness, ere he is aware. When
    thoughts
Of the last bitter hour come like a blight
Over thy spirit, and sad images
Of the stern agony, and shroud, and pall,
And breathless darkness, and the narrow
    house,
Make thee to shudder and grow sick at
    heart; —
Go forth, under the open sky, and list
To Nature's teachings, while from all
    around —

Earth and her waters, and the depths of
    air —
Comes a still voice: —
                      Yet a few days, and thee
The all-beholding sun shall see no more
In all his course; nor yet in the cold ground,
Where thy pale form was laid, with many
    tears,
Nor in the embrace of ocean, shall exist
Thy image. Earth, that nourished thee, shall
    claim
Thy growth, to be resolved to earth again,
And, lost each human trace, surrendering up
Thine individual being, shalt thou go
To mix forever with the elements,
To be a brother to the insensible rock
And to the sluggish clod, which the rude
    swain
Turns with his share, and treads upon. The
    oak
Shall send his roots abroad, and pierce thy
    mould.

    Yet not to thine eternal resting-place
Shalt thou retire alone, nor couldst thou
    wish
Couch more magnificent. Thou shalt lie
    down
With patriarchs of the infant world — with
    kings,
The powerful of the earth — the wise, the
    good,

Fair forms, and hoary seers of ages past,
All in one mighty sepulchre. The hills
Rock-ribbed and ancient as the sun, — the
     vales
Stretching in pensive quietness between;
The venerable woods — rivers that move
In majesty, and the complaining brooks
That make the meadows green; and, poured
     round all,
Old Ocean's gray and melancholy waste, —
Are but the solemn decorations all
Of the great tomb of man. The golden sun,
The planets, all the infinite host of heaven,
Are shining on the sad abodes of death
Through the still lapse of ages. All that tread
The globe are but a handful to the tribes
That slumber in its bosom. — Take the
     wings
Of morning, pierce the Barcan wilderness,
Or lose thyself in the continuous woods
Where rolls the Oregon, and hears no sound,
Save his own dashings — yet the dead are
     there:
And millions in those solitudes, since first
The flight of years began, have laid them
     down
In their last sleep — the dead reign there
     alone.
So shalt thou rest, and what if thou
     withdraw
In silence from the living, and no friend
Take note of thy departure? All that breathe

Will share thy destiny. The gay will laugh
When thou art gone, the solemn brood of
    care
Plod on, and each one as before will chase
His favorite phantom; yet all these shall
    leave
Their mirth and their employments, and
    shall come
And make their bed with thee. As the long
    train
Of ages glides away, the sons of men —
The youth in life's fresh spring, and he who
    goes
In the full strength of years, matron and
    maid,
The speechless babe, and the gray-headed
    man —
Shall one by one be gathered to thy side,
By those, who in their turn shall follow
    them.

    So live, that when thy summons comes to
    join
The innumerable caravan, which moves
To that mysterious realm, where each shall
    take
His chamber in the silent halls of death,
Thou go not, like the quarry-slave at night,
Scourged to his dungeon, but, sustained and
    soothed
By an unfaltering trust, approach thy grave

Like one who wraps the drapery of his
    couch
About him, and lies down to pleasant
    dreams.
                    William Cullen Bryant

The Mermaid Tavern

Souls of Poets dead and gone,
What Elysium have ye known,
Happy field or mossy cavern,
Choicer than the Mermaid Tavern,
Have ye tippled drink more fine
Than mine host's Canary wine?
Or are fruits of Paradise
Sweeter than those dainty pies
Of venison? O generous food!
Dressed as though bold Robin Hood
Would, with his maid Marian,
Sup and browse from horn and can.

I have heard that on a day
Mine host's sign-board flew away,
Nobody knew whither, till
An astrologer's old quill
To a sheepskin gave the story,
Said he saw you in your glory,
Underneath a new old sign
Sipping beverage divine,
And pledging with contented smack
The Mermaid in the Zodiac!

Souls of Poets dead and gone,
What Elysium have ye known,
Happy field or mossy cavern,
Choicer than the Mermaid Tavern?
John Keats

Each and All

Little thinks, in the field, yon red-cloaked
  clown
Of thee from the hill-top looking down;
The heifer that lows in the upland farm,
Far-heard, lows not thine ear to charm;
The sexton, tolling his bell at noon,
Deems not that great Napoleon
Stops his horse, and lists with delight,
Whilst his files sweep round yon Alpine
  height;
Nor knowest thou what argument
Thy life to thy neighbor's creed has lent.
All are needed by each one;
Nothing is fair or good alone.
I thought the sparrow's note from heaven,
Singing at dawn on the alder bough;
I brought him home, in his nest, at even;
He sings the song, but it cheers not now,
For I did not bring home the river and
  sky; —
He sang to my ear, — they sang to my eye.
The delicate shells lay on the shore:

The bubbles of the latest wave
Fresh pearls to their enamel gave,
And the bellowing of the savage sea
Greeted their safe escape to me.
I wiped away the weeds and foam,
I fetched my sea-born treasures home;
But the poor, unsightly, noisome things
Had left their beauty on the shore
With the sun and the sand and the wild
    uproar.
The lover watched his graceful maid,
As 'mid the virgin train she strayed,
Nor knew her beauty's best attire
Was woven still by the snow-white choir.
At last she came to his hermitage,
Like the bird from the woodlands to the
    cage; —
The gay enchantment was undone,
A gentle wife, but fairy none.
Then I said, ''I covet truth;
Beauty is unripe childhood's cheat;
I leave it behind with the games of
    youth:'' —

As I spoke, beneath my feet
The ground-pine curled its pretty wreath,
Running over the club-moss burrs;
I inhaled the violet's breath;
Around me stood the oaks and firs;
Pine-cones and acorns lay on the ground;
Over me soared the eternal sky,
Full of light and of deity;

394

Again I saw, again I heard,
The rolling river, the morning bird; —
Beauty through my senses stole;
I yielded myself to the perfect whole.
                    Ralph Waldo Emerson

The Village Blacksmith

Under a spreading chestnut-tree
    The village smithy stands;
The smith, a mighty man is he,
    With large and sinewy hands;
And the muscles of his brawny arms
    Are strong as iron bands.

His hair is crisp, and black, and long,
    His face is like the tan;
His brow is wet with honest sweat,
    He earns whate'er he can,
And looks the whole world in the face,
    For he owes not any man.

Week in, week out, from morn till night,
    You can hear his bellows blow;
You can hear him swing his heavy sledge
    With measured beat and slow,
Like a sexton ringing the village bell,
    When the evening sun is low.

And children coming home from school
    Look in at the open door;

They love to see the flaming forge,
  And hear the bellows roar,
And catch the burning sparks that fly
  Like chaff from a threshing-floor.

He goes on Sunday to the church,
  And sits among his boys;
He hears the parson pray and preach,
  He hears his daughter's voice,
Singing in the village choir,
  And it makes his heart rejoice.

It sounds to him like her mother's voice,
  Singing in Paradise!
He needs must think of her once more,
  How in the grave she lies;
And with his hard, rough hand he wipes
  A tear out of his eyes.

Toiling, — rejoicing, — sorrowing,
  Onward through life he goes;
Each morning sees some task begin,
  Each evening sees its close;
Something attempted, something done,
  Has earned a night's repose.

Thanks, thanks to thee, my worthy friend,
  For the lesson thou hast taught!
Thus at the flaming forge of life
  Our fortunes must be wrought;
Thus on its sounding anvil shaped
  Each burning deed and thought!
            Henry Wadsworth Longfellow

It Is Too Late!

It is too late! Ah, nothing is too late
Till the tired heart shall cease to palpitate.
Cato learned Greek at eighty; Sophocles
Wrote his grand Oedipus, and Simonides
Bore off the prize of verse from his
    compeers,
When each had numbered more than
    fourscore years,
And Theophrastus, at fourscore and ten,
Had but begun his "Characters of Men."
Chaucer, at Woodstock with the
    nightingales,
At sixty wrote the Canterbury Tales;
Goethe at Weimar, toiling to the last,
Completed Faust when eighty years were
    past.

Henry Wadsworth Longfellow

The Lost Occasion

Some die too late and some too soon,
At early morning, heart of noon,
Or the chill evening twilight. Thou,
Whom the rich heavens did so endow
With eyes of power and Jove's own brow,

With all the massive strength that fills
Thy home-horizon's granite hills,
With rarest gifts of heart and head
From manliest stock inherited,
New England's stateliest type of man,
In port and speech Olympian;
Whom no one met, at first, but took
A second awed and wondering look
(As turned, perchance, the eyes of Greece
On Phidias' unveiled masterpiece);
Whose words in simplest homespun clad,
The Saxon strength of Cædmon's had,
With power reserved at need to reach
The Roman forum's loftiest speech,
Sweet with persuasion, eloquent
In passion, cool in argument,
Or, ponderous, falling on thy foes
As fell the Norse god's hammer blows,
Crushing as if with Talus' flail
Through Error's logic-woven mail,
And failing only when they tried
The adamant of the righteous side. —
Thou, foiled in aim and hope, bereaved
Of old friends, by the new deceived,
Too soon for us, too soon for thee,
Beside thy lonely Northern sea,
Where long and low the marsh-lands spread,
Laid wearily down thy august head.

Thou shouldst have lived to feel below
Thy feet Disunion's fierce upthrow;
The late-sprung mine that underlaid

Thy sad concessions vainly made.
Thou shouldst have seen from Sumter's wall
The star-flag of the Union fall,
And armed rebellion pressing on
The broken lines of Washington!
No stronger voice than thine had then
Called out the utmost might of men,
To make the Union's charter free
And strengthen law by liberty.
How had that stern arbitrament
To thy gray age youth's vigor lent,
Shaming ambition's paltry prize
Before thy disillusioned eyes:
Breaking the spell about thee wound
Like the green withes that Samson bound:
Redeeming in one effort grand,
Thyself and thy imperilled land!
Ah, cruel fate, that closed to thee,
O sleeper by the Northern sea,
The gates of opportunity!
God fills the gaps of human need,
Each crisis brings its word and deed.
Wise men and strong we did not lack;
But still, with memory turning back,
In the dark hours we thought of thee,
And thy lone grave beside the sea.

Above that grave the east winds blow,
And from the marsh-lands drifting slow
The sea-fog comes, with evermore
The wave-wash of a lonely shore,
And sea-bird's melancholy cry,

As Nature fain would typify
The sadness of a closing scene,
The loss of that which should have been.
But, where thy native mountains bare
Their foreheads to diviner air,
Fit emblem of enduring fame.
One lofty summit keeps thy name.
For thee the cosmic forces did
The rearing of that pyramid,
The prescient ages shaping with
Fire, flood, and frost thy monolith.
Sunrise and sunset lay thereon
With hands of light their benison,
The stars of midnight pause to set
Their jewels in its coronet.
And evermore that mountain mass
Seems climbing from the shadowy pass
To light, as if to manifest
Thy nobler self, thy life at best!
                    John Greenleaf Whittier

A Dream Within a Dream

Take this kiss upon the brow!
And, in parting from you now,
Thus much let me avow —
You are not wrong, who deem
That my days have been a dream:
Yet if hope has flown away
In a night, or in a day,
In a vision, or in none,

Is it therefore the less *gone?*
All that we see or seem
Is but a dream within a dream.

I stand amid the roar
Of a surf-tormented shore,
And I hold within my hand
Grains of the golden sand —
How few! yet how they creep
Through my fingers to the deep,
While I weep — while I weep!
O God! can I not grasp
Them with a tighter clasp?
O God! can I not save
One from the pitiless wave?
Is *all* that we see or seem
But a dream within a dream?

Edgar Allan Poe

The Visionary

Silent is the house: all are laid asleep:
One alone looks out o'er the snow-wreaths
   deep,
Watching every cloud, dreading every
   breeze
That whirls the wildering drift, and bends
   the groaning trees.

Cheerful is the hearth, soft the matted floor;

Not one shivering gust creeps through pane
  or door;
The little lamp burns straight, its rays shoot
  strong and far:
I trim it well, to be the wanderer's guiding-
  star.

Frown, my haughty sire! chide, my angry
  dame;
Set your slaves to spy; threaten me with
  shame:
But neither sire nor dame, nor prying serf
  shall know,
What angel nightly tracks that waste of
  frozen snow.

What I love shall come like visitant of air,
Safe in secret power from lurking human
  snare;
Who loves me, no word of mine shall e'er
  betray,
Though for faith unstained my life must
  forfeit pay.

Burn, then, little lamp; glimmer straight and
  clear —
Hush! a rustling wing stirs, methinks, the
  air:
He for whom I wait, thus ever comes to me;
Strange Power! I trust thy might; trust thou
  my constancy.

Emily Brontë

Myself

I celebrate myself, and sing myself,
And what I assume you shall assume,
For every atom belonging to me as good
    belongs to you.
I loaf and invite my soul,
I lean and loaf at my ease observing a spear
    of summer grass.

My tongue, every atom of my blood, formed
    from this soil, this air,
Born here of parents born here from parents
    the same, and their parents the same,
I, now thirty-seven years old in perfect
    health begin,
Hoping to cease not till death.

Creeds and schools in abeyance,
Retiring back awhile sufficed at what they
    are, but never forgotten,
I harbor for good or bad, I permit to speak
    at every hazard,
Nature without check for original energy.

Walt Whitman

To Think of Time

I

To think of time — of all that retrospection,
To think of to-day, and the ages continued
  henceforward.

Have you guess'd you yourself would not
  continue?
Have you dreaded these earth-beetles?
Have you fear'd the future would be nothing
  to you?

Is to-day nothing? is the beginningless past
  nothing?
If the future is nothing they are just as
  surely nothing.

To think that the sun rose in the east — that
  men and women were flexible, real, alive
  — that every thing was alive,
To think that you and I did not see, feel,
  think, nor bear our part,
To think that we are now here and bear our
  part.

II

Not a day passes, not a minute or second
  without an accouchement,
Not a day passes, not a minute or second
  without a corpse.

404

The dull nights go over and the dull days
also,
The soreness of lying so much in bed goes
over,

The physician after long putting off gives
the silent and terrible look for an answer,
The children come hurried and weeping, and
the brothers and sisters are sent for,
Medicines stand unused on the shelf, (the
camphor-smell has long pervaded the
rooms,)
The faithful hand of the living does not
desert the hand of the dying,
The twitching lips press lightly on the
forehead of the dying,
The breath ceases and the pulse of the heart
ceases,
The corpse stretches on the bed and the
living look upon it,
It is palpable as the living are palpable.
The living look upon the corpse with their
eyesight,
But without eyesight lingers a different
living and looks curiously on the corpse.

III
To think the thought of death merged in the
thought of materials,
To think of all these wonders of city and
country, and others taking great interest in

them, and we are taking no interest in
them.
To think how eager we are in building our
houses,
To think others shall be just as eager, and
we quite indifferent.
(I see one building the house that serves him
a few years, or seventy or eighty years at
most,
I see one building the house that serves him
longer than that.)
Slow-moving and black lines creep over the
whole earth — they never cease — they
are the burial lines,
He that was President was buried, and he
that is now President shall surely be
buried.

IV

A reminiscence of the vulgar fate,
A frequent sample of the life and death of
workmen,
Each after his kind.
Cold dash of waves at the ferry-wharf, posh
and ice in the river, half-frozen mud in the
streets,
A gray discouraged sky overhead, the short
last daylight of December,
A hearse and stages, the funeral of an old
Broadway stage-driver, the cortege mostly
drivers.

Steady the trot to the cemetery, duly rattles the death-bell,

The gate is pass'd, the new-dug grave is halted at, the living alight, the hearse uncloses,

The coffin is pass'd out, lower'd and settled, the whip is laid on the coffin, the earth is swiftly shovel'd in,

The mound above is flatted with the spades — silence,

A minute — no one moves or speaks — it is done,

He is decently put away — is there any thing more?

He was a good fellow, free-mouth'd, quick-temper'd, not bad-looking,

Ready with life or death for a friend, fond of women, gambled, ate hearty, drank hearty,

Had known what it was to be flush, grew low-spirited toward the last, sicken'd, was help'd by a contribution,

Died, aged forty-one years — and that was his funeral.

Thumb extended, finger uplifted, apron, cape, gloves, strap, wet-weather clothes, whip carefully chosen,

Boss, spotter, starter, hostler, somebody loafing on you, you loafing on somebody, headway, man before and man behind,

Good day's work, bad day's work, pet

stock, mean stock, first out, last out, turning-in at night,
To think that these are so much and so nigh to other drivers, and he there takes no interest in them.

Walt Whitman

I Never Lost as Much But Twice

I never lost as much but twice,
And that was in the sod.
Twice have I stood a beggar
Before the door of God!

Angels — twice descending
Reimbursed my store —
Burglar! Banker — Father!
I am poor once more!

Emily Dickinson

I Years Had Been from Home

I Years had been from Home
And now before the Door
I dared not enter, lest a Face
I never saw before

Stare stolid into mine
And ask my Business there —
"My Business but a Life I left

408

Was such remaining there?''

I leaned upon the Awe —
I lingered with Before —
The Second like an Ocean rolled
And broke against my ear —

I laughed a crumbling Laugh
That I could fear a Door
Who Consternation compassed
And never winced before.

I fitted to the Latch
My Hand, with trembling care
Lest back the awful Door should spring
And leave me in the Floor —

Then moved my Fingers off
As cautiously as Glass
And held my ears, and like a Thief
Fled gasping from the House —
Emily Dickinson

There's a Certain Slant of Light

There's a certain Slant of light,
Winter Afternoons —
That oppresses, like the Heft
Of Cathedral Tunes —

Heavenly Hurt, it gives us —

We can find no scar,
But internal difference,
Where the Meanings, are —

None may teach it — Any —
'Tis the Seal Despair —
An imperial affliction
Sent us of the Air —

When it comes, the Landscape listens —
Shadows — hold their breath —
When it goes, 'tis like the Distance
On the look of Death —

Emily Dickinson

The Soul Selects Her Own Society

The Soul selects her own Society —
Then — shuts the Door —
To her divine Majority —
Present no more —

Unmoved — she notes the Chariots —
    pausing —
At her low Gate —
Unmoved — an Emperor be kneeling
Upon her Mat —

I've known her — from an ample nation —
Choose One —

Then — close the Valves of her attention —
Like Stone —

Emily Dickinson

The Pedigree of Honey

The pedigree of Honey
Does not concern the Bee,
Nor lineage of Ecstasy
Delay the Butterfly
On spangled journeys to the peak
Of some perceiveless thing —
The right of way to Tripoli
A more essential thing.

Emily Dickinson

I Died for Beauty — But Was Scarce

I died for Beauty — but was scarce
Adjusted in the Tomb
When One who died for Truth, was lain
In an adjoining Room —

He questioned softly "Why I failed"?
"For Beauty", I replied —
"And I — for Truth — Themself are
  One —
We Brethren, are", He said —

And so, as Kinsmen, met a Night —
We talked between the Rooms —
Until the Moss had reached our lips —
And covered up — our names —

Emily Dickinson

"Hope" Is the Thing with Feathers

"Hope" is the thing with feathers —
That perches in the soul —
And sings the tune without the words —
And never stops — at all —

And sweetest — in the Gale — is heard —
And sore must be the storm —
That could abash the little Bird
That kept so many warm —

I've heard it in the chillest land —
And on the strangest Sea —
Yet, never, in Extremity,
It asked a crumb — of Me.

Emily Dickinson

The Garden of Proserpine

Here, where the world is quiet;
  Here, where all trouble seems
Dead winds' and spent waves' riot
  In doubtful dreams of dreams;

I watch the green field growing
For reaping folk and sowing,
For harvest-time and mowing,
  A sleepy world of streams.

I am tired of tears and laughter,
  And men that laugh and weep;
Of what may come hereafter
  For men that sow to reap:
I am weary of days and hours,
Blown buds of barren flowers,
Desires and dreams and powers
  And everything but sleep.

Here life has death for neighbor,
  And far from eye or ear
Wan waves and wet winds labor,
  Weak ships and spirits steer;
They drive adrift, and whither
They wot not who make thither;
But no such winds blow hither,
  And no such things grow here.

No growth of moor or coppice,
  No heather-flower or vine,
But bloomless buds of poppies,
  Green grapes of Proserpine,
Pale beds of blowing rushes,
Where no leaf blooms or blushes
Save this whereout she crushes
  For dead men deadly wine.

Pale, without name or number,
  In fruitless fields of corn,
They bow themselves and slumber
  All night till light is born;
And like a soul belated,
In hell and heaven unmated,
By cloud and mist abated
  Comes out of darkness morn.

Though one were strong as seven,
  He too with death shall dwell,
Nor wake with wings in heaven,
  Nor weep for pains in hell;
Though one were fair as roses,
His beauty clouds and closes;
And well though love reposes,
  In the end it is not well.

Pale, beyond porch and portal,
  Crowned with calm leaves, she stands
Who gathers all things mortal
  With cold immortal hands;
Her languid lips are sweeter
Than love's who fears to greet her,
To men that mix and meet her
  From many times and lands.

She waits for each and other,
  She waits for all men born;
Forgets the earth her mother,
  The life of fruits and corn;
And spring and seed and swallow

Take wing for her and follow
Where summer song rings hollow
    And flowers are put to scorn.

There go the loves that wither,
    The old loves with wearier wings;
And all dead years draw thither,
    And all disastrous things;
Dead dreams of days forsaken,
Blind buds that snows have shaken,
Wild leaves that winds have taken,
    Red strays of ruined springs.

We are not sure of sorrow;
    And joy was never sure;
To-day will die to-morrow;
    Time stoops to no man's lure;
And love, grown faint and fretful,
With lips but half regretful
Sighs, and with eyes forgetful
    Weeps that no loves endure.

From too much love of living,
    From hope and fear set free,
We thank with brief thanksgiving
    Whatever gods may be
That no life lives for ever;
That dead men rise up never;
That even the weariest river
    Winds somewhere safe to sea.

Then star nor sun shall waken,

Nor any change of light:
  Nor sound of waters shaken,
    Nor any sound or sight:
Nor wintry leaves nor vernal,
Nor days nor things diurnal;
Only the sleep eternal
    In an eternal night.
                    Algernon Charles Swinburne

You Never Can Tell

You never can tell when you send a word
    Like an arrow shot from a bow
By an archer blind, be it cruel or kind,
    Just where it may chance to go.
It may pierce the breast of your dearest
        friend,
    Tipped with its poison or balm,
To a stranger's heart in life's great mart
    It may carry its pain or its calm.

You never can tell when you do an act
    Just what the result will be,
But with every deed you are sowing a seed,
    Though the harvest you may not see.
Each kindly act is an acorn dropped
    In God's productive soil;
You may not know, but the tree shall grow
    With shelter for those who toil.

You never can tell what your thoughts will
    do
    In bringing you hate or love,
For thoughts are things, and their airy wings
    Are swifter than carrier doves.
They follow the law of the universe —
    Each thing must create its kind,
And they speed o'er the track to bring you
    back
    Whatever went out from your mind.

Ella Wheeler Wilcox

The Two Glasses

There sat two glasses filled to the brim,
On a rich man's table, rim to rim;
One was ruddy and red as blood,
And one as clear as the crystal flood.

Said the glass of wine to the paler brother:
"Let us tell the tales of the past to each
    other;
I can tell of banquet and revel and mirth,
And the proudest and grandest souls on earth
Fell under my touch as though struck by
    blight,
Where I was king, for I ruled in might;
From the heads of kings I have torn the
    crown,
From the heights of fame I have hurled men
    down:

I have blasted many an honored name;
I have taken virtue and given shame;
I have tempted the youth with a sip, a taste,
That has made his future a barren waste.
Greater, far greater than king am I,
Or than any army beneath the sky.
I have made the arm of the driver fail,
And sent the train from the iron rail;
I have made good ships go down at sea,
And the shrieks of the lost were sweet to
   me,
For they said, 'Behold how great you be!
Fame, strength, wealth, genius before you
   fall,
For your might and power are over all.'
Ho! ho! pale brother,'' laughed the wine,
''Can you boast of deeds as great as mine?''

Said the water glass: ''I cannot boast
Of a king dethroned or a murdered host;
But I can tell of a heart once sad,
By my crystal drops made light and glad;
Of thirsts I've quenched, of brows I've
   laved,
Of hands I have cooled, and souls I have
   saved;
I have leaped through the valley, dashed
   down the mountain,
Flowed in the river and played in the
   fountain,
Slept in the sunshine and dropped from the
   sky,

And everywhere gladdened the landscape
  and eye.
I have eased the hot forehead of fever and
  pain;
I have made the parched meadows grow
  fertile with grain;
I can tell of the powerful wheel of the mill,
That ground out the flour and turned at my
  will.
I can tell of manhood debased by you,
That I have lifted and crowned anew.
I cheer, I help, I strengthen and aid;
I gladden the heart of man and maid;
I set the chained wine-captive free;
And all are better for knowing me.''

These are the tales they told each other,
The glass of wine and the paler brother,
As they sat together filled to the brim,
On the rich man's table, rim to rim.
Ella Wheeler Wilcox

The Man with the Hoe

Bowed by the weight of centuries he leans
Upon his hoe and gazes on the ground,
The emptiness of ages in his face,
And on his back the burden of the world.
Who made him dead to rapture and despair,
A thing that grieves not and that never
  hopes,

419

Stolid and stunned, a brother to the ox?
Who loosened and let down this brutal jaw?
Whose was the hand that slanted back this
  brow?
Whose breath blew out the light within this
  brain?

Is this the Thing the Lord God made and
  gave
To have dominion over sea and land;
To trace the stars and search the heavens for
  power;
To feel the passion of Eternity?
Is this the dream He dreamed who shaped
  the suns
And marked their ways upon the ancient
  deep?
Down all the caverns of Hell to their last
  gulf
There is no shape more terrible than this —
More tongued with censure of the world's
  blind greed —
More filled with signs and portents for the
  soul —
More packt with danger to the universe.

What gulfs between him and the seraphim!
Slave of the wheel of labor, what to him
Are Plato and the swing of Pleiades?
What the long reaches of the peaks of song,
The rift of dawn, the reddening of the rose?

Through this dread shape the suffering ages
   look;
Time's tragedy is in that aching stoop;
Through this dread shape humanity betrayed,
Plundered, profaned, and disinherited,
Cries protest to the Judges of the World,
A protest that is also prophecy.

O masters, lords and rulers in all lands,
Is this the handiwork you give to God,
This monstrous thing distorted and soul-
   quenched?
How will you ever straighten up this shape;
Touch it again with immortality;
Give back the upward looking and the light;
Rebuild in it the music and the dream;
Make right the immemorial infamies,
Perfidious wrongs, immedicable woes?

O masters, lords and rulers in all lands,
How will the Future reckon with this man?
How answer his brute question in that hour
When whirlwinds of rebellion shake all
   shores?
How will it be with kingdoms and with
   kings —
With those who shaped him to the thing he
   is —
When this dumb terror shall rise to judge the
   world,
After the silence of the centuries?

Edwin Markham

Victory in Defeat

Defeat may serve as well as victory
To shake the soul and let the glory out.
When the great oak is straining in the wind,
The boughs drink in new beauty, and the
    trunk
Sends down a deeper root on the windward
    side.
Only the soul that knows the mighty grief
Can know the mighty rapture. Sorrows come
To stretch out spaces in the heart for joy.

Edwin Markham

Lord, Make a Regular Man Out of Me

This I would like to be — braver and
    bolder,
Just a bit wiser because I am older,
Just a bit kinder to those I may meet,
Just a bit manlier taking defeat;
This for the New Year my wish and my
    plea —
Lord, make a regular man out of me.

This I would like to be — just a bit finer,
More of a smiler and less of a whiner,
Just a bit quicker to stretch out my hand
Helping another who's struggling to stand,
This is my prayer for the New Year to be,

Lord, make a regular man out of me.

This I would like to be — just a bit fairer,
Just a bit better, and just a bit squarer,
Not quite so ready to censure and blame,
Quicker to help every man in the game,
Not quite so eager men's failings to see,
Lord, make a regular man out of me.

This I would like to be — just a bit truer,
Less of the wisher and more of the doer,
Broader and bigger, more willing to give,
Living and helping my neighbor to live!
This for the New Year my prayer and my
     plea —
Lord, make a regular man out of me.

Edgar A. Guest

Myself

I have to live with myself, and so
I want to be fit for myself to know,
I want to be able, as days go by,
Always to look myself straight in the eye;
I don't want to stand, with the setting sun,
And hate myself for things I have done.

I don't want to keep on a closet shelf
A lot of secrets about myself,
And fool myself, as I come and go,
Into thinking that nobody else will know

The kind of a man I really am;
I don't want to dress up myself in sham.

I want to go out with my head erect,
I want to deserve all men's respect;
But here in the struggle for fame and pelf
I want to be able to like myself.
I don't want to look at myself and know
That I'm bluster and bluff and empty show.

I can never hide myself from me;
I see what others may never see;
I know what others may never know,
I never can fool myself, and so,
Whatever happens, I want to be
Self-respecting and conscience free.

Edgar A. Guest

Tell Him So

If you hear a kind word spoken
　Of some worthy soul you know,
It may fill his heart with sunshine
　If you only tell him so.

If a deed, however humble,
　Helps you on your way to go,
Seek the one whose hand has helped you,
　Seek him out and tell him so!

If your heart is touched and tender

Toward a sinner, lost and low,
It might help him to do better
If you'd only tell him so!

Oh, my sisters, oh, my brothers,
As o'er life's rough path you go,
If God's love has saved and kept you,
Do not fail to tell men so!

Unknown

Sculpture

I took a piece of plastic clay
And idly fashioned it one day.
And as my fingers pressed it, still
It moved and yielded to my will.

I came again when days were past:
The bit of clay was hard at last.
The form I gave it still it bore,
But I could change that form no more!

I took a piece of living clay,
And gently pressed it day by day,
And molded with my power and art
A young child's soft and yielding heart.

I came again when years had gone:
It was a man I looked upon.
He still that early impress bore,
And I could fashion it no more!

Unknown

The Measure of a Man

Not — "How did he die?" But — "How
    did he live?"
Not — "What did he gain?" But — "What
    did he give?"
These are the units to measure the worth
Of a man as a man, regardless of birth.

Not — "What was his station?" But —
    "Had he a heart?"
And — "How did he play his God-given
    part?
Was he ever ready with a word of good
    cheer,
To bring back a smile, to banish a tear?"

Not — "What was his church?" Nor —
    "What was his creed?"
But — "Had he befriended those really in
    need?"
Not — "What did the sketch in the
    newspaper say?"
But — "How many were sorry when he
    passed away?"

Unknown

Design

I found a dimpled spider, fat and white,
On a white heal-all, holding up a moth
Like a white piece of rigid satin cloth —
Assorted characters of death and blight
Mixed ready to begin the morning right,
Like the ingredients of a witches' broth —
A snow-drop spider, a flower like a froth,
And dead wings carried like a paper kite.
What had that flower to do with being
    white,
The wayside blue and innocent heal-all?
What brought the kindred spider to that
    height,
Then steered the white moth thither in the
    night?
What but design of darkness to appall? —
If design govern in a thing so small.

Robert Frost

Two Tramps in Mud Time

Out of the mud two strangers came
And caught me splitting wood in the yard.
And one of them put me off my aim
By hailing cheerily "Hit them hard!"
I knew pretty well why he dropped behind
And let the other go on a way.
I knew pretty well what he had in mind:

427

He wanted to take my job for pay.

Good blocks of beech it was I split,
As large around as the chopping block;
And every piece I squarely hit
Fell splinterless as a cloven rock.
The blows that a life of self-control
Spares to strike for the common good
That day, giving a loose to my soul,
I spent on the unimportant wood.

The sun was warm but the wind was chill.
You know how it is with an April day
When the sun is out and the wind is still,
You're one month on in the middle of May.
But if you so much as dare to speak,
A cloud comes over the sunlit arch,
A wind comes off a frozen peak,
And you're two months back in the middle
    of March.

A bluebird comes tenderly up to alight
And fronts the wind to unruffle a plume
His song so pitched as not to excite
A single flower as yet to bloom.
It is snowing a flake: and he half knew
Winter was only playing possum.
Except in color he isn't blue,
But he wouldn't advise a thing to blossom.

The water for which we may have to look
In summertime with a witching-wand,

In every wheelrut's now a brook,
In every print of a hoof a pond.
Be glad of water, but don't forget
The lurking frost in the earth beneath
That will steal forth after the sun is set
And show on the water its crystal teeth.

The time when most I loved my task
These two must make me love it more
By coming with what they came to ask.
You'd think I never had felt before
The weight of an ax-head poised aloft,
The grip on earth of outspread feet,
The life of muscles rocking soft
And smooth and moist in vernal heat.

Out of the woods two hulking tramps
(From sleeping God knows where last night,
But not long since in the lumber camps).
They thought all chopping was theirs of
    right.
Men of the woods and lumberjacks,
They judged me by their appropriate tool.
Except as a fellow handled an ax,
They had no way of knowing a fool.

Nothing on either side was said.
They knew they had but to stay their stay
And all their logic would fill my head:
As that I had no right to play
With what was another man's work for gain.
My right might be love but theirs was need.

And where the two exist in twain
Theirs was the better right — agreed.

But yield who will to their separation,
My object in living is to unite
My avocation and my vocation
As my two eyes make one in sight.
Only where love and need are one,
And the work is play for mortal stakes,
Is the deed ever really done
For Heaven and the future's sakes.

Robert Frost

West-Running Brook

''Fred, where is north?''

        ''North? North is there, my love.
The brook runs west.''

      ''West-Running Brook then call it.''
(West-Running Brook men call it to this
  day.)
''What does it think it's doing running west
When all the other country brooks flow east
To reach the ocean? It must be the brook
Can trust itself to go by contraries
The way I can with you — and you with
  me —
Because we're — we're — I don't know
  what we are.

What are we?''

  ''Young or new?''

    ''We must be something.
We've said we two. Let's change that to we
 three.
As you and I are married to each other,
We'll both be married to the brook. We'll
 build
Our bridge across it, and the bridge shall be
Our arm thrown over it asleep beside it.
Look, look, it's waving to us with a wave
To let us know it hears me.''

    ''Why, my dear,
That wave's been standing off this jut of
 shore —''
(The black stream, catching on a sunken
 rock,
Flung backward on itself in one white wave,
And the white water rode the black forever.
Not gaining but not losing, like a bird
White feathers from the struggle of whose
 breast
Flecked the dark stream and flecked the
 darker pool
Below the point, and were at last driven
 wrinkled
In a white scarf against the far-shore alders.)
''That wave's been standing off this jut of
 shore

431

Ever since rivers, I was going to say,
Were made in heaven. It wasn't waved to
  us."

"It wasn't, yet it was. If not to you,
It was to me — in an annunciation."

"Oh, if you take it off to lady-land,
As 't were the country of the Amazons
We men must see you to the confines of
And leave you there, ourselves forbid to
  enter —
It is your brook! I have no more to say."

"Yes, you have, too. Go on. You thought
  of something."

"Speaking of contraries, see how the brook
In that white wave runs counter to itself.
It is from that in water we were from
Long, long before we were from any
  creature.
Here we, in our impatience of the steps,
Get back to the beginning of beginnings,
The stream of everything that runs away.
Some say existence like a Pirouot
And Pirouette, forever in one place,
Stands still and dances, but it runs away;
It seriously, sadly, runs away
To fill the abyss's void with emptiness.
It flows beside us in this water brook,
But it flows over us. It flows between us

To separate us for a panic moment.
It flows between us, over us, and *with* us.
And it is time, strength, tone, light, life,
   and love —
And even substance lapsing unsubstantial:
The universal cataract of death
That spends to nothingness — and
   unresisted,
Save by some strange resistance in itself,
Not just a swerving, but a throwing back,
As if regret were in it and were sacred.
It has this throwing backward on itself
So that the fall of most of it is always
Raising a little, sending up a little.
Our life runs down in sending up the clock.
The brook runs down in sending up our life.
The sun runs down in sending up the brook.
And there is something sending up the sun.
It is this backward motion toward the
   source,
Against the stream, that most we see
   ourselves in,
The tribute of the current to the source.
It is from this in nature we are from.
It is most us."

                  "Today will be the day
You said so."

                  "No, today will be the day
You said the brook was called West-Running
   Brook."

"Today will be the day of what we both
    said."

Robert Frost

To Earthward

Love at the lips was touch
As sweet as I could bear;
And once that seemed too much;
I lived on air

That crossed me from sweet things,
The flow of — was it musk
From hidden grapevine springs
Down hill at dusk?

I had the swirl and ache
From sprays of honeysuckle
That when they're gathered shake
Dew on the knuckle.

I craved strong sweets, but those
Seemed strong when I was young;
The petal of the rose
It was that stung.

Now no joy but lacks salt
That is not dashed with pain
And weariness and fault;
I crave the stain

434

Of tears, the aftermark
Of almost too much love,
The sweet of bitter bark
And burning clove.

When stiff and sore and scarred
I take away my hand
From leaning on it hard
In grass and sand,

The hurt is not enough:
I long for weight and strength
To feel the earth as rough
To all my length.

Robert Frost

The Silken Tent

She is as in a field a silken tent
At midday when a sunny summer breeze
Has dried the dew and all its ropes relent,
So that in guys it gently sways at ease,
And its supporting central cedar pole,
That is its pinnacle to heavenward
And signifies the sureness of the soul,
Seems to owe naught to any single cord,
But strictly held by none, is loosely bound
By countless silken ties of love and thought
To everything on earth the compass round,
And only by one's going slightly taut

In the capriciousness of summer air
Is of the slightest bondage made aware.
Robert Frost

Prophecy

I shall lie hidden in a hut
   In the middle of an alder wood,
With the back door blind and bolted shut,
   And the front door locked for good.

I shall lie folded like a saint,
   Lapped in a scented linen sheet,
On a bedstead striped with bright-blue paint,
   Narrow and cold and neat.

The midnight will be glassy black
   Behind the panes, with wind about
To set his mouth against a crack
   And blow the candle out.

Elinor Wylie

What Are Years?

What is our innocence,
what is our guilt? All are
   naked, none is safe. And whence
is courage: the unanswered question,
the resolute doubt —

dumbly calling, deafly listening — that
is misfortune, even death,
    encourages others
    and in its defeat, stirs

    the soul to be strong? He
sees deep and is glad, who
    accedes to mortality
and in his imprisonment rises
upon himself as
the sea in a chasm, struggling to be
free and unable to be,
    in its surrendering
    finds its continuing.

    So he who strongly feels,
behaves. The very bird,
    grown taller as he sings, steels
his form straight up. Though he is captive,
his mighty singing
says, satisfaction is a lowly
thing, how pure a thing is joy.
    This is mortality,
    this is eternity.

Marianne Moore

Humor

Drinking

The thirsty earth soaks up the rain,
And drinks and gapes for drink again;
The plants suck in the earth, and are
With constant drinking fresh and fair;
The sea itself (which one would think
Should have but little need of drink)
Drinks ten thousand rivers up,
So filled that they o'erflow the cup.
The busy Sun (and one would guess
By 's drunken fiery face no less)
Drinks up the sea, and when he's done,
The Moon and Stars drink up the Sun:
They drink and dance by their own light,
They drink and revel all the night:
Nothing in Nature's sober found,
But an eternal health goes round.
Fill up the bowl, then, fill it high,
Fill all the glasses there — for why
Should every creature drink but I?
Why, man of morals, tell me why?

Abraham Cowley

Sally in Our Alley

Of all the girls that are so smart
  There's none like pretty Sally;
She is the darling of my heart,
  And she lives in our alley.
There is no lady in the land
  Is half so sweet as Sally;
She is the darling of my heart,
  And she lives in our alley.

Her father he makes cabbage nets,
  And through the streets does cry 'em;
Her mother she sells laces long
  To such as please to buy 'em;
But sure such folks could ne'er beget
  So sweet a girl as Sally!
She is the darling of my heart,
  And she lives in our alley.

When she is by, I leave my work,
  I love her so sincerely;
My master comes like any Turk,
  And bangs me most severely:
But let him bang his bellyful,
  I'll bear it all for Sally;
She is the darling of my heart,
  And she lives in our alley.

Of all the days that's in the week
  I dearly love but one day —

And that's the day that comes betwixt
    A Saturday and Monday;
For then I'm dressed all in my best
    To walk abroad with Sally;
She is the darling of my heart,
    And she lives in our alley.

My master carries me to church,
    And often am I blamèd
Because I leave him in the lurch
    As soon as text is namèd;
I leave the church in sermon-time
    And slink away to Sally;
She is the darling of my heart,
    And she lives in our alley.

When Christmas comes about again,
    Oh, then I shall have money;
I'll hoard it up, and box it all,
    I'll give it to my honey:
I would it were ten thousand pound,
    I'd give it all to Sally;
She is the darling of my heart,
    And she lives in our alley.

My master and the neighbors all
    Make game of me and Sally,
And, but for her, I'd better be
    A slave and row a galley;
But when my seven long years are out,
    O, then I'll marry Sally;

O, then we'll wed, and then we'll bed —
    But not in our alley!

Henry Carey

The Mad Gardener's Song

He thought he saw an Elephant,
    That practiced on a fife:
He looked again, and found it was
    A letter from his wife.
"At length I realize," he said,
    "The bitterness of Life!"

He thought he saw a Buffalo
    Upon the chimney-piece:
He looked again, and found it was
    His Sister's Husband's Niece,
"Unless you leave this house," he said,
    "I'll send for the Police!"

He thought he saw a Rattlesnake
    That questioned him in Greek:
He looked again, and found it was
    The Middle of Next Week.
"The one thing I regret," he said,
    "Is that it cannot speak!"

He thought he saw a Banker's Clerk
    Descending from the bus:
He looked again, and found it was
    A Hippopotamus.

"If this should stay to dine," he said,
  "There won't be much for us!"

He thought he saw a Kangaroo
  That worked a coffee-mill:
He looked again, and found it was
  A Vegetable-Pill.
"Were I to swallow this," he said,
  "I should be very ill!"

He thought he saw a Coach-and-Four
  That stood beside his bed:
He looked again, and found it was
  A Bear without a Head.
"Poor thing," he said, "poor silly thing!
  It's waiting to be fed!"

He thought he saw an Albatross
  That fluttered round the lamp:
He looked again, and found it was
  A Penny-Postage-Stamp.
"You'd best be getting home," he said,
  "The nights are very damp!"

He thought he saw a Garden-Door
  That opened with a key:
He looked again, and found it was
  A Double Rule of Three:
"And all its mystery," he said,
  "Is clear as day to me!"

He thought he saw an Argument

445

That proved he was the Pope:
He looked again, and found it was
   A Bar of Mottled Soap.
''A fact so dread,'' he faintly said,
   ''Extinguishes all hope!''

Lewis Carroll

The Game of Life

There's a game much in fashion — I think
   it's called Euchre
(Though I never have played it, for pleasure
   or lucre),
In which, when the cards are in certain
   conditions,
The players appear to have changed their
   positions,
And one of them cries, in a confident tone,
''I think I may venture to go it alone!''

While watching the game, 'tis a whim of the
   bard's
A moral to draw from that skirmish of cards,
And to fancy he finds in the trivial strife
Some excellent hints for the battle of Life,
Where — whether the prize be a ribbon or
   throne —
The winner is he who can go it alone!

When great Galileo proclaimed that the
   world

In a regular orbit was ceaselessly whirled,
And got — not a convert — for all of his
    pains,
But only derision and prison and chains,
"It moves, for all that!" was his answering
    tone,
For he knew, like the Earth, he could go it
    alone!

When Kepler, with intellect piercing afar,
Discovered the laws of each planet and star,
And doctors, who ought to have lauded his
    name,
Derided his learning, and blackened his
    fame,
"I can wait!" he replied, "till the truth you
    shall own";
For he felt in his heart he could go it alone!

Alas! for the player who idly depends,
In the struggle for life, upon kindred or
    friends;
Whatever the value of blessings like these,
They can never atone for inglorious ease,
Nor comfort the coward who finds, with a
    groan,
That his crutches have left him to go it
    alone!

There's something, no doubt, in the hand
    you may hold;

Health, family, culture, wit, beauty, and
    gold
The fortunate owner may fairly regard
As, each in its way, a most excellent card;
Yet the game may be lost, with all these for
    your own,
Unless you've the courage to go it alone!

In battle or business, whatever the game,
In law or in love, it is ever the same;
In the struggle for power, or the scramble
    for pelf,
Let this be your motto — Rely on yourself!
For, whether the prize be a ribbon or throne,
The victor is he who can go it alone!

                              John Godfrey Saxe

Early Rising

"God bless the man who first invented
    sleep!"
    So Sancho Panza said, and so say I:
And bless him, also, that he didn't keep
    His great discovery to himself; nor try
To make it — as the lucky fellow might —
A close monopoly by patent-right!

Yes; bless the man who first invented sleep
    (I really can't avoid the iteration);
But blast the man, with curses loud and
    deep,

Whate'er the rascal's name, or age, or
    station,
Who first invented, and went round
    advising,
That artificial cut-off, — Early Rising!

"Rise with the lark, and with the lark to
    bed,"
    Observes some solemn, sentimental owl;
Maxims like these are very cheaply said:
    But, ere you make yourself a fool or fowl,
Pray, just inquire about his rise and fall,
And whether larks have any beds at all!

The time for honest folks to be abed
    Is in the morning, if I reason right;
And he who cannot keep his precious head
    Upon his pillow till it's fairly light,
And so enjoy his forty morning winks,
Is up to knavery, or else — he drinks!

Thomson, who sang about the "Seasons,"
    said
    It was a glorious thing to *rise* in season;
But then he said it — lying — in his bed,
    At ten o'clock, A.M., — the very reason
He wrote so charmingly. The simple fact is,
His preaching wasn't sanctioned by his
    practice.

'Tis, doubtless, well to be sometimes
    awake, —

Awake to duty, and awake to truth, —
But when, alas! a nice review we take
  Of our best deeds and days, we find, in
    sooth,
The hours that leave the slightest cause to
    weep
Are those we passed in childhood, or asleep!

'Tis beautiful to leave the world awhile
  For the soft visions of the gentle night;
And free, at last, from mortal care or guile,
  To live as only in the angels' sight,
In sleep's sweet realm so cozily shut in,
Where, at the worst, we only *dream* of sin!

So let us sleep and give the Maker praise.
  I like the lad who, when his father
    thought
To clip his morning nap by hackneyed
    phrase
  Of vagrant worm by early songster
    caught,
Cried, "Served him right! — it's not at all
    surprising;
The worm was punished, sir, for early
    rising!"

                              John Godfrey Saxe

The Preacher's Vacation

The old man went to meetin', for the day
   was bright and fair,
Though his limbs were very totterin', and
   'twas hard to travel there;
But he hungered for the Gospel, so he
   trudged the weary way
On the road so rough and dusty, 'neath the
   summer's burning ray.

By and by he reached the building, to his
   soul a holy place;
Then he paused, and wiped the sweat drops
   off his thin and wrinkled face;
But he looked around bewildered, for the
   old bell did not toll,
And the doors were shut and bolted, and he
   did not see a soul.

So he leaned upon his crutches, and he said,
   "What does it mean?"
And he looked this way and that, till it
   seemed almost a dream;
He had walked the dusty highway, and he
   breathed a heavy sigh —
Just to go once more to meetin', ere the
   summons came to die.

But he saw a little notice, tacked upon the
   meetin' door,

So he limped along to read it, and he read it
    o'er and o'er.
Then he wiped his dusty glasses, and he
    read it o'er again,
Till his limbs began to tremble and his eyes
    began to pain.

As the old man read the notice, how it made
    his spirit burn!
"Pastor absent on vacation — church is
    closed till his return."
Then he staggered slowly backward, and he
    sat him down to think,
For his soul was stirred within him, till he
    thought his heart would sink.

So he mused along and wondered, to himself
    soliloquized —
"I have lived to almost eighty, and was
    never so surprised,
As I read that oddest notice, stickin' on the
    meetin' door,
'Pastor on vacation' — never heard the like
    before.

"Why, when I first jined the meetin', very
    many years ago,
Preachers traveled on the circuit, in the heat
    and through the snow;
If they got their clothes and vittels ('twas
    but little cash they got),

They said nothin' 'bout vacation, but were
   happy in their lot.

"Would the farmer leave his cattle, or the
   shepherd leave his sheep?
Who would give them care and shelter, or
   provide them food to eat?
So it strikes me very sing'lar when a man of
   holy hands
Thinks he needs to have vacation, and
   forsakes his tender lambs.

"Did St. Paul git such a notion? Did a
   Wesley or a Knox?
Did they in the heat of summer turn away
   their needy flocks?
Did they shut their meetin' house, just go
   and lounge about?
Why, they knew that if they did Satan
   certainly would shout.

"Do the taverns close their doors, just to
   take a little rest?
Why, 'twould be the height of nonsense, for
   their trade would be distressed.
Did you ever know it happen, or hear
   anybody tell,
Satan takin' a vacation, shuttin' up the doors
   of hell?

"And shall preachers of the gospel pack
   their trunks and go away,

453

Leavin' saints and dyin' sinners git along as
    best they may?
Are the souls of saints and sinners valued
    less than settlin' beer?
Or do preachers tire quicker than the rest of
    mortals here?

"Why it is I cannot answer, but my feelings
    they are stirred;
Here I've dragged my totterin' footsteps for
    to hear the Gospel Word,
But the preacher is a travelin' and the
    meetin' house is closed;
I confess it's very tryin', hard, indeed, to
    keep composed.

"Tell me, when I tread the valley and go up
    the shining height,
Will I hear no angels singin' — will I see no
    gleamin' light?
Will the golden harps be silent? Will I meet
    no welcome there?
Why, the thought is most distressin', would
    be more than I could bear.

"Tell me, when I reach the city over on the
    other shore,
Will I find a little notice tacked upon the
    golden door,
Tellin' me 'mid dreadful silence, writ in
    words that cut and burn —

'Jesus absent on vacation, heaven closed till
   his return.' ''
Unknown

To a Thesaurus

O precious codex, volume, tome,
   Book, writing, compilation, work
Attend the while I pen a pome,
   A jest, a jape, a quip, a quirk.

For I would pen, engross, indite,
   Transcribe, set forth, compose, address,
Record, submit — yea, even write
   An ode, an elegy to bless —

To bless, set store by, celebrate,
   Approve, esteem, endow with soul,
Commend, acclaim, appreciate,
   Immortalize, laud, praise, extol

Thy merit, goodness, value, worth,
   Expedience, utility —
O manna, honey, salt of earth,
   I sing, I chant, I worship thee!

How could I manage, live, exist,
   Obtain, produce, be real, prevail,
Be present in the flesh, subsist,
   Have place, become, breathe or inhale,

Without thy help, recruit, support,
    Opitulation, furtherance,
Assistance, rescue, aid, resort,
    Favor, sustention, and advance?

Alas! alack! and well-a-day!
    My case would then be dour and sad,
Likewise distressing, dismal, gray,
    Pathetic, mournful, dreary, bad.

* * *

Though I could keep this up all day,
    This lyric, elegiac song.
Meseems hath come the time to say
    Farewell! adieu! good-by! so long!
                                        Franklin P. Adams

A Chronicle

Once — but no matter when —
    There lived — no matter where —
A man, whose name — but then
    I need not that declare.

He — well, he had been born,
    And so he was alive;
His age — I details scorn —
    Was somethingty and five.

He lived — how many years
  I truly can't decide;
But this one fact appears:
  He lived — until he died.

"He died," I have averred,
  But cannot prove 'twas so,
But that he was interred,
  At any rate, I know.

I fancy he'd a son,
  I hear he had a wife:
Perhaps he'd more than one,
  I know not, on my life!

But whether he was rich,
  Or whether he was poor,
Or neither — both — or which,
  I cannot say, I'm sure.

I can't recall his name,
  Or what he used to do:
But then — well, such is fame!
  'Twill so serve me and you.

And that is why I thus
  About this unknown man
Would fain create a fuss,
  To rescue, if I can

From dark oblivion's blow,
  Some record of his lot:

But, ah! I do not know
  Who — where — when — why — or
    what.

In this brief pedigree
  A moral we should find —
But what it ought to be
  Has quite escaped my mind!

Unknown

When Father Carves the Duck

We all look on with anxious eyes,
  When father carves the duck,
And mother almost always sighs,
  When father carves the duck.
Then all of us prepare to rise,
And hold our bibs before our eyes,
And be prepared for some surprise,
  When father carves the duck.

He braces up and grabs a fork
  Whene'er he carves a duck,
And won't allow a soul to talk,
  Until he's carved the duck.
The fork is jabbed into the sides,
Across the breast the knife he slides,
While every careful person hides
  From flying chips of duck.

The platter's always sure to slip
    When father carves a duck,
And how it makes the dishes skip!
    Potatoes fly amuck!
The squash and cabbage leap in space,
We get some gravy in our face,
And father mutters Hindu grace
    Whene'er he carves a duck.

We then have learned to walk around
    The dining-room and pluck
From off the window-sills and walls
    Our share of father's duck.
While father growls and blows and jaws,
And swears the knife was full of flaws,
And mother jeers at him because
    He couldn't carve a duck.
                    Ernest Vincent Wright

Methuselah

Methuselah ate what he found on his plate,
And never, as people do now,
Did he note the amount of the calory count;
He ate it because it was chow.
He wasn't disturbed as at dinner he sat,
Devouring a roast or a pie,
To think it was lacking in granular fat
Or a couple of vitamins shy.
He cheerfully chewed each species of food,
Unmindful of troubles or fears

459

Lest his health might be hurt
By some fancy dessert;
And he lived over nine hundred years.

Unknown

The Jumblies

They went to sea in a sieve, they did;
  In a sieve they went to sea:
In spite of all their friends could say,
On a winter's morn, on a stormy day,
  In a sieve they went to sea.
And when the sieve turned round and round,
And everyone cried, ''You'll all be
    drowned!''
They called aloud, ''Our sieve ain't big,
But we don't care a button; we don't care a
    fig:
  In a sieve we'll go to sea!''
    Far and few, far and few,
      Are the lands where the Jumblies
        live:
      Their heads are green, and their hands
        are blue;
      And they went to sea in a sieve.

They sailed away in a sieve, they did,
  In a sieve they sailed so fast,
With only a beautiful pea-green veil
Tied with a ribbon, by way of a sail,

460

To a small tobacco-pipe mast.
And every one said who saw them go,
"Oh! won't they be soon upset; you know!
For the sky is dark, and the voyage is long;
And, happen what may, it's extremely
     wrong
   In a sieve to sail so fast.

The water it soon came in, it did;
   The water it soon came in:
So, to keep them dry, they wrapped their
     feet
In a pinky paper all folded neat;
   And they fastened it down with a pin.
And they passed the night in a crockery-jar;
And each of them said, "How wise we are!
Though the sky be dark, and the voyage be
     long,
Yet we never can think we were rash or
     wrong
   While round in our sieve we spin."

And all night long they sailed away;
   And, when the sun went down,
They whistled and warbled a moony song
To the echoing sound of a coppery gong,
   In the shade of the mountains brown,
   "O Timballoo! how happy we are
When we live in a sieve and crockery-jar!
And all night long, in the moonlight pale,
We sail away with a pea-green sail
   In the shade of the mountains brown."

They sailed to the Western Sea, they did, —
  To a land all covered with trees:
And they bought an owl, and a useful cart,
And a pound of rice, and a cranberry-tart,
  And a hive of silvery bees;
And they bought a pig, and some green
    jackdaws,
And a lovely monkey with lollipop paws,
And forty bottles of ring-bo-ree,
  And no end of Stilton cheese.

And in twenty years they all came back, —
  In twenty years or more;
And every one said, "How tall they've
    grown!
For they've been to the Lakes, and the
    Torrible Zone,
  And the hills of the Chankly Bore."
And they drank their health, and gave them
    a feast
Of dumplings made of beautiful yeast;
And every one said, "If we only live,
We, too, will go to sea in a sieve,
  To the hills of the Chankly Bore."
    Far and few, far and few,
      Are the lands where the Jumblies
        live.
    Their heads are green, and their hands
        are blue;
      And they went to sea in a sieve.

Edward Lear

Mr. and Mrs. Discobbolos

Mr. and Mrs. Discobbolos
    Climbed to the top of a wall,
  And they sate to watch the sunset sky
  And to hear the Nupiter Piffkin cry
    And the Biscuit Buffalo call.
They took up a roll and some Camomile tea,
And both were as happy as happy could
         be —
    Till Mrs. Discobbolos said, —
    "Oh! W! X! Y! Z!
    It has just come into my head —
Suppose we should happen to fall!!!!!
        Darling Mr. Discobbolos!

"Suppose we should fall down flumpetty
    Just like two pieces of stone!
  Onto the thorns, — or into the moat!
  What would become of your new green
        coat?
    And might you not break a bone?
It never occurred to me before —
That perhaps we shall never go down any
        more!"
    And Mrs. Discobbolos said —
    "Oh! W! X! Y! Z!
    What put it into your head
To climb up this wall? — my own
        Darling Mr. Discobbolos?"

463

Mr. Discobbolos answered, —
　　"At first it gave me pain, —
　And I felt my ears turn perfectly pink
　When your exclamation made me think
　　We might never get down again!
But now I believe it is wiser far
To remain for ever just where we are." —
　　And Mr. Discobbolos said,
　　"Oh! W! X! Y! Z!
　It has just come into my head —
We shall never go down again —
　　　　　　Dearest Mrs. Discobbolos!"

So Mr. and Mrs. Discobbolos
　　Stood up, and began to sing,
　"Far away from hurry and strife
　Here we will pass the rest of life,
　　Ding a dong, ding dong, ding!
We want no knives nor forks nor chairs,
No tables nor carpets nor household cares,
　　From worry of life we've fled —
　　Oh! W! X! Y! Z!
　There is no more trouble ahead
Sorrow or any such thing —
　　　　　For Mr. and Mrs. Discobbolos!"

Mr. and Mrs. Discobbolos
　　Lived on the top of the wall,
For twenty years, a month, and a day,
Till their hair had grown all pearly gray,
　　And their teeth began to fall.
They never were ill, or at all dejected,

By all admired, and by some respected,
   Till Mrs. Discobbolos said,
     "Oh! W! X! Y! Z!
   It has just come into my head,
We have no more room at all —
            Darling Mr. Discobbolos!

"Look at our six fine boys!
   And our six sweet girls so fair!
Upon this wall they have all been born,
And not one of the twelve has happened
     to fall
Through my maternal care!
Surely they should not pass their lives
Without any chance of husbands or wives!"
   And Mrs. Discobbolos said,
     "Oh! W! X! Y! Z!
   Did it never come into your head
That our lives must be lived elsewhere,
           Dearest Mr. Discobbolos?

"They have never been at a ball,
   Nor have even seen a bazaar!
Nor have heard folks say in a tone all
     hearty,
   "What loves of girls (at a garden party)
   Those Misses Discobbolos are!"
Morning and night it drives me wild
To think of the fate of each darling child!"
   But Mr. Discobbolos said,
     "Oh! W! X! Y! Z!

What has come to your fiddledum
            head!
What a runcible goose you are!
                Octopod Mrs. Discobbolos!''

Suddenly Mr. Discobbolos
    Slid from the top of the wall;
And beneath it he dug a dreadful trench,
And filled it with dynamite, gunpowder
            gench,
    And aloud he began to call —
"Let the wild bee sing,
And the blue bird hum!
For the end of your lives has certainly
            come!''
        And Mrs. Discobbolos said,
        "Oh! W! X! Y! Z!
    We shall presently all be dead,
On this ancient runcible wall,
                Terrible Mr. Discobbolos!''

Pensively, Mr. Discobbolos
    Sat with his back to the wall;
He lighted a match, and fired the train,
And the mortified mountain echoed again
    To the sound of an awful fall!
And all the Discobbolos family flew
In thousands of bits to the sky so blue,
        And no one was left to have said,
        "Oh! W! X! Y! Z!
    Has it come into anyone's head

That the end has happened to all
Of the whole of the Clan Discobbolos?''

The Nutcrackers and the Sugar-Tongs

I

The Nutcrackers sate by a plate on the table;
  The Sugar-tongs sate by a plate at his
    side;
And the Nutcrackers said, ''Don't you wish
  we were able
    Along the blue hills and green meadows
    to ride?
Must we drag on this stupid existence
  forever,
  So idle and weary, so full of remorse,
While every one else takes his pleasure, and
  never
    Seems happy unless he is riding a horse?

II

''Don't you think we could ride without
  being instructed?
  Without any saddle or bridle or spur?
Our legs are so long, and so aptly
  constructed,
  I'm sure that an accident could not occur.
Let us all of a sudden hop down from the
  table,

And hustle downstairs, and each jump on
    a horse!
Shall we try? Shall we go? Do you think we
    are able?''
The Sugar-tongs answered distinctly, ''Of
    course!''

III

So down the long staircase they hopped in a
    minute;
    The Sugar-tongs snapped, and the
    Crackers said ''Crack!''
The stable was open; the horses were in it:
    Each took out a pony, and jumped on his
    back.
The Cat in a fright scrambled out of the
    doorway;
    The Mice tumbled out of a bundle of hay;
The brown and white Rats, and the black
    ones from Norway,
    Screamed out, ''They are taking the
    horses away!''

IV

The whole of the household was filled with
    amazement:
    The Cups and the Saucers danced madly
    about;
The Plates and the Dishes looked out of the
    casement;
    The Saltcellar stood on his head with a
    shout;

The Spoons, with a chatter, looked out of
the lattice;
The Mustard-pot climbed up the
gooseberry-pies;
The Soup-ladle peeped through a heap of
veal-patties,
And squeaked with a ladle-like scream of
surprise.

V

The Frying-pan said, "It's an awful
delusion!"
The Tea-kettle hissed and grew black in
the face;
And they all rushed down stairs in the
wildest confusion,
To see the great Nutcracker-Sugar-tong
race.
And out of the stable, with screamings and
laughter,
(Their ponies were cream-coloured,
speckled with brown,)
The Nutcrackers first, and the Sugar-tongs
after,
Rode all round the yard, and then all
round the town.

VI

They rode through the street, and they rode
by the station;
They galloped away to the beautiful shore;

In silence they rode, and "made no
     observation,"
   Save this: "We will never go back any
     more!"
And still you might hear, till they rode out
     of hearing,
   The Sugar-tongs snap, and the Crackers
     say "Crack!"
Till, far in the distance their forms
     disappearing,
   They faded away; and they never came
     back!

Edward Lear

The Goat

There was a man, now please take note,
There was a man, who had a goat.
He lov'd that goat, indeed he did,
He lov'd that goat, just like a kid.

One day that goat felt frisk and fine,
Ate three red shirts from off the line.
The man he grabbed him by the back,
And tied him to a railroad track.

But when the train hove into sight,
That goat grew pale and green with fright.
He heaved a sigh, as if in pain,
Coughed up those shirts and flagged the train.

Unknown

If I Should Die To-Night

After Arabella Eugenia Smith

If I should die to-night
And you should come to my cold corpse and
    say,
Weeping and heartsick o'er my lifeless
    clay —
If I should die to-night,
And you should come in deepest grief and
    woe —
And say: "Here's that ten dollars that I
    owe,"
  I might arise in my large white cravat
  And say, "What's that?"

If I should die to-night
And you should come to my cold corpse and
    kneel,
Clasping my bier to show the grief you feel,
  I say, if I should die to-night
And you should come to me, and there and
    then
Just even hint at paying me that ten,
  I might arise the while,
  But I'd drop dead again.

Ben King

An Overworked Elocutionist

Once there was a little boy whose name was
  Robert Reese;
And every Friday afternoon he had to speak
  a piece.
So many poems thus he learned, that soon
  he had a store
Of recitations in his head and still kept
  learning more.

And now this is what happened: He was
  called upon one week
And totally forgot the piece he was about to
  speak.
His brain he cudgeled. Not a word remained
  within his head!
And so he spoke at random, and this is what
  he said:

"My beautiful, my beautiful, who standest
  proudly by,
It was the schooner Hesperus — the
  breaking waves dashed high!
Why is this Forum crowded? What means
  this stir in Rome?
Under a spreading chestnut tree, there is no
  place like home!

When freedom from her mountain height
  cried, 'Twinkle, little star,'

472

Shoot if you must this old gray head, King
  Henry of Navarre!
Roll on, thou deep and dark blue castled
  crag of Drachenfels,
My name is Norval, on the Grampian Hills,
  ring out, wild bells!

If you're waking, call me early, to be or not
  to be,
The curfew must not ring tonight! Oh,
  woodman, spare that tree!
Charge, Chester, charge! On, Stanley, on!
  and let who will be clever!
The boy stood on the burning deck, but I go
  on forever!''

His elocution was superb, his voice and
  gestures fine;
His schoolmates all applauded as he finished
  the last line.
''I see it doesn't matter,'' Robert thought,
  ''what words I say,
So long as I declaim with oratorical
  display.''

                                    Carolyn Wells

Antigonish

As I was going up the stair
I met a man who wasn't there!
He wasn't there again today!
I wish, I *wish* he'd stay away!
Hughes Mearns

Very Like a Whale

One thing that literature would be greatly the
  better for
Would be a more restricted employment by
  authors of simile and metaphor.
Authors of all races, be they Greeks,
  Romans, Teutons or Celts,
Can't seem just to say that anything is the
  thing it is but have to go out of their way
  to say that it is like something else.
What does it mean when we are told
That the Assyrian came down like a wolf on
  the fold?
In the first place, George Gordon Byron had
  had enough experience
To know that it probably wasn't just one
  Assyrian, it was a lot of Assyrians.
However, as too many arguments are apt to
  induce apoplexy and thus hinder
  longevity,

474

We'll let it pass as one Assyrian for the sake
of brevity.
Now then, this particular Assyrian, the one
whose cohorts were gleaming in purple
and gold,
Just what does the poet mean when he says
he came down like a wolf on the fold?
In heaven and earth more than is dreamed of
in our philosophy there are a great many
things,
But I don't imagine that among them there is
a wolf with purple and gold cohorts or
purple and gold anythings.
No, no, Lord Byron, before I'll believe that
this Assyrian was actually like a wolf I
must have some kind of proof;
Did he run on all fours and did he have a
hairy tail and a big red mouth and big
white teeth and did he say Woof woof?
Frankly I think it very unlikely, and all you
were entitled to say, at the very most,
Was that the Assyrian cohorts came down
like a lot of Assyrian cohorts about to
destroy the Hebrew host.
But that wasn't fancy enough for Lord
Byron, oh dear me no, he had to invent a
lot of figures of speech and then
interpolate them,
With the result that whenever you mention
Old Testament soldiers to people they say
Oh yes, they're the ones that a lot of

wolves dressed up in gold and purple ate
them.
That's the kind of thing that's being done all
the time by poets, from Homer to
Tennyson;
They're always comparing ladies to lilies
and veal to venison,
And they always say things like that the
snow is a white blanket after a winter
storm.
Oh it is, is it, all right then, you sleep under
a six-inch blanket of snow and I'll sleep
under a half-inch blanket of unpoetical
blanket material and we'll see which one
keeps warm,
And after that maybe you'll begin to
comprehend dimly
What I mean by too much metaphor and
simile.

Ogden Nash

Reflections on Ice-Breaking

Candy
Is dandy

But liquor
Is quicker.

Ogden Nash

So That's Who I Remind Me Of

When I consider men of golden talents,
I'm delighted, in my introverted way,
To discover, as I'm drawing up the balance,
How much we have in common, I and they.

Like Burns, I have a weakness for the
   bottle,
Like Shakespeare, little Latin and less
   Greek;
I bite my fingernails like Aristotle;
Like Thackeray, I have a snobbish streak.

I'm afflicted with the vanity of Byron,
I've inherited the spitefulness of Pope;
Like Petrarch, I'm a sucker for a siren,
Like Milton, I've a tendency to mope.

My spelling is suggestive of a Chaucer;
Like Johnson, well, I do not wish to die
(I also drink my coffee from the saucer);
And if Goldsmith was a parrot, so am I.

Like Villon, I have debits by the carload,
Like Swinburne, I'm afraid I need a nurse;
By my dicing is Christopher out-Marlowed,
And I dream as much as Coleridge, only
   worse.

In comparison with men of golden talents,

I am all a man of talent ought to be;
I resemble every genius in his vice, however
    heinous —
Yet I write so much like me.

Ogden Nash

Portrait of the Artist as a Prematurely Old Man

It is common knowledge to every schoolboy
    and even every Bachelor of Arts,
That all sin is divided into two parts.
One kind of sin is called a sin of
    commission, and that is very important,
And it is what you are doing when you are
    doing something you ortant,
And the other kind of sin is just the opposite
    and is called a sin of omission and is
    equally bad in the eyes of all right-
    thinking people, from Billy Sunday to
    Buddha,
And it consists of not having done
    something you shudda.
I might as well give you my opinion of these
    two kinds of sin as long as, in a way,
    against each other we are pitting them,
And that is, don't bother your head about
    sins of commission because however
    sinful, they must at least be fun or else
    you wouldn't be committing them.

It is the sin of omission, the second kind of
    sin,
That lays eggs under your skin.
The way you get really painfully bitten
Is by the insurance you haven't taken out
    and the checks you haven't added up the
    stubs of and the appointments you haven't
    kept and the bills you haven't paid and the
    letters you haven't written.
Also, about sins of omission there is one
    particularly painful lack of beauty,
Namely, it isn't as though it had been
    a riotous red letter day or night every time
    you neglected to do your duty;
You didn't get a wicked forbidden thrill
Every time you let a policy lapse or forgot
    to pay a bill;
You didn't slap the lads in the tavern on the
    back and loudly cry Whee,
Let's all fail to write just one more letter
    before we go home, and this round of
    unwritten letters is on me.
No, you never get any fun
Out of the things you haven't done,
But they are the things that I do not like to
    be amid,
Because the suitable things you didn't do
    give you a lot more trouble than the
    unsuitable things you did.
The moral is that it is probably better not to
    sin at all, but if some kind of sin you
    must be pursuing,

Well, remember to do it by doing rather than by not doing.

Ogden Nash

Various Themes

They Flee from Me

They flee from me that sometime did me
  seek,
With naked foot stalking in my chamber.
I have seen them gentle, tame, and meek,
That now are wild, and do not remember
That some time they put themselves in
  danger
To take bread at my hand; and now they
  range,
Busily seeking with a continual change.

Thanked be fortune, it hath been otherwise
Twenty times better; but once, in speciall,
In thin array, after a pleasant guise,
When her loose gown from her shoulders did
  fall,
And she me caught in her arms long and
  small,
Therewith all sweetly did me kiss,
And softly said, Dear heart, how like you
  this?

It was no dream; I lay broad awaking.
But all is turned now through my gentleness

Into a strange fashion of forsaking;
And I have leave to go of her goodness,
And she also to use newfangleness.
But since that I so kindly am served,
I fain would know what *she* hath deserved.

Sir Thomas Wyatt

A Thing of Beauty

A thing of beauty is a joy for ever:
Its loveliness increases; it will never
Pass into nothingness; but still will keep
A bower quiet for us, and a sleep
Full of sweet dreams, and health, and quiet
   breathing.
Therefore, on every morrow, are we
   wreathing
A flowery band to bind us to the earth,
Spite of despondence, of the inhuman dearth
Of noble natures, of the gloomy days,
Of all the unhealthy and o'er-darkened ways
Made for our searching: yes, in spite of all,
Some shape of beauty moves away the pall
From our dark spirits. Such the sun, the
   moon,
Trees old and young, sprouting a shady boon
For simple sheep; and such are daffodils
With the green world they live in; and clear
   rills
That for themselves a cooling covert make

'Gainst the hot season; the mid-forest brake,
Rich with a sprinkling of fair musk-rose
   blooms:
And such too is the grandeur of the dooms
We have imagined for the mighty dead;
All lovely tales that we have heard or read:
An endless fountain of immortal drink,
Pouring unto us from the heaven's brink.
Nor do we merely feel these essences
For one short hour; no, even as the trees
That whisper round a temple become soon
Dear as the temple's self, so does the moon,
The passion poesy, glories infinite,
Haunt us till they become a cheering light
Unto our souls, and bound to us so fast,
That, whether there be shine, or gloom
   o'ercast,
They always must be with us, or we die.

From *Endymion*
John Keats

On Seeing the Elgin Marbles

My spirit is too weak — mortality
Weighs heavily on me like unwilling sleep,
And each imagined pinnacle and steep
Of godlike hardship, tells me I must die
Like a sick Eagle looking at the sky.
Yet 'tis a gentle luxury to weep
That I have not the cloudy winds to keep,

Fresh for the opening of the morning's eye.

Such dim-conceivèd glories of the brain
Bring round the heart an undescribable feud;
So do these wonders a most dizzy pain,
That mingles Grecian grandeur with the rude
Wasting of old Time — with a billowy
  main —
A sun — a shadow of a magnitude.

John Keats

The Solitary Reaper

Behold her, single in the field,
Yon solitary Highland Lass!
Reaping and singing by herself;
Stop here, or gently pass!
Alone she cuts and binds the grain,
And sings a melancholy strain;
O listen! for the Vale profound
Is overflowing with the sound.

No nightingale did ever chant
More welcome notes to weary bands
Of travellers in some shady haunt,
Among Arabian sands:
A voice so thrilling ne'er was heard
In spring-time from the Cuckoo-bird,
Breaking the silence of the seas
Among the farthest Hebrides.

Will no one tell me what she sings? —
Perhaps the plaintive numbers flow
For old, unhappy, far-off things,
And battles long ago:
Or is it some more humble lay,
Familiar matter of to-day?
Some natural sorrow, loss, or pain,
That has been, and may be again?

Whate'er the theme, the maiden sang
As if her song could have no ending;
I saw her singing at her work,
And o'er the sickle bending; —
I listened, motionless and still;
And, as I mounted up the hill,
The music in my ear I bore
Long after it was heard no more.

William Wordsworth

Ulalume

The skies they were ashen and sober;
   The leaves they were crispèd and sere,
   The leaves they were withering and sere;
It was night in the lonesome October
   Of my most immemorial year;
It was hard by the dim lake of Auber,
   In the misty mid region of Weir:
It was down by the dank tarn of Auber,
   In the ghoul-haunted woodland of Weir.

Here once, through an alley Titanic
　　Of cypress, I roamed with my Soul —
　　Of cypress, with Psyche, my Soul.
These were days when my heart was
　　　volcanic
　　As the scoriac rivers that roll,
　　As the lavas that restlessly roll
Their sulphurous currents down Yaanek
　　In the ultimate climes of the pole,
That groan as they roll down Mount Yaanek
　　In the realms of the boreal pole.

Our talk had been serious and sober,
　　But our thoughts they were palsied and
　　　sere,
　　Our memories were treacherous and sere,
For we knew not the month was October,
　　And we marked not the night of the year,
　　(Ah, night of all nights in the year!)
We noted not the dim lake of Auber
　　(Though once we had journeyed down
　　　here),
Remembered not the dank tarn of Auber
　　Nor the ghoul-haunted woodland of Weir.

And now, as the night was senescent
　　And star-dials pointed to morn,
　　As the star-dials hinted of morn,
At the end of our path a liquescent
　　And nebulous lustre was born,
Out of which a miraculous crescent

Arose with a duplicate horn,
Astarte's bediamonded crescent
Distinct with its duplicate horn.

And I said — "She is warmer than Dian:
She rolls through an ether of sighs,
She revels in a region of sighs:
She has seen that the tears are not dry on
These cheeks, where the worm never dies,
And has come past the stars of the Lion
To point us the path to the skies,
To the Lethean peace of the skies:
Come up, in despite of the Lion,
To shine on us with her bright eyes:
Come up through the lair of the Lion,
With love in her luminous eyes."

But Psyche, uplifting her finger,
Said — "Sadly this star I mistrust,
Her pallor I strangely mistrust:
Oh, hasten! — oh, let us not linger!
Oh, fly! — let us fly! — for we must."
In terror she spoke, letting sink her
Wings until they trailed in the dust;
In agony sobbed, letting sink her
Plumes till they trailed in the dust,
Till they sorrowfully trailed in the dust.

I replied — "This is nothing but dreaming:
Let us on by this tremulous light!
Let us bathe in this crystalline light!
Its sibyllic splendor is beaming

With hope and in beauty to-night:
  See, it flickers up the sky through the
    night!
Ah, we safely may trust to its gleaming,
  And be sure it will lead us aright:
We safely may trust to a gleaming
That cannot but guide us aright,
Since it flickers up to Heaven through the
    night."

Thus I pacified Psyche and kissed her,
  And tempted her out of her gloom,
  And conquered her scruples and gloom;
And we passed to the end of the vista,
  But were stopped by the door of a tomb,
  By the door of a legended tomb;
And I said — "What is written, sweet
    sister,
  On the door of this legended tomb?"
  She replied — "Ulalume — Ulalume —
  'Tis the vault of thy lost Ulalume!"

Then my heart it grew ashen and sober
  As the leaves that were crispèd and sere,
  As the leaves that were withering and
    sere,
And I cried — "It was surely October
  On this very night of last year
  That I journeyed — I journeyed down
    here,
  That I brought a dread burden down here:
  On this night of all nights in the year,

Ah, what demon has tempted me here?
Well I know, now, this dim lake of Auber,
  This misty mid region of Weir:
Well I know, now, this dank tarn of Auber,
  This ghoul-haunted woodland of Weir.''

Edgar Allan Poe

Israfel

*And the angel Israfel, whose heart strings
are a lute, and who has the sweetest voice of
all God's creatures.* — Koran

In Heaven a spirit doth dwell
  ''Whose heart-strings are a lute;''
None sing so wildly well
As the angel Israfel,
And the giddy stars (so legends tell)
Ceasing their hymns, attend the spell
  Of his voice, all mute.

Tottering above
  In her highest noon,
  The enamoured moon
Blushes with love.
While, to listen, the red levin
(With the rapid Pleiads, even,
Which were seven,)
Pauses in Heaven.

And they say (the starry choir
  And the other listening things)
That Israfeli's fire
Is owing to that lyre
  By which he sits and sings —
The trembling living wire
Of those unusual strings.

But the skies that angel trod,
  Where deep thoughts are a duty —
Where Love's a grown-up God —
  Where the Houri glances are
Imbued with all the beauty
  Which we worship in a star.

Therefore, thou art not wrong,
  Israfeli, who despisest
An unimpassioned song:
To thee the laurels belong,
  Best bard, because the wisest!
Merrily live, and long!

The ecstasies above
  With thy burning measures suit —
Thy grief, thy joy, thy hate, thy love,
  With the fervour of thy lute
  Well may the stars be mute!
Yes, Heaven is thine; but this
  Is a world of sweets and sours;
  Our flowers are merely — flowers,
And the shadow of thy perfect bliss
  Is the sunshine of ours.

If I could dwell
Where Israfel
    Hath dwelt, and he where I,
He might not sing so wildly well
    A mortal melody,
While a bolder note than this might swell
    From my lyre within the sky.

Edgar Allan Poe

The Conqueror Worm

Lo! 'tis a gala night
    Within the lonesome latter years!
An angel throng, bewinged, bedight
    In veils, and drowned in tears,
Sit in a theatre, to see
    A play of hopes and fears,
While the orchestra breathes fitfully
    The music of the spheres.

Mimes, in the form of God on high,
    Mutter and mumble low,
And hither and thither fly —
    Mere puppets they, who come and go
At bidding of vast formless things
    That shift the scenery to and fro,
Flapping from out their Condor wings
    Invisible Woe!

That motley drama — oh, be sure
   It shall not be forgot!
With its Phantom chased for evermore,
   By a crowd that seize it not,
Through a circle that ever returneth in
   To the self-same spot.
And much of Madness, and more of Sin,
   And Horror the soul of the plot.

But see, amid the mimic rout
   A crawling shape intrude!
A blood-red thing that writhes from out
   The scenic solitude!
It writhes! — it writhes! — with mortal
     pangs
   The mimes become its food,
And seraphs sob at vermin fangs
   In human gore imbued.

Out — out are the lights — out all!
   And, over each quivering form,
The curtain, a funeral pall,
   Comes down with the rush of a storm,
While the angels, all pallid and wan,
   Uprising, unveiling, affirm
That the play is the tragedy, "Man,"
   And its hero the Conqueror Worm.

Edgar Allan Poe

Ring Out, Wild Bells

Ring out, wild bells, to the wild sky,
  The flying cloud, the frosty light:
  The year is dying in the night;
Ring out, wild bells, and let him die.

Ring out the old, ring in the new,
  Ring, happy bells, across the snow:
  The year is going, let him go;
Ring out the false, ring in the true.

Ring out the grief that saps the mind,
  For those that here we see no more;
  Ring out the feud of rich and poor,
Ring in redress to all mankind.

Ring out a slowly dying cause,
  And ancient forms of party strife;
  Ring in the nobler modes of life,
With sweeter manners, purer laws.

Ring out the want, the care, the sin,
  The faithless coldness of the times;
  Ring out, ring out my mournful rhymes,
But ring the fuller minstrel in.

Ring out false pride in place and blood,
  The civic slander and the spite;
  Ring in the love of truth and right,
Ring in the common love of good.

Ring out old shapes of foul disease,
　Ring out the narrowing lust of gold;
　Ring out the thousand wars of old,
Ring in the thousand years of peace.

Ring in the valiant man and free,
　The larger heart, the kindlier hand;
　Ring out the darkness of the land,
Ring in the Christ that is to be.
　　　　　　　Alfred, Lord Tennyson

Locksley Hall

Comrades, leave me here a little, while as
　yet 'tis early morn:
Leave me here, and when you want me,
　sound upon the bugle horn.
'Tis the place, and all around it, as of old,
　the curlews call,
Dreary gleams about the moorland flying
　over Locksley Hall;
Locksley Hall, that in the distance overlooks
　the sandy tracts,
And the hollow ocean-ridges roaring into
　cataracts.

Many a night from yonder ivied casement,
　ere I went to rest,
Did I look on great Orion sloping slowly to
　the West.

Many a night I saw the Pleiads, rising thro'
   the mellow shade,
Glitter like a swarm of fire-flies tangled in a
   silver braid.
Here about the beach I wander'd, nourishing
   a youth sublime
With the fairy tales of science, and the long
   result of Time;
When the centuries behind me like a fruitful
   land reposed;
When I clung to all the present for the
   promise that it closed:
When I dipt into the future far as human eye
   could see;
Saw the Vision of the world, and all the
   wonder that would be. —

In the Spring a fuller crimson comes upon
   the robin's breast;
In the Spring the wanton lapwing gets
   himself another crest;
In the Spring a livelier iris changes on the
   burnish'd dove;
In the Spring a young man's fancy lightly
   turns to thoughts of love.

Then her cheek was pale and thinner than
   should be for one so young,
And her eyes on all my motions with a mute
   observance hung,
And I said, ''My cousin Amy, speak, and
   speak the truth to me,

497

Trust me, cousin, all the current of my
  being sets to thee.''
On her pallid cheek and forehead came a
  colour and a light,
As I have seen the rosy red flushing in the
  northern night.
And she turn'd — her bosom shaken with a
  sudden storm of sighs —
All the spirit deeply dawning in the dark of
  hazel eyes —
Saying, ''I have hid my feelings, fearing
  they should do me wrong;''
Saying, ''Dost thou love me, cousin?''
  weeping, ''I have loved thee long.''

Love took up the glass of Time, and turn'd
  it in his glowing hands;
Every moment, lightly shaken, ran itself in
  golden sands.
Love took up the harp of Life, and smote on
  all the chords with might;
Smote the chord of Self; that, trembling,
  pass'd in music out of sight.
Many a morning on the moorland did we
  hear the copses ring,
And her whisper throng'd my pulses with
  the fullness of the Spring.
Many an evening by the waters did we
  watch the stately ships,
And our spirits rush'd together at the
  touching of the lips.

O my cousin, shallow-hearted! O my Amy,
mine no more!
O the dreary, dreary moorland! O the
barren, barren shore!
Falser than all fancy fathoms, falser than all
songs have sung,
Puppet to a father's threat, and servile to a
shrewish tongue!
Is it well to wish thee happy? — having
known me — to decline
On a range of lower feelings and a narrower
heart than mine!
Yet it shall be: thou shalt lower to his level
day by day,
What is fine within thee growing coarse to
sympathize with clay.

As the husband is, the wife is: thou art
mated with a clown,
And the grossness of his nature will have
weight to drag thee down.
He will hold thee, when his passion shall
have spent its novel force,
Something better than his dog, a little dearer
than his horse.
What is this? his eyes are heavy: think not
they are glazed with wine.
Go to him: it is thy duty: kiss him: take his
hand in thine.
It may be my lord is weary, that his brain is
over-wrought:

Soothe him with thy finer fancies, touch him
   with thy lighter thought.

He will answer to the purpose, easy things
   to understand —
Better thou wert dead before me, tho' I slew
   thee with my hand!
Better thou and I were lying, hidden from
   the heart's disgrace,
Roll'd in one another's arms, and silent in a
   last embrace.
Cursed be the social wants that sin against
   the strength of youth!
Cursed be the social lies that warp us from
   the living truth!
Cursed be the sickly forms that err from
   honest Nature's rule!
Cursed be the gold that gilds the straiten'd
   forehead of the fool!

Well — 'tis well that I should bluster! —
   Hadst thou less unworthy proved —
Would to God — for I had loved thee more
   than ever wife was loved.
Am I mad, that I should cherish that which
   bears but bitter fruit?
I will pluck it from my bosom, tho' my
   heart be at the root.
Never, tho' my mortal summers to such
   length of years should come
As the many-winter'd crow that leads the
   clanging rookery home.

Where is comfort? in division of the records
    of the mind?
Can I part her from herself, and love her, as
    I knew her, kind?

I remember one that perish'd: sweetly did
    she speak and move:
Such a one do I remember, whom to look at
    was to love.
Can I think of her as dead, and love her for
    the love she bore?
No — she never loved me truly: love is love
    for evermore.
Comfort? comfort scorn'd of devils! this is
    truth the poet sings,
That a sorrow's crown of sorrow is
    remembering happier things.

Drug thy memories, less thou learn it, lest
    thy heart be put to proof,
In the dead unhappy night, and when the
    rain is on the roof.
Like a dog, he hunts in dreams, and thou art
    staring at the wall,
Where the dying night-lamp flickers, and the
    shadows rise and fall.
Then a hand shall pass before thee, pointing
    to his drunken sleep,
To thy widow'd marriage-pillows, to the
    tears that thou wilt weep.
Thou shalt hear the "Never, never,"
    whisper'd by the phantom years,

And a song from out the distance in the
   ringing of thine ears;
And an eye shall vex thee, looking ancient
   kindness on thy pain.
Turn thee, turn thee on thy pillow: get thee
   to thy rest again.
Nay, but Nature brings thee solace; for a
   tender voice will cry.
'Tis a purer life than thine; a lip to drain thy
   trouble dry.
Baby lips will laugh me down: my latest
   rival brings thee rest.
Baby fingers, waxen touches, press me from
   the mother's breast.
O, the child too clothes the father with a
   dearness not his due.
Half is thine and half is his: it will be
   worthy of the two.

O, I see thee old and formal, fitted to thy
   petty part,
With a little hoard of maxims preachng
   down a daughter's heart.
''They were dangerous guides the feelings
   — she herself was not exempt —
Truly, she herself had suffer'd'' — Perish in
   thy self-contempt!
Overlive it — lower yet — be happy!
   wherefore should I care?
I myself must mix with action, lest I wither
   by despair.

What is that which I should turn to, lighting
    upon days like these?
Every door is barr'd with gold, and opens
    but to golden keys.
Every gate is throng'd with suitors, all the
    markets overflow.
I have but an angry fancy: what is that
    which I should do?

I had been content to perish, falling on the
    foeman's ground,
When the ranks are roll'd in vapour, and the
    winds are laid with sound.
But the jingling of the guinea helps the hurt
    that Honour feels,
And the nations do but murmur, snarling at
    each other's heels.
Can I but relive in sadness? I will turn that
    earlier page.
Hide me from my deep emotion, O thou
    wondrous Mother-Age!

Make me feel the wild pulsation that I felt
    before the strife,
When I heard my days before me, and the
    tumult of my life;
Yearning for the large excitement that the
    coming years would yield,
Eager-hearted as a boy when first he leaves
    his father's field,
And at night along the dusky highway near
    and nearer drawn,

Sees in heaven the light of London flaring
    like a dreary dawn;
And his spirit leaps within him to be gone
    before him then,
Underneath the light he looks at, in among
    the throngs of men;
Men, my brothers, men the workers, ever
    reaping something new:
That which they have done but earnest of the
    things that they shall do:
For I dipt into the future, far as human eye
    could see,
Saw the Vision of the world, and all the
    wonder that would be;
Saw the heavens fill with commerce,
    argosies of magic sails,
Pilots of the purple twilight, dropping down
    with costly bales;
Heard the heavens fill with shouting, and
    there rain'd a ghastly dew
From the nation's airy navies grappling in
    the central blue;
Far along the world-wide whisper of the
    south-wind rushing warm,
With the standards of the peoples plunging
    thro' the thunder storm;
Till the war-drum throbb'd no longer, and
    the battle flags were furl'd
In the Parliament of man, the Federation of
    the world.
There the common sense of most shall hold
    a fretful realm in awe,

And the kindly earth shall slumber, lapt in
    universal law.

So I triumphed, ere my passions sweeping
    thro' me left me dry,
Left me with the palsied heart, and left me
    with the jaundiced eye;
Eye, to which all order festers, all things
    here are out of joint,
Science moves, but slowly slowly, creeping
    on from point to point:
Slowly comes a hungry people, as a lion,
    creeping nigher,
Glares at one that nods and winks behind a
    slowly-dying fire.
Yet I doubt not thro' the ages one increasing
    purpose runs,
And the thoughts of men are widen'd with
    the process of the suns.

What is that to him that reaps not harvest of
    his youthful joys,
Tho' the deep heart of existence beat for
    ever like a boy's?
Knowledge comes, but wisdom lingers, and
    I linger on the shore,
And the individual withers, and the world is
    more and more.
Knowledge comes, but wisdom lingers, and
    he bears a laden breast,
Full of sad experience, moving toward the
    stillness of his rest.

Hark my merry comrades call me, sounding
  on the bugle-horn.
They to whom my foolish passion were a
  target for their scorn:
Shall it not be scorn to me to harp on such a
  moulder'd string?
I am shamed thro' all my nature to have
  loved so slight a thing.
Weakness to be wroth with weakness!
  woman's pleasure, woman's pain —
Nature made them blinder motions bounded
  in a shallower brain:
Woman is the lesser man, and all thy
  passions, match'd with mine,
Are as moonlight unto sunlight, and as water
  unto wine —

Here at least, where nature sickens, nothing.
  Ah, for some retreat
Deep in yonder shining Orient, where my
  life began to beat;
Where in wild Mahratta-battle fell my father
  evil-starr'd; —
I was left a trampled orphan, and a selfish
  uncle's ward.
Or to burst all links of habit — there to
  wander far away,
On from island unto island at the gateways
  of the day.
Larger constellations burning, mellow moons
  and happy skies,

Breadths of tropic shade and palms in
    cluster, knots of Paradise.
Never comes the trader, never floats an
    European flag,
Slides the bird o'er lustrous woodland,
    swings the trailer from the crag;
Droops the heavy-blossom'd bower, hangs
    the heavy-fruited tree —
Summer isles of Eden lying in dark-purple
    spheres of sea.

There methinks would be enjoyment more
    than in this march of mind,
In the steamship, in the railway, in the
    thoughts that shake mankind.
There the passions cramp'd no longer shall
    have scope and breathing-space:
I will take some savage woman, she shall
    rear my dusky race.
Iron-jointed, supple-sinew'd, they shall dive,
    and they shall run,
Catch the wild goat by the hair, and hurl
    their lances in the sun;
Whistle back the parrot's call, and leap the
    rainbows of the brooks,
Not with blinded eyesight poring over
    miserable books —

Fool, again the dream, the fancy! but I *know*
    my words are wild,
But I count the gray barbarian lower than
    the Christian child.

I, to herd with narrow foreheads, vacant of
    our glorious gains,
Like a beast with lower pleasures, like a
    beast with lower pains!
Mated with a squalid savage — what to me
    were sun or clime?
I the heir of all the ages, in the foremost
    files of time —
I that rather held it better men should perish
    one by one,
Than that earth should stand at gaze like
    Joshua's moon in Ajalon!

Not in vain the distance beacons. Forward,
    forward let us range.
Let the great world spin for ever down the
    ringing grooves of change.
Thro' the shadow of the globe we swept into
    the younger day:
Better fifty years of Europe than a cycle of
    Cathay.
Mother-Age (for mine I knew not) held me
    as when life begun:
Rift the hills, and roll the waters, flash the
    lightnings, weigh the Sun —
O, I see the crescent promise of my spirit
    hath not set.
Ancient founts of inspiration well thro' all
    my fancy yet.

Howsoever these things be, a long farewell
    to Locksley Hall!

Now for me the woods may wither, now for
   me the rooftree fall.
Comes a vapour from the margin,
   blackening over heath and holt,
Cramming all the blast before it, in its breast
   a thunderbolt.
Let it fall on Locksley Hall, with rain or
   hail, or fire or snow;
For the mighty wind arises, roaring seaward,
   and I go.

Alfred, Lord Tennyson

Days of Birth

Monday's child is fair of face,
Tuesday's child is full of grace,
Wednesday's child is full of woe,
Thursday's child has far to go,
Friday's child is loving and giving,
Saturday's child works for its living,
   And a child that's born on the Sabbath day
Is fair and wise and good and gay.

Unknown

Rabbi Ben Ezra

Grow old along with me!
The best is yet to be,
The last of life, for which the first was
   made:

Our times are in his hand
Who saith, "A whole I planned,
Youth shows but half; trust God: see all, nor
 be afraid!"

Not that, amassing flowers,
Youth sighed, "Which rose make ours,
Which lily leave and then as best recall?"
Not that, admiring stars,
It yearned, "Nor Jove, nor Mars;
Mine be some figured flame which blends,
 transcends them all!"

Not for such hopes and fears
Annulling youth's brief years,
Do I remonstrate: folly wide the mark!
Rather I prize the doubt
Low kinds exist without,
Finished and finite clods, untroubled by a
 spark.

Poor vaunt of life indeed,
Were man but formed to feed
On joy, to solely seek and find and feast:
Such feasting ended, then
As sure an end to men;
Irks care the crop-full bird? Frets doubt the
 maw-crammed beast?

Rejoice we are allied
To that which doth provide
And not partake, effect and not receive!

A spark disturbs our clod;
Nearer we hold of God
Who gives, than of his tribes that take, I
    must believe.

Then, welcome each rebuff
That turns earth's smoothness rough,
Each sting that bids nor sit nor stand but go!
Be our joys three-parts pain!
Strive, and hold cheap the strain;
Learn, nor account the pang; dare, never
    grudge the throe!

For thence, — a paradox
Which comforts while it mocks, —
Shall life succeed in that it seems to fail:
What I aspired to be,
And was not, comforts me:
A brute I might have been, but would not
    sink i' the scale.

What is he but a brute
Whose flesh has soul to suit,
Whose spirit works lest arms and legs want
    play?
To man, propose this test —
Thy body at its best,
How far can that project thy soul on its lone
    way?

Yet gifts should prove their use:
I own the Past profuse

Of power each side, perfection every turn:
Eyes, ears took in their dole,
Brain treasured up the whole;
Should not the heart beat once "How good
   to live and learn"?

Not once beat "Praise be thine!
I see the whole design,
I, who saw power, see now love perfect too:
Perfect I call thy plan:
Thanks that I was a man!
Maker, remake, complete — I trust what
   thou shalt do!"

For pleasant is this flesh;
Our soul, in its rose-mesh
Pulled ever to the earth, still yearns for rest:
Would we some prize might hold
To match those manifold
Possessions of the brute, — gain most, as
   we did best!

Let us not always say,
"Spite of this flesh to-day
I strove, made head, gained ground upon the
   whole!"
As the bird wings and sings,
Let us cry, "All good things
Are ours, nor soul helps flesh more, now,
   than flesh helps soul!"

Therefore I summon age

To grant youth's heritage,
Life's struggle having so far reached its
    term:
Thence shall I pass, approved
A man, for aye removed
From the developed brute; a god, though in
    the germ.

And I shall thereupon
Take rest, ere I be gone
Once more on my adventure brave and new:
Fearless and unperplexed,
When I wage battle next,
What weapons to select, what armour to
    indue.

Youth ended, I shall try
My gain or loss thereby;
Leave the fire ashes, what survives is gold:
And I shall weigh the same,
Give life its praise or blame:
Young, all lay in dispute: I shall know,
    being old.

For note, when evening shuts,
A certain moment cuts
The deed off, calls the glory from the grey:
A whisper from the west
Shoots — "Add this to the rest,
Take it and try its worth: here dies another
    day."

So, still within this life,
Though lifted o'er its strife,
Let me discern, compare, pronounce at last,
"This rage was right i' the main,
That acquiescence vain:
The Future I may face now I have proved
   the Past."

For more is not reserved
To man, with soul just nerved
To act to-morrow what he learns to-day:
Here, work enough to watch
The Master work, and catch
Hints of the proper craft, tricks of the tool's
   true play.

As it was better, youth
Should strive, through acts uncouth,
Toward making, than repose on aught found
   made:
So, better, age, exempt
From strife, should know, than tempt
Further. Thou waitedst age: wait death nor
   be afraid!

Enough now, if the Right
And Good and Infinite
Be named here, as thou callest thy hand
   thine own,
With knowledge absolute,
Subject to no dispute

From fools that crowded youth, nor let thee
    feel alone.

Be there, for once and all,
Severed great minds from small,
Announced to each his station in the Past!
Was I, the world arraigned,
Were they, my soul disdained,
Right? Let age speak the truth and give us
    peace at last.

Now, who shall arbitrate?
Ten men love what I hate,
Shun what I follow, slight what I receive;
Ten, who in ears and eyes
Match me: we all surmise,
They this thing, and I that: whom shall my
    soul believe?

Not on the vulgar mass
Called ''work,'' must sentence pass,
Things done, that took the eye and had the
    price;
O'er which, from level stand,
The low world laid its hand,
Found straightway to its mind, could value
    in a trice:

But all, the world's coarse thumb
And finger failed to plumb,
So passed in making up the main account;
All instincts immature,

515

All purposes unsure,
That weighed not as his work, yet swelled
   the man's amount:

Thoughts hardly to be packed
Into a narrow act,
Fancies that broke through language and
   escaped;
All I could never be,
All, men ignored in me,
This, I was worth to God, whose wheel the
   pitcher shaped.

Ay, note that Potter's wheel,
That metaphor! and feel
Why time spins fast, why passive lies our
   clay, —
Thou, to whom fools propound,
When the wine makes its round,
"Since life fleets, all is change; the Past
   gone, seize to-day!"

Fool! All that is, at all,
Last ever, past recall;
Earth changes, but thy soul and God stand
   sure:
What entered into thee,
That was, is, and shall be:
Time's wheel runs back or stops: Potter and
   clay endure.

He fixed thee 'mid this dance

Of plastic circumstance,
This Present, thou, forsooth, would fain
   arrest:
Machinery just meant
To give thy soul its bent,
Try thee and turn thee forth, sufficiently
   impressed.

What though the earlier grooves,
Which ran the laughing loves
Around thy base, no longer pause and press?
What though, about thy rim,
Skull-things in order grim
Grow out, in graver mood, obey the sterner
   stress?

Look not thou down but up!
To uses of a cup,
The festal board, lamp's flash and trumpet's
   peal,
The new wine's foaming flow,
The Master's lips aglow!
Thou, heaven's consummate cup, what
   needst thou with earth's wheel?

But I need, now as then,
Thee, God, who mouldest men,
And since, not even while the whirl was
   worst,
Did I — to the wheel of life
With shapes and colors rife,

Bound dizzily — mistake my end, to slake
  thy thirst:

So, take and use thy work.
Amend what flaws may lurk,
What strain o' the stuff, what warpings past
  the aim!
My times be in thy hand!
Perfect the cup as planned!
Let age approve of youth, and death
  complete the same!

                    Robert Browning

Echoes

To W. A.

Or ever the knightly years were gone
  With the old world to the grave,
I was a King in Babylon
  And you were a Christian Slave.

I saw, I took, I cast you by,
  I bent and broke your pride.
You loved me well, or I heard them lie,
  But your longing was denied.
Surely I knew that by and by
  You cursed your gods and died.

And a myriad suns have set and shone

Since then upon the grave
Decreed by the King in Babylon
  To her that had been his Slave.

The pride I trampled is now my scathe,
  For it tramples me again.
The old resentment lasts like death,
  For you love, yet you refrain.
I break my heart on your hard unfaith,
  And I break my heart in vain.

Yet not for an hour do I wish undone
  The deed beyond the grave,
When I was a King in Babylon
  And you were a Virgin Slave.
              William Ernest Henley

With Rue My Heart Is Laden

With rue my heart is laden
  For golden friends I had,
For many a rose-lipt maiden
  And many a lightfoot lad.

By brooks too broad for leaping
  The lightfoot boys are laid:
The rose-lipt girls are sleeping
  In fields where roses fade.
              A. E. Housman

A Minuet on Reaching the Age of Fifty

Old Age, on tiptoe, lays her jewelled hand
Lightly in mine. — Come, tread a stately
      measure
Most gracious partner, nobly posed and
      bland.
  Ours be no boisterous pleasure,
But smiling conversation, with quick glance
And memories dancing lightlier than we
      dance,

  Friends who a thousand joys
Divide and double, save one joy supreme
  Which many a pang alloys.
  Let wanton girls and boys
Cry over lovers' woes and broken toys.
Our waking life is sweeter than their dream.

Dame Nature, with unwitting hand,
Has sparsely strewn the black abyss with
      lights
Minute, remote, and numberless. We stand
  Measuring far depths and heights,
  Arched over by a laughing heaven,
Intangible and never to be scaled.
If we confess our sins, they are forgiven.
  We triumph, if we know we failed.

  Tears that in youth you shed.

Congealed to pearls, now deck your silvery
      hair;
   Sighs breathed for loves long dead
Frosted the glittering atoms of the air
    Into the veils you wear
Round your soft bosom and most queenly
      head;
    The shimmer of your gown
Catches all tints of autumn, and the dew
Of gardens where the damask roses blew;

The myriad tapers from these arches hung
    Play on your diamonded crown;
And stars, whose light angelical caressed
    Your virgin days,
Gave back in your calm eyes their holier
      rays.
   The deep past living in your breast
   Heaves these half-merry sighs;
   And the soft accents of your tongue
   Breathe unrecorded charities.

    Hasten not; the feast will wait.
This is a master-night without a morrow.
No chill and haggard dawn, with after-
     sorrow,
    Will snuff the spluttering candle out,
Or blanch the revellers homeward straggling
     late.
    Before the rout

Wearies or wanes, will come a calmer
    trance.
Lulled by the poppied fragrance of this
    bower,
    We'll cheat the lapsing hour,
And close our eyes, still smiling, on the
    dance.

George Santayana

The Second Coming

Turning and turning in the widening gyre
The falcon cannot hear the falconer;
Things fall apart; the centre cannot hold;
Mere anarchy is loosed upon the world,
The blood-dimmed tide is loosed, and
    everywhere
The ceremony of innocence is drowned;
The best lack all conviction, while the worst
Are full of passionate intensity.

Surely some revelation is at hand;
Surely the Second Coming is at hand.
The Second Coming! Hardly are those words
    out
When a vast image out of *Spiritus Mundi*
Troubles my sight: somewhere in sands of
    the desert
A shape with lion body and the head of a
    man,

A gaze blank and pitiless as the sun,
Is moving its slow thighs, while all about it
Reel shadows of the indignant desert birds.
The darkness drops again; but now I know
That twenty centuries of stony sleep
Were vexed to nightmare by a rocking
  cradle,
And what rough beast, its hour come round
  at last,
Slouches towards Bethlehem to be born?
William Butler Yeats

Among School Children

I walk through the long schoolroom
  questioning,
A kind old nun in a white hood replies;
The children learn to cipher and to sing,
To study reading-books and history,
To cut and sew, be neat in everything
In the best modern way — the children's
  eyes
In momentary wonder stare upon
A sixty year old smiling public man.

I dream of a Ledæan body, bent
Above a sinking fire, a tale that she
Told of a harsh reproof; or trivial event
That changed some childish day to
  tragedy —

Told, and it seemed that our two natures
    blent
Into a sphere from youthful sympathy,
Or else, to alter Plato's parable,
Into the yolk and white of the one shell.

And thinking of that fit of grief or rage
I look upon one child or t'other there
And wonder if she stood so at that age —
For even daughters of the swan can share
Something of every paddler's heritage —
And had that color upon cheek or hair;
And thereupon my heart is driven wild:
She stands before me as a living child.

Her present image floats into the mind —
Did quattrocento finger fashion it
Hollow of cheek as though it drank the wind
And took a mess of shadows for its meat?
And I though never of Ledæan kind
Had pretty plumage once — enough of that,
Better to smile on all that smile, and show
There is a comfortable kind of old
    scarecrow.

What youthful mother, a shape upon her lap
Honey of generation had betrayed.
And that must sleep, shriek, struggle to
    escape
As recollection or the drug decide,
Would think her son, did she but see that
    shape

With sixty or more winters on its head,
A compensation for the pang of his birth,
Or the uncertainty of his setting forth?

Plato thought nature but a spume that plays
Upon a ghostly paradigm of things;
Soldier Aristotle played the taws
Upon the bottom of a king of kings;
World-famous golden-thighed Pythagoras
Fingered upon a fiddle stick or strings
What a star sang and careless Muses heard:
Old clothes upon old sticks to scare a bird.

Both nuns and mothers worship images,
But those the candles light are not as those
That animate a mother's reveries,
But keep a marble or a bronze repose.
And yet they too break hearts — O
   Presences
That passion, piety or affection knows,
And that all heavenly glory symbolize —
O self-born mockers of man's enterprise;

Labor is blossoming or dancing where
The body is not bruised to pleasure soul,
Nor beauty born out of its own despair,
Nor blear-eyed wisdom out of midnight oil.
O chestnut tree, great rooted blossomer,
Are you the leaf, the blossom or the bole?
O body swayed to music, O brightening
   glance,

How can we know the dancer from the
  dance?
                                 William Butler Yeats

The Listeners

"Is there anybody there?" said the
  Traveller,
  Knocking on the moonlit door;
And his horse in the silence champed the
  grasses
  Of the forest's ferny floor;
And a bird flew up out of the turret,
  Above the Traveller's head;
And he smote upon the door again a second
  time;
  "Is there anybody there?" he said.
But no one descended to the Traveller;
  No head from the leaf-fringed sill
Leaned over and looked into his grey eyes,
  Where he stood perplexed and still.
But only a host of phantom listeners
  That dwelt in the lone house then
Stood listening in the quiet of the moonlight
  To that voice from the world of men:
Stood thronging the faint moonbeams on the
  dark stair,
  That goes down to the empty hall,
Hearkening in an air stirred and shaken
  By the lonely Traveller's call.

And he felt in his heart their strangeness,
  Their stillness answering his cry,
While his horse moved, cropping the dark
    turf,
  'Neath the starred and leafy sky;
For he suddenly smote on the door, even
  Louder, and lifted his head:
"Tell them I came, and no one answered
  That I kept my word," he said.
Never the least stir made the listeners,
  Though every word he spake
Fell echoing through the shadowiness of the
    still house
  From the one man left awake:
Ay, they heard his foot upon the stirrup,
  And the sound of iron on stone,
And how the silence surged softly backward,
  When the plunging hoofs were gone.

Walter De La Mare

The Forgotten Man

Not on our golden fortunes builded high —
Not on our boasts that soar into the sky —
Not upon these is resting in this hour
The fate of the future; but upon the power
Of him who is forgotten — yes, on him
Rest all our hopes reaching from rim to rim.
In him we see all of earth's toiling bands,

527

With crooked backs, scarred faces, shattered
  hands.

He seeks no office and he asks no praise
For all the patient labor of his days.
He is the one supporting the huge weight;
He is the one guarding the country's gate.
He bears the burdens of these earthly ways:
We pile the debts, he is the one who pays.
He is the one who holds the solid power
To steady nations in their trembling hour.
Behold him as he silently goes by,
For it is at his word that nations die.

Shattered with loss and lack,
He is the one who holds upon his back
The continent and all its mighty loads —
This toiler makes possible the roads
On which the gilded thousands travel free —
Makes possible our feasts, our roaring
  boards,
Our pomps, our easy days, our golden
  hoards.
He gives stability to nations:
He makes possible our nation, sea to sea.
His strength makes possible our college
  walls —
Makes possible our legislative halls —
Makes possible our churches soaring high
With spires, the fingers pointing to the sky.

Shall then this man go hungry, here in lands

Blest by his honor, builded by his hands?
Do something for him: let him never be
Forgotten: let him have his daily bread:
He who has fed us, let him now be fed.
Let us remember all his tragic lot —
Remember, or else be ourselves forgot!
All honor to the one that in this hour
Cries to the world as from a lighted
    tower —
Cries for the Man Forgotten. Honor the one
Who asks for him a glad place in the sun.
He is a voice for the voiceless. Now,
    indeed,
We have a tongue that cries the mortal need.
                              Edwin Markham

The Vampire

A fool there was and he made his prayer
(Even as you and I!)
To a rag and a bone and a hank of hair,
(We called her the woman who did not
    care),
But the fool he called her his lady fair —
(Even as you and I!)

*Oh, the years we waste and the tears we
    waste,
And the work of our head and hand
Belong to the woman who did not know*

(And now we know that she never could know)
And did not understand!

A fool there was and his goods he spent,
(Even as you and I!)
Honour and faith and a sure intent
(And it wasn't the least what the lady
    meant),
But a fool must follow his natural bent
(Even as you and I!)

Oh, the toil we lost and the spoil we lost
And the excellent things we planned
Belong to the woman who didn't know why
(And now we know that she never knew why)
And did not understand!

The fool was stripped to his foolish hide,
(Even as you and I!)
Which she might have seen when she threw
    him aside —
(But it isn't on record the lady tried)
So some of him lived but the most of him
    died —
(Even as you and I!)

''And it isn't the shame and it isn't the
*   blame*
That stings like a white-hot brand —
It's coming to know that she never knew why

(Seeing, at last, she could never know why)
And never could understand!''

(Seeing, at last, she could never know why)
And never could understand!''
                                        Rudyard Kipling

George Crabbe

Give him the darkest inch your shelf allows,
Hide him in lonely garrets, if you will —
But his hard, human pulse is throbbing still
With the sure strength that fearless truth
    endows
In spite of all fine science disavows,
Of his plain excellence and stubborn skill
There yet remains what fashion cannot kill,
Though years have thinned the laurel from
    his brows.

Whether or not we read him, we can feel
From time to time the vigor of his name
Against us like a finger for the shame
And emptiness of what our souls reveal
In books that are as altars where we kneel
To consecrate the flicker, not the flame.
                        Edwin Arlington Robinson

Mr. Flood's Party

Old Eben Flood, climbing alone one night
Over the hill between the town below
And the forsaken upland hermitage

531

That held as much as he should ever know
On earth again of home, paused warily.
The road was his with not a native near;
And Eben, having leisure, said aloud,
For no man else in Tilbury Town to hear:

"Well, Mr. Flood, we have the harvest
    moon
Again, and we may not have many more;
The bird is on the wing, the poet says,
And you and I have said it here before.
Drink to the bird." He raised up to the light
The jug that he had gone so far to fill,
And answered huskily: "Well, Mr. Flood,
Since you propose it, I believe I will."

Alone, as if enduring to the end
A valiant armor of scarred hopes outworn,
He stood there in the middle of the road
Like Roland's ghost winding a silent horn.
Below him, in the town among the trees,
Where friends of other days had honored
    him,
A phantom salutation of the dead
Rang thinly till old Eben's eyes were dim.

Then, as a mother lays her sleeping child
Down tenderly, fearing it may awake,
He set the jug down slowly at his feet
With trembling care, knowing that most
    things break;
And only when assured that on firm earth

532

It stood, as the uncertain lives of men
Assuredly did not, he paced away,
And with his hand extended paused again:

"Well, Mr. Flood, we have not met like this
In a long time, and many a change has come
To both of us, I fear, since last it was
We had a drop together. Welcome home!"
Convivially returning with himself,
Again he raised the jug up to the light;
And with an acquiescent quaver said:
"Well, Mr. Flood, if you insist, I might.

"Only a very little, Mr. Flood —
For auld lang syne. No more, sir; that will
    do."
So, for the time, apparently it did,
And Eben evidently thought so too;
For soon amid the silver loneliness
Of night he lifted up his voice and sang,
Secure, with only two moons listening,
Until the whole harmonious landscape
    rang —

"For auld lang syne." The weary throat
    gave out,
The last word wavered, and the song was
    done.
He raised again the jug regretfully
And shook his head, and was again alone.
There was not much that was ahead of him,
And there was nothing in the town below —

Where strangers would have shut the many
    doors
That many friends had opened long ago.
                    Edwin Arlington Robinson

The Red Wheelbarrow

so much depends
upon

a red wheel
barrow

glazed with rain
water

beside the white
chickens.

William Carlos Williams

The Men That Don't Fit In

There's a race of men that don't fit in,
    A race that can't stay still;
So they break the hearts of kith and kin,
    And they roam the world at will.
They range the field and they rove the flood,
    And they climb the mountain's crest;

Theirs is the curse of the gypsy blood,
    And they don't know how to rest.

If they just went straight they might go far;
    They are strong and brave and true;
But they're always tired of the things that
        are,
    And they want the strange and new.
They say: "Could I find my proper groove,
    What a deep mark I would make!"
So they chop and change, and each fresh
        move
    Is only a fresh mistake.

And each forgets, as he strips and runs
    With a brilliant, fitful pace,
It's the steady, quiet, plodding ones
    Who win in the lifelong race.
And each forgets that his youth has fled,
    Forgets that his prime is past,
Till he stands one day, with a hope that's
        dead,
    In the glare of the truth at last.

He has failed, he has failed; he has missed
        his chance;
    He has just done things by half.
Life's been a jolly good joke on him,
    And now is the time to laugh.
Ha, ha! He is one of the Legion Lost;
    He was never meant to win;

He's a rolling stone, and it's bred in the
    bone;
  He's a man who won't fit in.

                   Robert W. Service

Cargoes

Quinquireme of Nineveh from distant Ophir
Rowing home to haven in sunny Palestine,
With a cargo of ivory,
And apes and peacocks,
Sandalwood, cedarwood, and sweet white
  wine.

Stately Spanish galleon coming from the
  Isthmus,
Dipping through the Tropics by the palm-
  green shores,
With a cargo of diamonds,
Emeralds, amethysts,
Topazes, and cinnamon, and gold moidores.

Dirty British coaster with a salt-caked smoke
  stack
Butting through the Channel in the mad
  March days,
With a cargo of Tyne coal,
Road-rail, pig-lead,
Firewood, iron-ware, and cheap tin trays.

                   John Masefield

Out Fishin'

A feller isn't thinkin' mean,
  Out fishin';
His thoughts are mostly good an' clean,
  Out fishin'.
He doesn't knock his fellow men,
Or harbor any grudges then;
A feller's at his finest when
  Out fishin'.

The rich are comrades to the poor,
  Out fishin';
All brothers of a common lure
  Out fishin'.
The urchin with the pin an' string
Can chum with millionaire and king;
Vain pride is a forgotten thing,
  Out fishin'.

A feller gits a chance to dream,
  Out fishin',
He learns the beauties of a stream,
  Out fishin';
An' he can wash his soul in air
That isn't foul with selfish care,
An' relish plain and simple fare,
  Out fishin'.

A feller has no time for hate,
  Out fishin';

He isn't eager to be great,
  Out fishin'.
He isn't thinkin' thoughts of pelf,
Or goods stacked high upon a shelf,
But he is always just himself,
  Out fishin'.

A feller's glad to be a friend,
  Out fishin';
A helpin' hand he'll always lend,
  Out fishin'.
The brotherhood of rod an' line
An' sky and stream is always fine;
Men come real close to God's design,
  Out fishin'.

A feller isn't plotting schemes,
  Out fishin';
He's only busy with his dreams,
  Out fishin'.
His livery is a coat of tan,
His creed — to do the best he can;
A feller's always mostly man,
  Out fishin'.

Edgar A. Guest

Peregrine

Liar and bragger,
He had no friend
Except a dagger

And a candle-end;
The one he read by;
The one scared cravens;
And he was fed by
The Prophet's ravens.
Such haughty creatures
Avoid the human;
They fondle nature's
Breast, not woman —
A she-wolf's puppies —
A wild-cat's pussy-fur:
Their stirrup-cup is
The pride of Lucifer.
A stick he carried,
Slept in a lean-to;
He'd never married,
And he didn't mean to.
He'd tried religion
And found it pleasant;
He relished a pigeon
Stewed with a pheasant
In an iron kettle;
He built stone ovens.
He'd never settle
In any province.
He made pantries
Of Vaux and Arden
And the village gentry's
Kitchen-garden.
Fruits within yards
Were his staples;
He drank whole vineyards

From Rome to Naples,
Then went to Brittany
For the cider.
He could sit any
Horse, a rider
Outstripping Cheiron's
Canter and gallop.
Pau's environs
The pubs of Salop,
Wells and Bath inns
Shared his pleasure
With taverns of Athens;
The Sultan's treasure
He'd seen in Turkey;
He'd known London
Bright and murky.
His bones were sunned on
Paris benches
Beset by sparrows;
Roman trenches,
Cave-men's barrows,
He liked, impartial;
He liked an Abbey.
His step was martial;
Spent and shabby
He wasn't broken;
A dozen lingoes
He must have spoken.
As a king goes
He went, not minding
That he lived seeking

540

And never finding.
He'd visit Peking
And then be gone soon
To the far Canaries.
He'd cross a monsoon
To chase vagaries.
He loved a city
And a street's alarums;
Parks were pretty
And so were bar-rooms.
He loved fiddles;
He talked with rustics;
Life was riddles
And queer acrostics.
His sins were serried,
His virtues garish;
His corpse was buried
In a country parish.
Before he went hence —
God knows where —
He spoke this sentence
With a princely air:
"The noose draws tighter;
This is the end;
I'm a good fighter,
But a bad friend:
I've played the traitor
Over and over;
I'm a good hater,
But a bad lover."

Elinor Wylie

Little Things

Little drops of water,
   Little grains of sand,
Make the mighty ocean
  ,And the pleasant land.

Thus the little minutes,
   Humble though they be,
Make the mighty ages
   Of eternity.
       Julia A. Fletcher

Directive

Back out of all this now too much for us,
Back in a time made simple by the loss
Of detail, burned, dissolved, and broken off
Like graveyard marble sculpture in the
   weather,
There is a house that is no more a house
Upon a farm that is no more a farm
And in a town that is no more a town.
The road there, if you'll let a guide direct
   you
Who only has at heart your getting lost,
May seem as if it should have been a
   quarry —
Great monolithic knees the former town

Long since gave up pretence of keeping
    covered.
And there's a story in a book about it:
Besides the wear of iron wagon wheels
The ledges show lines ruled southeast
    northwest,
The chisel work of an enormous Glacier
That braced his feet against the Arctic Pole.
You must not mind a certain coolness from
    him
Still said to haunt this side of Panther
    Mountain.
Nor need you mind the serial ordeal
Of being watched from forty cellar holes
As if by eye pairs out of forty firkins.
As for the woods' excitement over you
That sends light rustle rushes to their leaves,
Charge that to upstart inexperience.
Where were they all not twenty years ago?
They think too much of having shaded out
A few old pecker-fretted apple trees.
Make yourself up a cheering song of how
Someone's road home from work this once
    was,
Who may be just ahead of you on foot
Or creaking with a buggy load of grain.
The height of the adventure is the height
Of country where two village cultures faded
Into each other. Both of them are lost.
And if you're lost enough to find yourself
By now, pull in your ladder road behind you
And put a sign up CLOSED to all but me.

Then make yourself at home. The only field
Now left's no bigger than a harness gall.
First there's the children's house of make
    believe,
Some shattered dishes underneath a pine,
The playthings in the playhouse of the
    children.
Weep for what little things could make them
    glad.
Then for the house that is no more a house,
But only a belilaced cellar hole,
Now slowly closing like a dent in dough.
This was no playhouse but a house in
    earnest.
Your destination and your destiny's
A brook that was the water of the house,
Cold as a spring as yet so near its source,
Too lofty and original to rage.
(We know the valley streams that when
    aroused
Will leave their tatters hung on barb and
    thorn.)
I have kept hidden in the instep arch
Of an old cedar at the waterside
A broken drinking goblet like the Grail
Under a spell so the wrong ones can't find
    it,
So can't get saved, as Saint Mark says they
    mustn't.
(I stole the goblet from the children's
    playhouse.)

Here are your waters and your watering
  place,
Drink and be whole again beyond confusion.
Robert Frost

Chicago

Hog Butcher for the World,
Tool Maker, Stacker of Wheat,
Player with Railroads and the Nation's
  Freight Handler;
Stormy, husky, brawling,
City of the Big Shoulders:
They tell me you are wicked, and I believe
  them; for I have seen your painted
  women under the gas lamps luring the
  farm boys.
And they tell me you are crooked, and I
  answer: Yes, it is true I have seen the
  gunman kill and go free to kill again.
And they tell me you are brutal, and my
  reply is: On the faces of women and
  children I have seen the marks of
  wanton hunger.
And having answered so I turn once more to
  those who sneer at this my city, and I
  give them back the sneer and say to
  them:
Come and show me another city with lifted
  head singing so proud to be alive and
  coarse and strong and cunning.

Flinging magnetic curses amid the toil of
    piling job on job, here is a tall bold
    slugger set vivid against the little soft
    cities;
Fierce as a dog with tongue lapping for
    action, cunning as a savage pitted
    against the wilderness,
    Bareheaded,
    Shoveling,
    Wrecking,
    Planning,
    Building, breaking, rebuilding,
Under the smoke, dust all over his mouth,
    laughing with white teeth,
Under the terrible burden of destiny laughing
    as a young man laughs,
Laughing even as an ignorant fighter laughs
    who has never lost a battle,
Bragging and laughing that under his wrist is
    the pulse, and under his ribs the heart of
    the people,
                Laughing!
Laughing the stormy, husky, brawling
    laughter of youth; half-naked, sweating,
    proud to be Hog-butcher, Toolmaker,
    Stacker of Wheat, Player with
    Railroads, and Freight-handler to the
    Nation.

                         Carl Sandburg

Cool Tombs

When Abraham Lincoln was shoveled into
   the tombs, he forgot the copperheads and
   the assassin . . . in the dust, in the cool
   tombs.

And Ulysses Grant lost all thought of con
   men and Wall Street, cash and collateral
   turned ashes . . . in the dust, in the cool
   tombs.

Pocahontas' body, lovely as a poplar, sweet
   as a red haw in November or a pawpaw in
   May, did she wonder? does she
   remember? . . . in the dust, in the cool
   tombs?

Take any streetful of people buying clothes
   and groceries, cheering a hero or throwing
   confetti and blowing tin horns . . . tell
   me if the lovers are losers . . . tell me if
   any get more than the lovers . . . in the
   dust . . . in the cool tombs.

Carl Sandburg

Sunday Morning

Complacencies of the peignoir, and late
Coffee and oranges in a sunny chair,
And the green freedom of a cockatoo
Upon a rug mingle to dissipate
The holy hush of ancient sacrifice.
She dreams a little, and she feels the dark
Encroachment of that old catastrophe,
As a calm darkens among water-lights.
The pungent oranges and bright, green
   wings
Seem things in some procession of the dead,
Winding across wide water, without sound.
The day is like wide water, without sound,
Stilled for the passing of her dreaming feet
Over the sea, to silent Palestine,
Dominion of the blood and sepulchre.

Why should she give her bounty to the
   dead?
What is divinity if it can come
Only in silent shadows and in dreams?
Shall she not find in comforts of the sun,
In pungent fruit and bright, green wings, or
   else
In any balm or beauty of the earth,
Things to be cherished like the thought of
   heaven?
Divinity must live within herself:
Passions of rain, or moods in falling snow;

Grievings in loneliness, or unsubdued
Elations when the forest blooms; gusty
Emotions on wet roads on autumn nights;
All pleasures and all pains, remembering
The bough of summer and the winter
    branch.
These are the measures destined for her
    soul.

Jove in the clouds had his inhuman birth.
No mother suckled him, no sweet land gave
Large-mannered motions to his mythy mind.
He moved among us, as a muttering king,
Magnificent, would move among his hinds,
Until our blood, commingling, virginal,
With heaven, brought such requital to desire
The very hinds discerned it, in a star.
Shall our blood fail? Or shall it come to be
The blood of paradise? And shall the earth
Seem all of paradise that we shall know?
The sky will be much friendlier then than
    now,
A part of labor and a part of pain,
And next in glory to enduring love,
Not this dividing and indifferent blue.

She says, "I am content when wakened
    birds,
Before they fly, test the reality
Of misty fields, by their sweet questionings;
But when the birds are gone, and their warm
    fields

Return no more, where, then, is paradise?''
There is not any haunt of prophecy,
Nor any old chimera of the grave,
Neither the golden underground, nor isle
Melodious, where spirits gat them home,
Nor visionary south, nor cloudy palm
Remote on heaven's hill, that has endured
As April's green endures; or will endure
Like her remembrance of awakened birds,
Or her desire for June and evening, tipped
By the consummation of the swallow's
   wings.

She says, ''But in contentment I still feel
The need of some imperishable bliss.''
Death is the mother of beauty; hence from
   her,
Alone, shall come fulfilment to our dreams
And our desires. Although she strews the
   leaves
Of sure obliteration on our paths,
The path sick sorrow took, the many paths
Where triumph rang its brassy phrase, or
   love
Whispered a little out of tenderness,
She makes the willow shiver in the sun
For maidens who were wont to sit and gaze
Upon the grass, relinquished to their feet.
She causes boys to pile new plums and pears
On disregarded plate. The maidens taste
And stray impassioned in the littering
   leaves.

Is there no change of death in paradise?
Does ripe fruit never fall? Or do the boughs
Hang always heavy in that perfect sky,
Unchanging, yet so like our perishing earth,
With rivers like our own that seek for seas
They never find, the same receding shores
That never touch with inarticulate pang?
Why set the pear upon those river-banks
Or spice the shores with odors of the plum?
Alas, that they should wear our colors there,
The silken weavings of our afternoons,
And pick the strings of our insipid lutes!
Death is the mother of beauty, mystical,
Within whose burning bosom we devise
Our earthly mothers waiting, sleeplessly.

Supple and turbulent, a ring of men
Shall chant in orgy on a summer morn
Their boisterous devotion to the sun,
Not as a god, but as a god might be,
Naked among them, like a savage source.
Their chant shall be a chant of paradise,
Out of their blood, returning to the sky;
And in their chant shall enter, voice by
    voice,
The windy lake wherein their lord delights,
The trees, like serafin, and echoing hills,
That choir among themselves long
    afterward.
They shall know well the heavenly
    fellowship

Of men that perish and of summer morn.
And whence they came and whither they
   shall go
The dew upon their feet shall manifest.

She hears, upon that water without sound,
A voice that cries, ''The tomb in Palestine
Is not the porch of spirits lingering.
It is the grave of Jesus, where He lay.''
We live in an old chaos of the sun,
Or old dependency of day and night,
Or island solitude, unsponsored, free,
Of that wide water, inescapable.
Deer walk upon our mountains, and the
   quail
Whistle about us their spontaneous cries;
Sweet berries ripen in the wilderness;
And, in the isolation of the sky,
At evening, casual flocks of pigeons make
Ambiguous undulations as they sink,
Downward to darkness, on extended wings.
Wallace Stevens

what if a much of a which of a wind

what if a much of a which of a wind
gives the truth to summer's lie;
bloodies with dizzying leaves the sun
and yanks immortal stars awry?
Blow king to beggar and queen to seem

(blow friend to fiend:blow space to time)
— when skies are hanged and oceans
    drowned,
the single secret will still be man

what if a keen of a lean wind flays
screaming hills with sleet and snow:
strangles valleys by ropes of thing
and stifles forests in white ago?
Blow hope to terror;blow seeing to blind
(blow pity to envy and soul to mind)
— whose hearts are mountains,roots are
    trees,
it's they shall cry hello to the spring

what if a dawn of a doom of a dream
bites this universe in two,
peels forever out of his grave
and sprinkles nowhere with me and you?
Blow soon to never and never to twice
(blow life to isn't:blow death to was)
— all nothing's only our hugest home;
the most who die,the more we live

E. E. Cummings

To Brooklyn Bridge

How many dawns, chill from his rippling
    rest
The seagull's wings shall dip and pivot him,

Shedding white rings of tumult, building
  high
Over the chained bay waters Liberty —

Then, with inviolate curve, forsake our eyes
As apparitional as sails that cross
Some page of figures to be filed away;
— Till elevators drop us from our day . . .

I think of cinemas, panoramic sleights
With multitudes bent toward some flashing
  scene
Never disclosed, but hastened to again,
Foretold to other eyes on the same screen;

And Thee, across the harbor, silver-paced
As though the sun took step of thee, yet left
Some motion ever unspent in thy stride, —
Implicitly thy freedom staying thee!

Out of some subway scuttle, cell or loft
A bedlamite speeds to thy parapets,
Tilting there momently, shrill shirt
  ballooning,
A jest falls from the speechless caravan.

Down Wall, from girder into street noon
  leaks,
A rip-tooth of the sky's acetylene;
All afternoon the cloud-flown derricks
  turn. . .

Thy cables breathe the North Atlantic still.

And obscure as that heaven of the Jews,
Thy guerdon . . . Accolade thou dost
   bestow
Of anonymity time cannot raise:
Vibrant reprieve and pardon thou dost show.

O harp and altar, of the fury fused,
(How could mere toil align thy choiring
   strings!)
Terrific threshold of the prophet's pledge,
Prayer of pariah, and the lover's cry, —

Again the traffic lights that skim thy swift
Unfractioned idiom, immaculate sigh of
   stars,
Beading thy path — condense eternity:
And we have seen night lifted in thine arms.

Under thy shadow by the piers I waited;
Only in darkness is thy shadow clear.
The City's fiery parcels all undone,
Already snow submerges an iron year . . .

O Sleepless as the river under thee,
Vaulting the sea, the prairies' dreaming sod,
Unto us lowliest sometime sweep, descend
And of the curveship lend a myth to God.

Hart Crane

The End of the World

Quite unexpectedly, as Vasserot
The armless ambidextrian was lighting
A match between his great and second toe,
And Ralph the lion was engaged in biting
The neck of Madame Sossman while the
    drum
Pointed, and Teeny was about to cough
In waltz-time swinging Jocko by the
    thumb —
Quite unexpectedly the top blew off:

And there, there overhead, there, there hung
    over
Those thousands of white faces, those dazed
    eyes,
There in the starless dark the poise, the
    hover,
There with vast wings across the cancelled
    skies,
There in the sudden blackness the black pall
Of nothing, nothing, nothing — nothing at
    all.

Archibald MacLeish

The Force That Through the Green Fuse Drives the Flower

The force that through the green fuse drives
    the flower
Drives my green age; that blasts the roots of
    trees
Is my destroyer.
And I am dumb to tell the crooked rose
My youth is bent by the same wintry fever.

The force that drives the water through the
    rocks
Drives my red blood; that dries the mouthing
    streams
Turns mine to wax.
And I am dumb to mouth unto my veins
How at the mountain spring the same mouth
    sucks.

The hand that whirls the water in the pool
Stirs the quicksand; that ropes the blowing
    wind
Hauls my shroud sail.
And I am dumb to tell the hanging man
How of my clay is made the hangman's
    lime.

The lips of time leech to the fountain head;
Love drips and gathers, but the fallen blood
Shall calm her sores.

And I am dumb to tell a weather's wind
How time has ticked a heaven round the
   stars.

And I am dumb to tell the lover's tomb
How at my sheet goes the same crooked
   worm.
                      Dylan Thomas

Poetry

I, too, dislike it: there are things that are
            important
     beyond all this fiddle.
Reading it, however, with a perfect
         contempt for it, one
     discovers in
it after all, a place for the genuine.
    Hands that can grasp, eyes
    that can dilate, hair that can rise
       if it must, these things are important not
       because a

high-sounding interpretation can be put upon
       them but
    because they are
useful. When they become so derivative
      as to become
    unintelligible,
the same thing may be said for all of us,
      that we

do not admire what
we cannot understand: the bat
 holding on upside down or in quest of
 something to

eat, elephants pushing, a wild horse taking a
 roll, a tire-
less-wolf under
a tree, the immovable critic twitching his
 skin like a
 horse that feels a flea, the base-
ball fan, the statistician —
 nor is it valid
  to discriminate "against business
  documents and

school-books"; all these phenomena are
  important. One
 must make a distinction
however: when dragged into prominence
 by half poets,
 the result is not poetry.
nor till the poets among us can be
 "literalists of
 the imagination" — above
  insolence and triviality and can
  present

for inspection, imaginary gardens with
  real toads in
  them, shall we have

it. In the meantime, if you demand on
the one hand,
the raw material of poetry in
all its rawness and
that which is on the other hand
genuine, then you are interested in
poetry.

Marianne Moore

Index of Authors

Adams, Franklin P., 455
Aiken, Conrad, 156
Allen, Alice E., 263
Allen, Elizabeth Akers, 258
Bangs, John Kendrick, 241
Blake, William, 164, 227, 327, 328, 373
Bourdillon, Francis W., 151
Bradstreet, Anne, 113
Bridges, Robert, 144
Brontë, Emily, 274, 401
Brown, Thomas Edward, 208
Browning, Elizabeth Barrett, 125, 126
Browning, Ophelia Guyon, 351
Browning, Robert, 24, 35, 132, 198, 273, 509
Bryant, William Cullen, 182, 276, 331, 388
Bulwer-Lytton, Robert, 44
Burns, Robert, 118, 165
Byrom, John, 326
Byron, Lord, George Gordon, 3, 120, 175
Carey, Henry, 442
Carroll, Lewis, 444
Cary, Phoebe, 261
Clarke, Joseph I. C., 305
Clough, Arthur Hugh, 335
Coleridge, Samuel Taylor, 232
Collier, Thomas Stephens, 39
Cowley, Abraham, 441

Crane, Hart, 158, 553
Cummings, E.E., 552
De La Mare, Walter, 526
Dickinson, Emily, 205, 408, 409, 410, 411, 412
Doane, George Washington, 336
Donne, John, 106, 108, 109, 318
Drayton, Michael, 100
Dyer, Sir Edward, 363
Ehrmann, Max, 357
Emerson, Ralph Waldo, 190, 191, 298, 393
Fields, James T., 66
Finch, Frances Miles, 303
Fletcher, Julia A., 542
Foss, Sam Walter, 355
Freneau, Philip, 163
Frost, Robert, 214, 215, 216, 427, 430, 434, 435, 542
Galsworthy, John, 284
Godolphin, Sidney, 324
Gray, Thomas, 370
Guest, Edgar A., 155, 247, 249, 422, 423, 537
Gulistan of Moslih Eddin Saadi, 363
Hall, Mary Lee, 359
Hamilton, Robert Browning, 278
Henley, William Ernest, 308, 518
Herbert, George, 321, 323
Herrick, Robert, 112, 225, 319
Holmes, Oliver Wendell, 237
Hood, Thomas, 187
Hope, Laurence, 147
Hopkins, Gerard Manley, 208, 337
Housman, A.E., 209, 284, 519
Jackson, Helen Hunt, 206
Jonson, Ben, 111
Keats, John, 123, 124, 183, 392, 484, 485
Kilmer, Joyce, 255, 286

King, Ben, 471
Kingsley, Charles, 239
Kipling, Rudyard, 60, 242, 350, 529
Landor, Walter Savage, 231
Lawrence, D. H., 252
Lear, Edward, 460, 463, 467
Longfellow, Henry Wadsworth, 6, 192, 193, 195,
  395, 397
Lowell, Amy, 210
Lowell, James Russell, 41, 43, 134, 200
MacLeish, Archibald, 556
Malone, Walter, 354
Markham, Edwin, 339, 342, 419, 422, 527
Marlowe, Christopher, 101, 102
Marston, Philip Bourke, 283
Marvell, Andrew, 114, 115
Masefield, John, 536
Mearns, Hughes, 474
Melville, Herman, 199, 301
Millay, Edna St. Vincent, 157, 221
Miller, Alice Duer, 312
Milton, John, 270, 366
Moore, Marianne, 436, 558
Moore, Thomas, 233, 235, 297
Morris, George P., 5
Nash, Ogden, 474, 476, 477, 478
Newman, John Henry, 333
Noyes, Alfred, 85
Parry, Joseph, 152
Poe, Edgar Allan, 126, 130, 400, 487, 491, 493
Pope, Alexander, 271, 367
Raleigh, Sir Walter, 267
Riley, James Whitcomb, 50, 146
Robinson, Edwin Arlington, 531
Rossetti, Christina Georgina, 142, 143, 206
Rossetti, Dante Gabriel, 136, 141

Rowswell, A. K., 288
Sandburg, Carl, 312, 545, 547
Santayana, George, 520
Saxe, John Godfrey, 446, 448
Service, Robert W., 67, 72, 534
Shakespeare, William, 102, 103, 104, 105, 106,
    364, 365
Shelley, Percy Bysshe, 121, 122, 178, 384
Shirley, James, 267
Sidney, Sir Philip, 99
Spenser, Edmund, 98
Stevens, Wallace, 217, 548
Stevenson, Robert Louis, 57, 146, 282
Swain, Charles, 260
Swinburne, Algernon Charles, 143, 240, 412
Taylor, Jane, 256
Teasdale, Sara, 153
Tennyson, Alfred, Lord, 18, 131, 196, 197, 236,
    495, 496
Thomas, Dylan, 292, 557
Thompson, Francis, 342
Thoreau, Henry David, 198, 334
Thorpe, Rose Hartwick, 53
Trowbridge, John Townsend, 75
Untermeyer, Louis, 253
Van Dyke, Henry, 310
Vaughan, Henry, 268, 325
Wallace, William Ross, 253
Waller, Edmund, 113, 227
Wells, Carolyn, 472
Whitman, Walt, 202, 203, 403, 404
Whittier, John Greenleaf, 12, 279, 397
Wilcos, Ella Wheeler, 338, 416, 417
Willard, Emma, 353
Williams, William Carlos, 220, 289, 534

Wordsworth, William, 119, 167, 168, 228, 272, 375, 486
Wright, Ernest Vincent, 458
Wyatt, Sir Thomas, 483
Wylie, Elinor, 154, 436, 538
Yeats, William Butler, 244, 522, 523

Index of Titles

Along the Road, 278
America for Me, 310
Among School Children, 523
Antigonish, 474
Ashes of Life, 157
At the Round Earth's Imagined Corners, 318
Auguries of Innocence, 328
Auld Lang Syne, 118
Autumn, 187
Aux Italiens, 44
Back to Griggsby's Station, 50
The Ballad of East and West, 60
Ballad of the Tempest, 66
The Barrel-Organ, 85
Batter My Heart, 318
Becoming a Dad, 249
A Bird Came Down the Walk, 205
A Birthday, 142
The Blessed Damozel, 136
Blow, Bugle, Blow, 196
The Blue and the Gray, 303
The Blue-Bird, 199
Break, Break, Break, 197
Bright Star, Would I Were Steadfast as Thou Art,
    124
The Canonization, 109
Cargoes, 536

Chicago, 545
A Child's Laughter, 240
Christmas at Sea, 57
A Chronicle, 456
Cleopatra Dying, 39
The Cloud, 178
The Collar, 321
Composed Upon Westminster Bridge, 167
Concord Hymn, 298
The Conqueror Worm, 493
Cool Tombs, 547
A Creed, 342
The Cremation of Sam McGee, 67
Curfew Must Not Ring Tonight, 53
Darius Green and His Flying-Machine, 75
Days of Birth, 509
The Death of the Flowers, 276
Death the Leveller, 267
The Definition of Love, 114
Desideria, 272
Design, 427
The Destruction of Sennacherib, 3
Directive, 542
A Dream Within a Dream, 400
Drinking, 441
Each and All, 393
Early Rising, 448
Echoes, 518
Emily Geiger, 299
The End of the World, 556
England, My England, 308
Even Such Is Time, 267
Evening Contemplation, 336
Fable, 191
Farewell to Love, 100
The Fighting Race, 305

The Fire of Drift-wood, 193
The First Day, 143
The First Snowfall, 43
First Time He Kissed Me, 125
The Flea, 106
Flow Gently, Sweet Afton, 165
For Annie, 126
The force that through the green fuse drives the
    flower, 557
The Forgotten Man, 527
A Friend's Greeting, 155
The Game of Life, 446
The Garden, 115
The Garden of Proserpine, 412
George Crabbe, 531
Go from Me, 126
The Goat, 470
God's Grandeur, 337
God's World, 221
Grass, 203
Grass, 312
The Hand That Rocks the Cradle Is the Hand That
    Rules the World, 253
The Harp That Once Through Tara's Halls, 297
Helen, 101
His Litany to the Holy Spirit, 319
Home, 247
Home Is Where There Is One to Love Us, 260
"Hope" Is the Thing with Feathers, 412
The Hound of Heaven, 342
The Hour Glass, 111
The House by the Side of the Road, 355
The House with Nobody in It, 286
How the Great Guest Came, 339
How They Brought the Good News from Ghent to
    Aix, 35

Hyacinths to Feed Thy Soul, 363
Hymn to Intellectual Beauty, 384
Hymn to the Night, 192
I Died for Beauty — But Was Scarce, 411
I Have Loved England, 312
I Never Lost as Much But Twice, 408
I Will Not Let Thee Go, 144
I Years Had Been from Home, 408
If I Should Die To-Night, 471
The Indian Serenade, 121
Inspiration, 334
Inversnaid, 208
Israfel, 491
It Is a Beauteous Evening, Calm and Free, 167
It Is Too Late!, 397
The Jumblies, 460
Kashmiri Song, 147
Know Then Thyself, 367
The Lady of Shalott, 18
The Lamb, 327
Lead, Kindly Light, 333
Light, 151
Lilacs, 210
The Listeners, 526
Little Things, 542
Locksley Hall, 496
Long, Long Be My Heart with Such Memories
    Filled, 233
Lord, Make a Regular Man Out of Me, 422
The Lost Occasion, 397
Love Not Me, 97
Loveliest of Trees, 209
Love's Philosophy, 122
Love Song, 154
Loving in Truth, 99
The Mad Gardener's Song, 444

The Main-Truck; Or a Leap for Life, 5
The Man with the Hoe, 419
The March into Virginia, 301
Maud Muller, 12
The Measure of a Man, 426
The Men That Don't Fit In, 534
The Mermaid Tavern, 392
Methuselah, 459
Mid-Rapture, 141
A Minuet on Reaching the Age of Fifty, 520
Mowing, 215
Mr. and Mrs. Discobbolos, 463
Mr. Flood's Party, 531
Music I Heard, 156
My Dog, 241
My Garden, 208
My Grandmother's Love Letters, 158
My Love, 134
My Love in Her Attire, 97
My Mind to Me a Kingdom Is, 363
My Mother, 256
My Mother's Garden, 263
My November Guest, 216
My Spirit Longeth for Thee, 326
Myself, 403
Myself, 423
Nature, 198
New Friends and Old Friends, 152
Night, 373
A Noiseless Patient Spider, 202
Not Marble, nor the Gilded Monuments, 103
Not Thou But I, 283
Nurse's Song, 227
The Nutcrackers and the Sugar-Tongs, 467
October's Bright Blue Weather, 206

Ode (Intimations of Immortality from Recollections of Early Childhood), 375
Ode on a Distant Prospect of Eton College, 370
Ode to a Nightingale, 183
Oft in the Stilly Night, 235
Old Age, 227
The Old Man Dreams, 237
On a Girdle, 113
On His Deceased Wife, 270
On His Seventy-Fifth Birthday, 231
On Seeing the Elgin Marbles, 485
On Time, 366
One Day I Wrote Her Name, 98
One Word Is Too Often Profaned, 122
Opportunity, 354
Optimism, 338
Out Fishin', 537
An Overworked Elocutionist, 472
The Pasture, 214
The Pedigree of Honey, 411
Peregrine, 538
Piano, 252
The Pied Piper of Hamelin, 24
Pippa's Song, 198
Poetry, 558
Portrait of the Artist as a Prematurely Old Man, 478
The Power of the Dog, 242
Pray Without Ceasing, 351
A Prayer, 357
Prayer, 323
A Prayer for My Daughter, 244
Prayer for This House, 253
The Preacher's Vacation, 451
Prophecy, 436
Prospice, 273
Psalm 23: The Lord Is My Shepherd, 317

Queen-Ann's-Lace, 220
Rabbi Ben Ezra, 509
Recessional, 350
The Red Wheelbarrow, 534
Reflections on Ice-Breaking, 476
A Refusal to Mourn the Death, by Fire, of a Child
   in London, 292
Remembrance, 274
The Retreat, 325
Ring Out, Wild Bells, 495
Rock Me to Sleep, 258
Rocked in the Cradle of the Deep, 353
Romance, 146
Rondel, 143
Roofs, 255
Sally in Our Alley, 442
Sculpture, 425
The Sea, 175
The Second Coming, 522
She Was a Phantom of Delight, 119
Should You Go First, 288
The Silken Tent, 435
The Skeleton in Armor, 6
A Slumber Did My Spirit Seal, 272
The Snow-Storm, 190
So Might It Be, 284
So That's Who I Remind Me of, 477
So, We'll Go No More A-Roving, 120
The Solitary Reaper, 486
Song, 131
Sonnet, 98
The Soul Selects Her Own Society, 410
The Spell of the Yukon, 72
Spring Night, 153
Sunday Morning, 548
Suppose, 261

Sweet and Low, 236
Sweet Disorder, 112
Tell Him So, 424
Telling the Bees, 279
Thanatopsis, 388
A Thanksgiving to God for His House, 225
There Is No God, 335
There's A Certain Slant of Light, 409
They Are All Gone, 268
They Flee from Me, 483
They That Have Power to Hurt, 364
A Thing of Beauty, 484
Thirteen Ways of Looking at a Blackbird, 217
The Tide Rises, the Tide Falls, 195
Tintern Abbey, 168
To a Thesaurus, 455
To a Waterfowl, 331
To an Athlete Dying Young, 284
To Brooklyn Bridge, 553
To Earthward, 434
To Electra, 112
To My Dear and Loving Husband, 113
To One in Paradise, 130
To Spring, 164
To Think of Time, 404
Tract, 289
Tree at My Window, 216
Turn Again to Life, 359
The Two Glasses, 417
Two Tramps in Mud Time, 427
Ulalume, 487
A Valediction Forbidding Mourning, 108
The Vampire, 529
Verses Written in 1872, 282
Very Like a Whale, 474
Victory in Defeat, 422

The Village Blacksmith, 395
The Visionary, 401
Vital Spark of Heavenly Flame, 271
We Are Seven, 228
West-Running Brook, 430
What Are Years?, 436
what if a much of a which of a wind, 552
What Is So Rare As a Day in June, 200
When Father Carves the Duck, 458
When Forty Winters, 365
When I Consider Everything That Grows, 106
When I Have Fears That I May Cease to Be, 123
When I Have Seen by Time's Fell Hand, 104
When in the Chronicle of Wasted Time, 105
When She Comes Home, 146
Who Ever Loved, That Loved Not at First Sight?,
   102
Who Is Silvia?, 102
The Wild Honey Suckle, 163
Will You Love Me When I'm Old?, 151
The Wind, 206
Wise Men and Shepherds, 324
With Rue My Heart is Laden, 519
A Woman's Last Word, 132
The Yellow Violet, 182
You Never Can Tell, 416
Young and Old, 239
Youth and Age, 232
Yussouf, 41

Index of First Lines

A bird came down the walk —, 205
A child said What is the grass? fetching it to me
  with full, 203
A feller isn't thinkin' mean, 537
A fool there was and he made his prayer, 529
A garden is a lovesome thing, God wot!, 208
A noiseless patient spider, 202
A simple child, 228
A slumber did my spirit seal;, 272
A stranger came one night to Yussouf's tent, 41
A sweet disorder in the dress, 112
A thing of beauty is a joy for ever:, 484
All the bells of heaven may ring, 240
Among twenty snowy mountains, 217
And what is so rare as a day in June?, 200
Announced by all the trumpets of the sky, 190
As I was going up the stair, 474
As virtuous men pass mildly away, 108
At Paris it was, at the opera there; —, 44
At the round earth's imagined corners, blow, 318
Back out of all this now too much for us, 542
Backward, turn backward, O time, in your flight,
  258
Batter my heart, three personed God; for you, 318
Before the cathedral in grandeur rose, 339
Behold her, single in the field, 486
Beneath yon Larkspur's azure bells, 199

Blessing on the hand of women!, 253

Bowed by the weight of centuries he leans, 419

Break, break, break, 197

Bright star, would I were steadfast as thou art —, 124

By the flow of the inland river, 303

By the rude bridge that arched the flood, 298

Candy, 476

Cold in the earth, and the deep snow piled above thee!, 274

Complacencies of the peignoir, and late, 548

Comrades, leave me here a little, while as yet 'tis early morn:, 496

Consider this small dust, here in the glass, 111

Death, when you come to me, tready with a footstep, 284

Defeat may serve as well as victory, 422

Did all the lets and bars appear, 301

Earth has not anything to show more fair:, 167

Even such is Time, which takes in trust, 267

Fair flower, that dost so comely grow, 163

Farewell! — but whenever you welcome the hour, 233

Farewell! thou art too dear for my possessing, 364

Fear death? — to feel the fog in my throat, 273

First time he kissed me, he but only kiss'd, 125

Five years have past; five summers, with the length, 168

Flow gently, sweet Afton, among thy green braes!, 165

Fly envious Time, till thou run out thy race, 366

For God's sake hold your tongue, and let me love, 109

"Fred, where is north?", 430

From fairest creatures we desire increase, 365

Give him the darkest inch your shelf allows, 531

Go from me. Yet I feel that I shall stand, 126
"God bless the man who first invented sleep!", 448
God of our fathers, known of old —, 350
Grow old along with me!, 509
Had I concealed my love, 154
Hamelin Town's in Brunswick, 24
Happy those early days, when I, 325
He thought he saw an Elephant, 444
Her body is not so white as, 220
Her heart is like her garden, 263
Here is the place; right over the hill, 279
Here, where the world is quiet;, 412
Hog Butcher for the World, 545
Home's not merely four square walls, 260
"Hope" is the thing with feathers —, 412
How many dawns, chill from his ripling rest, 553
How vainly men themselves amaze, 115
I arise from dreams of thee, 121
I bring fresh showers for the thirsting flowers, 178
I celebrate myself, and sing myself, 403
I dare not ask a kiss, 112
I died for Beauty — but was scarce, 411
I fled Him, down the nights and down the days;,
    342
I found a dimpled spider, fat and white., 427
I have no dog, but it must be, 241
I have to live with myself, and so, 423
I have loved England, dearly and deeply, 312
I heard the trailing garments of the Night, 192
I never lost as much but twice, 408
I saw old Autumn in the misty morn, 187
I shall lie hidden in a hut, 436
I sprang to the stirrup, and Joris, and he;, 35
I strove with none; for none was worth my strife.,
    231
I struck the board, and cried, "No more;, 321

I, too, dislike it: there are things that are important, 558
I took a piece of plastic clay, 425
I walk through the long schoolroom questioning, 523
I walked a mile with Pleasure;, 278
I wanted the gold, and I sought it;, 72
I will make you brooches and toys for your delight, 146
I will not let thee go., 144
I will teach you my townspeople, 289
I wish I could remember the first day, 143
I would ask of you, my darling, 151
I Years had been from Home, 408
I'd like to be the sort of friend that you have been to me;, 155
If ever there lived a Yankee lad, 75
If ever two were one, then surely we., 113
If I should die and leave you here a while, 359
If I should die to-night, 471
If of thy mortal goods thou art bereft, 363
If with light head erect I sing, 334
If you hear a kind word spoken, 424
I'm going out to clean the pasture spring;, 214
In Heaven a spirit doth dwell, 491
In the hour of my distress, 319
"Is there anybody there?" said the Traveller, 526
It is a beauteous evening, calm and free;, 167
It is common knowledge to every schoolboy and even every, 478
It is too late! Ah, nothing is too late, 397
It lies not in our power to love or hate, 102
It must have been for one of us, my own, 283
It takes a heap o' livin' in a house t' make it home, 247
Kissing her hair, I sat against her feet, 143

Know then thyself, presume not God to scan, 367
Lead, kindly Light, amid the encircling gloom, 333
Let me do my work each day;, 357
Let's contend no more, Love, 132
Liar and bragger, 538
Lilacs, 210
Little drops of water, 542
Little Lamb, who made thee?, 327
Little thinks, in the field, yon red-cloaked clown, 393
Lo! 'tis a gala night, 493
Lord, thou hast given me a cell, 225
Lord, when the wise men came from far, 324
Love at the lips was touch, 434
Love has gone and left me, and the days are all alike., 157
Love not me for comely grace, 97
Loveliest of trees, the cherry now, 209
Loving in truth, and fain in verse my love to show, 99
Make new friends, but keep the old;, 152
Mark but this flea, and mark in this, 106
Maud Muller on a summer's day, 12
May nothing evil cross this door, 253
Men call you fair, and you do credit it, 98
Methought I saw my late espoused Saint, 270
Methuselah ate what he found on his plate, 459
Monday's child is fair of face, 509
Mr. and Mrs. Discobbolos, 463
Music I heard with you was more than music, 156
My heart aches, and a drowsy numbness pains, 183
My heart is like a singing bird, 142
My love in her attire doth show her wit, 97
My love is of a birth as rare, 114
My mind to me a kingdom is, 363
My Sorrow, when she's here with me, 216

579

My spirit is too weak — mortality, 485
My spirit longeth for thee, 326
Never until the mankind making, 292
Not as all other women are, 134
Not — "How did he die?" But — "How did he
    live?", 426
Nor marble, nor the gilded monuments, 103
Not on our golden fortunes builded high —, 527
Now Sam McGee was from Tennessee, where the
    cotton blooms and, 67
Now sleeps the crimson petal, now the white; 131
O nature! I do not aspire, 198
A precious codex, volume, tome, 455
O suns and skies and clouds of June, 206
O Thou with dewy locks, who lookest down, 164
O world, I cannot hold thee close enough!, 221
Of all the girls that are so smart, 442
Oft in the stilly night, 235
Oh East is East, and West is West, and never the
    twain shall meet, 60
Oh for one hour of youthful joy!, 237
Old Age, on tiptoe, lays her jewelled hand, 520
Old Eben Flood, climbing alone one night, 531
Old Ironsides at anchor lay, 5
Old women say that men don't know, 249
On either side the river lie, 18
Once — but no matter when —, 456
Once more the storm is howling, and half hid, 244
Once there was a little boy whose name was Robert
    Reese;, 472
One day I wrote her name upon the strand, 98
One thing that literature would be greatly the better
    for, 474
One word is too often profaned, 122
Or ever the knightly years were gone, 518
Out of the mud two strangers came, 427

Pale hands I love beside the Shalimar, 147
Pap's got his patent right, and rich as all creation;, 50
Pile the bodies high at Austerlitz and Waterloo., 312
Prayer, the Church's banquet, Angels' age, 323
Quinquireme of Nineveh from distant Ophir, 536
Quite unexpectedly, as Vasserot, 556
"Read out the names!" and Burke sat back, 305
Ring out, wild bells, to the wild sky, 495
Rocked in the cradle of the deep, 353
She is as in a field a silken tent, 435
She was a Phantom of delight, 119
Should auld acquaintance be forgot, 118
Should you go first and I remain, 288
Silent is the house: all are laid asleep:, 401
Since there's no help, come let us kiss and part;, 100
Sinks the sun below the desert, 39
Slowly England's sun was setting o'er the hilltops far away, 53
so much depends, 534
So, we'll go no more a-roving, 120
Softly, in the dusk, a woman is singing to me;, 252
Softly now the light of day, 336
Some die too late and some too soon, 397
Souls of Poets dead and gone, 392
"Speak! speak! thou fearful guest!, 6
Suppose, my little lady, 261
Surprised by joy — impatient as the Wind, 272
Sweet and low, sweet and low, 236
Take this kiss upon the brow!, 400
Talk happiness. The world is sad enough, 338
Thank Heaven! the crisis —, 126
That which her slender waist confined, 113

The Assyrian came down like the wolf on the fold, 3

The awful shadow of some unseen Power, 384

The blessed damozel leaned out, 136

The force that through the green fuse drives the flower, 557

The fountains mingle with the river, 122

The glories of our blood and state, 267

The harp that once through Tara's halls, 297

The Lord is my shepherd; I shall not want., 317

The melancholy days are come, the saddest of the year, 276

The mountain and the squirrel, 191

The night has a thousand eyes, 151

The Nutcrackers sat by a plate on the table;, 467

The old man went to meetin', for the day was bright and fair, 451

The park is filled with night and fog, 153

The pedigree of Honey, 411

The road is wide and the stars are out and the breath of the night is, 255

The seas are quiet when the winds give o'er;, 227

The sheets were frozen hard, and they cut the naked hand;, 57

The skies they were ashen and sober;, 487

The soul selects her own Society —, 410

The snow had begun in the gloaming, 43

The splendour falls on castle walls, 196

The sun descending in the West, 373

The thirsty earth soaks up the rain, 441

The tide rises, the tide falls, 195

The time you won your town the race, 284

The world is charged with the grandeur of God., 337

The year's at the spring, 198

There are hermit souls that live withdrawn, 355

There are no stars tonight, 158
There is a destiny that makes us brothers;, 342
There is a pleasure in the pathless woods, 175
'There is no God,' the wicked saith, 335
There is sorrow enough in the natural way, 242
There sat two glasses filled to the brim, 417
There was a man, now please take note, 470
There was a time when meadow, grove, and stream, 375
There was never a sound beside the wood but one, 215
There's a barrel-organ caroling across a golden street, 85
There's a certain Slant of light, 409
There's a game much in fashion — I think it's called Euchre, 446
There's a race of men that don't fit in, 534
They are all gone into the world of light!, 268
They do me wrong who say I come no more, 354
They flee from me that sometime did me seek, 483
They went to sea in a sieve, they did;, 460
This darksome burn, horseback brown, 208
This I would like to be — graver and bolder, 422
Thou lovely and beloved, thou my love;, 141
Thou wast all that to me, love, 130
Though he that, ever kind and true, 282
'Tis fine to see the Old World, and travel up and down, 310
To him who in the love of Nature holds, 388
To see a World in a grain of sand, 328
To think of time — of all that retrospection, 404
Tree at my window, window tree, 216
Turning and turning in the widening gyre, 522
'Twas in the days of the Revolution, —, 299
Unanswered yet the prayer your lips have pleaded, 351

Under a spreading chestnut-tree, 395
Verse, a breeze 'mid blossoms straying, 232
Vital spark of heavenly flame!, 271
Was this the face that launched a thousand ships, 101
We all look on with anxious eyes, 458
We sat within the farm-house old, 193
We were crowded in the cabin, 66
What have I done for you, 308
what if a much of a which of a wind, 552
What is our innocence, 436
When Abraham Lincoln was shoveled into the tombs, he, 547
When all the world is young, lad, 239
When beechen buds begin to swell, 182
When I consider everything that grows, 106
When I consider men of golden talents, 477
When I have fears that I may cease to be, 123
When I have seen by Time's fell hand defaced, 104
When in the chronicle of wasted time, 105
When she comes home again! A thousand ways, 146
When the voices of children are heard on the green, 227
Whenever I walk to Suffern along the Erie track, 286
Whither, midst falling dew, 331
Who fed me from her gentle breast, 256
Who has seen the wind?, 206
Who is Silvia? what is she, 102
With rue my heart is laden, 519
Ye distant spires, ye antique towers, 370
You never can tell when you send a word, 416

A note on the text
Large print edition designed by
Lynn Harmet
Composed in 16 pt Times Roman
on a Mergenthaler Linotron 202
by Modern Graphics, Inc.

The publishers hope that this
Large Print book has brought
you pleasurable reading.
Each title is designed to make
the text as easy to see as possible.
G.K. Hall Large Print books are
available from your library and
your local bookstore. Or you can
receive information on upcoming
and current Large Print books by
mail and order directly from the
publisher. Just send your name
and address to:

G.K. Hall & Co.
70 Lincoln Street
Boston, Mass. 02111

or call, toll-free:

1-800-343-2806